SWANSEA CITY
Seasons in the Sun
1981-82 & 1982-83

DESERT ISLAND FOOTBALL HISTORIES

SWANSEA CITY

Seasons in the Sun
1981-82 & 1982-83

Series Editor: Clive Leatherdale

Terry Grandin

DESERT ISLAND BOOKS

First published in 2005
by
DESERT ISLAND BOOKS LIMITED
7 Clarence Road, Southend on Sea, Essex SS1 1AN
United Kingdom
www.desertislandbooks.com

© 2005 Terry Grandin

British Library Cataloguing-in-Publication Data
A catalogue record for this book is available from the British Library

ISBN 1-905328-02-8

Printed in Great Britain
by
Biddles Ltd, King's Lynn

The photographs in this book were kindly provided by
the Huw Evans Picture Agency

CONTENTS

FOREWORD

I was lucky enough to have played a small part in the fastest rise up the divisions by any club in the history of the Football League. When John Toshack first spoke to me about joining the Swans they had already left the Fourth and Third Divisions far behind.

I was with Wrexham at the time and the thought of being part of Tosh's revolution appealed to me very much. I had no hesitation in signing and made my Swansea debut on 1 December 1979, strangely enough back at the Racecourse against the club I had just left. Within two seasons we had reached the very top.

Such was the impact of the Swans' style of play that no fewer than six of our players were selected to play for Wales in one game, and I was fortunate to be numbered amongst those. There were also many times when ten of the eleven on duty for the club were all internationals.

The phenomenal rise up the divisions has long been a talking point for Swansea fans, who enjoyed great days as Arsenal, Manchester United and even Liverpool were put to the sword. Yet perhaps even more talked about was the rapid descent back down the divisions, which almost took the club into extinction.

This book gives an accurate account of the good days on the way up – and pulls no punches as events conspired to send the club spinning back down at an even faster rate.

The reasons for the fall from grace are set out clearly and readers can make up their own minds as to why the Swans found themselves back in Division Four less than three years after playing top-flight football.

Yes, we did live the dream when Swansea City matched the best teams in the land. So if you are a football fan like me, sit back and enjoy the exploits of team-mates of mine like Alan Curtis, Leighton James, Bob Latchford, Nigel Stevenson, the late Robbie James, and all the others who helped give the Swans their seasons in the sun.

DAVID GILES
(Swansea City and Wales: now radio and TV summariser and pundit)

AUTHOR'S NOTE

My first visit to the Vetch Field was on 26 March 1960, when Cardiff City were the visitors. An exciting game ended 3-3, with Brayley Reynolds scoring twice and Dixie Hale firing in the other. I was already a football 'nut' by then, but that match confirmed to me that there would never be anything to beat the 'beautiful game'.

When I was asked to write this book by Clive Leatherdale of Desert Island Books, I had to think long and hard before accepting. Although, like most fans, I knew many of the events depicted in the following chapters, I realised that to tell the true story would need many hours of research. This is where my occupation as a sports journalist and statistician came in handy, because for the last seven seasons I have been covering all Swansea's home games in my role of freelance reporter.

The impressive start to the 2004-05 season at the magnificent new Liberty Stadium makes it hard to remember that as recently as May 2003 the club needed to win its final game of the season against Hull to retain its League membership. Perhaps nothing changes in this game we all love.

There have been many highs and lows in the Swans' 85-year existence but nothing could compare with the rapid rise up the divisions and subsequent fall from grace related in this story.

A task of this magnitude could not have been accomplished without assistance, and I owe special thanks to my good friend David Giles, or 'Gilo' as he has been known since his playing days. He gave me an insight into what it was like to be a player in those heady days as the club reached the very top. I am also very grateful to him for allowing me to reproduce several of his personal photographs, and also for writing the Foreword to this book.

I could not have illustrated this tale without access to the vast photographic library of the Huw Evans Picture Agency. Huw allowed me to sift through hundreds of Swansea photos and my only problem was how to whittle my 150 possibles down to those eventually used. My thanks to Huw for his valued assistance and patience. Thanks also to Richard Shepherd for making his collection of programmes and statistics available, and to Swansea supporters Colin Jones, Ugo Valerio and Peter Gilbert for their contribution.

I am reasonably competent on the computer, but thankfully my son Jason is far more so. I am indebted to his help, particularly with the statistical summaries and photographs.

This book is dedicated to my young grandchildren Ella, Freya, Lauren, Tillie and Max in the knowledge that they are growing up in homes where football is still regarded as the 'beautiful game'.

TERRY GRANDIN

1
THE ONLY WAY IS UP
(August 1974 – February 1978)

The fans were edgy, and not only the Swansea supporters. Nearly 19,000 were packed into Deepdale and 10,000 of them had made the long and arduous trip up to Lancashire from south-west Wales. The stakes were high and it was a test of nerve as well as skill: victory for the Swans would earn them promotion to Division One, while 'Proud' Preston were desperate for a win to stave off relegation to Division Three.

Manager John Toshack was fully aware that although the Swans had beaten Preston 3-0 earlier in that 1980-81 season, the final game on 2 May would be completely different. He couldn't think of a harder match to finish the campaign.

He then proceeded to make one of the toughest decisions of his short managerial career by again leaving out skipper John Mahoney. The kick-off was just two hours away. Someone had to miss out to allow for the return of Jeremy Charles up front, and the experienced Wales international midfielder was the unlucky player singled out. 'It was a game he wanted to play in more than any other,' said Toshack, 'and don't forget that we are cousins and grew up in the same Cardiff streets.'

The decision was made because Preston had little creative flair, lacking a particular player to be marked out of the game, which was a job Mahoney would have relished. It also proved that Toshack had no favourites in his squad.

Tommy Craig was given the captaincy and he led his side out onto the Deepdale pitch in front of the television cameras, the bright sunlight and the expectant supporters. Swansea were in their change strip of light blue shirts with dark blue sleeves.

Within half an hour they had the fans roaring with approval and one foot in the First Division after goals from Leighton James and the skipper. Confidence was high at the start, both on and off the field, and when James cut in from the left to unleash a dipping shot that deceived Roy Tunks in the home goal it set visiting pulses racing. Two minutes later the unmarked Craig tapped home the second and Swans fans could be forgiven for thinking that the job was done.

But Preston were managed by 1966 World Cup star Nobby Stiles and he had never given up on any lost causes during an illustrious career with Manchester United and England. Back came North End in the second half and Swansea were forced on the defensive for long periods. The chanting from the away fans grew a little fainter and at last the home support found their voices. When Scotland Under-23 international Alex Bruce halved the deficit with just over ten minutes remaining it was time for much chewing of Welsh fingernails. Home supporters raised the volume as they sensed that something could be pulled out of the fire and the threat of Third Division football was no longer the certainty for them that it had appeared to be at half-time.

A shot drifted just wide of the Swansea post, Dave Stewart blocked another goalbound effort, Nigel Stevenson headed clear, and the ball was hacked upfield at every opportunity by the blue-shirted Swans as they hung on with the seconds ticking away.

Then came the moment that made the long trip north worthwhile. Jeremy Charles sidefooted into the corner of the net from close range to put the result beyond doubt and send the Swans soaring into the First Division for the first time in their sixty-year history.

When the referee blew the final whistle the celebrations began. First on the field was Toshack, who made straight for eighteen-year-old Dudley Lewis, the youngest member of his victorious side. After embracing each other, every player ran to the Swansea supporters to soak up the cheers and adulation.

The dressing room was awash with champagne as the team, management and directors toasted an amazing achievement. Three of those on the field that day – Wyndham Evans, Robbie James and Jeremy Charles – had been with the Swans in the dark days of the Fourth Division just three seasons earlier. In the midst of it all was a guest at the match, none other than Toshack's mentor at Liverpool, the great Bill Shankly: 'What John has done at this club is amazing,' he said. 'He is not manager of the month' (a reference to the award won by Toshack in April), 'he is manager of the century.'

Chairman Malcolm Struel was already thinking ahead to life amongst the elite: 'Providing we sell the expected number of season tickets and providing gates are good we will find the money to strengthen the squad. We have never said no to the manager and hopefully we won't have to in the future.' Prophetic words indeed from the man who had masterminded the leap from the basement.

While the Swans celebrated sneaking into that third promotion place, pushing aside Blackburn on goal-difference, Preston were now staring at the drop into Division Three. They still had to play Derby County in their final match, which they won 2-1, but Cardiff City's 0-0 draw with West Ham meant it was double Welsh delight as the Bluebirds stayed ahead of Preston, also on goal-differnce, to send Stiles' team down.

Much had been achieved by Swansea City in a short space of time, both on and off the field. With most people's thoughts now focused on playing the likes of Manchester United, Liverpool and Arsenal in the coming season, few looked back to the miserable times of 1975. It was then that the Swans finished third from bottom of the Fourth Division and were forced to go cap in hand to the Football League and apply for re-election for the first time since joining the League in 1920.

Harry Gregg was manager at the start of that 1974-75 season. The former Manchester United and Northern Ireland keeper had taken over from Roy Bentley two years previously but there had been little improvement in the Swans' fortunes. Attendances had dipped below the 3,000 mark, making finances tight and Chairman Struel struggled to keep the club afloat: 'Television is the main cause of a decline in attendances,' he said, although recognising that the game must be improved as a spectacle to bring the fans back in.

One of the means of saving money was a proposal to withdraw the reserves from the Combination League, but this resulted in protests from supporters: 'There are no sacred cows when we are fighting for our lives,' suggested a harassed Struel.

That 1974-75 season had started poorly for the Swans with defeat at Darlington compounded by the dismissal of seventeen-year-old full-back Stephen Thomas. He was sent off for punching Darlo's Colin Sinclair, which also resulted in Gregg becoming involved in heated exchanges with the North-Eastern side's officials.

Thomas, who worked at Baglan Steelworks and was yet to be offered even a part-time contract, was the first of a number of Swansea players to be dismissed that season. Gregg tried introducing a code of conduct, but by the turn of the year the Swans had the unenviable record of the most dismissals of any Football League side (22) since the resumption of play following the Second World War.

The Annual Shareholders Meeting held in October 1974 painted a harsh picture: the club showed a massive deficit of £223,657 in the last financial year, with further losses already incurred.

As far as Gregg was concerned, the administration side of the club meant nothing to him: 'I am sick and tired of hearing about the club's financial state. I would much rather talk about the practical side of football. Manliness has been taken out of the game and we are now pandering to the demands of Europe and changing our game to that played on the Continent which, after all, is only being played by a bunch of fairies.' Clearly Gregg was upset at having so many players sent off, and obviously had scant regard for European footballers.

To make matters worse, the Swans slumped 1-3 in a Cup replay at non-league Kettering. Graham Atkinson, brother of the more famous Ron, broke his leg after a challenge from young Robbie James and it ended his career. James had returned to Swansea after going on loan to Arsenal in November. In fact he only stayed at Highbury for two days before returning to west Wales to stake a claim for a first-team place.

The New Year started badly with a home defeat by Workington, one of only four sides below the Swans. Paul Bevan became the seventh player sent off when they met Scunthorpe but, thanks to a goal from James and a penalty save from loan keeper Steve Potter, they won 1-0 to give themselves a little respite.

On 23 January, Gregg parted company with the Swans to take up a post with Crewe. Long-serving clubman Harry Griffiths took over as 'caretaker' manager. It was a surprise appointment as it was expected that John Charles, the youth team coach, would be given the role. One week later Struel announced that the City Council had purchased the Vetch Field for £50,000 and given the club a grant of £150,000 to help clear the massive overdraft:

'If further financial pressure forces us out of the League, the terms of the sale would mean that we would have to surrender the lease to the council with vacant possession,' he informed the Swansea public. 'If League football was ever lost, tenure at the Vetch Field would cease. It is a bad deal for the club but if they hadn't come in with their offer we would have been out of the League by now.'

Hardly the words to inspire the new manager or the players, especially as by the end of February they were only one place above the re-election positions. Griffiths, who had clocked up 27 years with the Swans, had improved the quality of play and the discipline, although as yet the results still left a lot to be desired.

With seven games left, Griffiths was offered the manager's job on a permanent basis, on the day the Swans lost 1-2 at home to Reading. Only one point was gained in the last four matches to leave the club having to apply for re-election after finishing 22nd out of 24.

The lowest attendance that season was the 1,428 for the visit of Scunthorpe, while the average home crowd was 2,070. Only Workington, Southport and Rochdale posted a lower total. Clearly the chairman would need a lot of hard work to raise sufficient votes from his counterparts to keep the club in the Football League, and also in existence.

Struel and Griffiths composed a letter which they sent to every League club, stating the reasons why they should receive their vote. They then personally canvassed as many chairmen as they could. The initiative paid off, with Swansea receiving the most number of votes of the clubs applying for re-election. League football was saved, for the time being at least. Much more needed to be done to avoid such a near-catastrophe ever happening again.

Griffiths desperately wanted to strengthen the side for 1975-76 but he was told that he had to operate with only fifteen full-time professionals. He knew that if the team could play attractive football then the crowds would increase, but by the start of the season only 503 season tickets had been purchased.

Despite this, and the news that a further £40,000 had been lost during that ill-fated season, Griffiths spent £1,000 in purchasing goalkeeper Stephen Potter who had been on loan at the Vetch. Joining him were Geoff Bray, Paul Harris, Andy Leitch and George Smith, a tough-tackling half-back who came on a free transfer from Cardiff City.

The first game of 1975-76 saw the visit of Tranmere, and a diving header by Wyndham Evans after five minutes gave the Swans an early lead. Rovers had Mark Palios, late of the Football Association, in their ranks, while leading their line was on-loan striker Tommy Tynan. The visitors fought back to draw 1-1 but it was still an encouraging start.

Gates began to improve and when Newport came to the Vetch in September, 4,456 were present for the best home crowd since the visit of Bradford City back in February 1974.

Swansea's lack of goals forced Griffiths to seek a target man and in October nineteen-year-old Tynan joined the club on loan. He was still on Liverpool's books, having been hand-picked by Bill Shankly when only fifteen, and he was their Central League side's leading scorer for the previous two seasons. He celebrated his arrival with a goal on his debut against Doncaster. Tynan looked to be the answer to Swansea's problems, as up until then, with twelve games gone, they had only bagged thirteen goals. Defensively there were few problems, because over the same period they had only conceded a similar amount.

Unfortunately, after also finding the net in a 3-1 victory over Bradford City, Tynan walked out, claiming personal reasons. His two goals had come in six games.

Results improved and sixth position was reached in the autumn. The Boxing Day crowd of 4,091 for the 4-2 win over Watford showed that the policy of entertaining football, as against 'win at all costs', was beginning to have an effect on support.

The only cloud on the horizon was the poor away form. While they were unbeaten at home, the Swans had yet to win a match on their travels, but Griffiths was confident that the corner had been turned. He proudly pointed out the wealth of young talent at the club such as Alan Curtis, Robbie James, Jeremy Charles, Nigel Stevenson, and a few others who were also knocking on the first-team door.

In February, promotion-chasing Reading were put to the sword 5-1, Swansea's biggest League win in two years, and they followed that with victory at Torquay to register their first away success of the season. The game in Devon was noteworthy in that Robbie James became the first player to achieve 100 League games, all of them for Swansea, before reaching his nineteenth birthday.

There was more good news when Curtis was selected to play for Wales against England. Five long years had elapsed since a Swansea player had represented his country.

The poor away record meant that the Swans were well off the pace in the spring and they finished eleventh, though this was a marked improvement on what had gone before. The lowest attendance during 1975-76 was 1,311 for the final game, against Brentford, but the average was up on the previous term to 2,865, a rise of almost 50 per cent, but there was still much to do both on and off the field.

During the close season, John Charles resigned as youth team manager and the job was taken on by Roy Saunders. Griffiths signed the experienced players he felt he needed – Eddie May from Wrexham, Les Chappell from Doncaster, Gil Reece and Gary Moore. But they were all upstaged by sixteen-year-old Jeremy Charles, who made a wonderful start to 1976-77 and his own Football League career by scoring within two minutes of coming on as a substitute against Newport. He also added a second as the Swans blitzed their neighbours 4-1.

For Alan Curtis it would be an important time in his career, and he reckoned that it was 'make or break' for the club. 'I believed there would be sweeping changes throughout the club if we failed to win promotion that season,' said the Rhondda-born striker. 'I felt it could be my last season as a Division Four player if we didn't go up.'

After eleven matches the Swans were joint third, but once again lack of success away from home hampered their progress. November's 0-1 defeat at Halifax was their fifth loss in eight away starts.

A brief foray in the League Cup lightened the mood and 13,600 watched visitors Bolton of Division One held 1-1, with Curtis netting the Swans' goal. Although the away leg resulted in a 1-5 defeat, Swansea earned praise for the manner in which they had played against opposition three divisions above them.

Pride comes before a fall and after two good performances against the Trotters, the Swans played host to Minehead in the first round of the FA

Cup. Few would have expected a 0-1 defeat, with the non-leaguers' goal coming from a former Swan, Andy Leitch.

Promotion, however, had not been disregarded. In February plans were put in motion for a 'mad dash for promotion'. Sadly, the following match saw a 1-2 defeat at Doncaster, and the Swans slumped to thirteenth place.

In the meantime, the first phase of an ambitious floodlight improvement scheme had been carried out at a cost of £7,500, and the Vice-Presidents Club actively sought more financial aid to bring the floodlights up to European standard. Chairman Struel was confident the club was moving in the right direction. 'I am convinced that we are on the right lines although we face a hard task to win promotion this year.'

Crowds were up around the 5,000 mark and, with 38 games played, the Swans were only four points off a promotion spot with two games in hand. Over 10,000 were present when Rochdale were beaten 3-2 and in the last home match of the campaign almost 11,000 turned up to see if the Swans could overturn Watford. Unfortunately the Hornets led 4-0 by half-time. A second-half strike by Charles did little to appease the disappointed home fans.

The final League table showed Swansea fifth, one point off promotion and destined for at least another term in the basement division. The lowest attendance for 1976-77 was the 2,392 recorded for the visit of Scunthorpe, while the season's average had jumped to 5,315. Alan Curtis was voted Division Four 'Player of the Year' by managers of clubs in the division. But could he be persuaded to stay?

The pundits obviously valued all the good work done by the genial Griffiths. Swansea were quoted as favourites to gain promotion in 1977-78 along with Watford. Three new players arrived – Neil Davids from Norwich, Keith Barber from Luton, and Kevin Moore from Blackpool.

A double strike by Curtis gave the Swans a 2-1 victory over Barnsley in one of their opening games but Eddie May was man of the match after breaking up a number of dangerous raids by the Tykes in front of a crowd totalling 6,739.

Four undefeated games constituted Swansea's best start to a season for fifteen years, and many fans were already beginning to believe that this could be their year. Attendances were on the up and the commercial side of the club was going well. Supporters Club officials even opened up a kiosk at the ground on match-days to enrol new members.

The directors led from the front by attending almost every match, both home and away. The previous season, Chairman Struel and Vice-Chairman Tom Phillips had only missed one away fixture.

There was a downside to the good start, however, as it brought the scouts flocking to the Vetch to run their eyes over young talent blossoming at the club, although Curtis was still the main focus of attention. 'None of our young stars are leaving Swansea City,' Struel was forced to say publicly. 'They are not for sale and that is that.'

On hearing rumours that West Ham were prepared to pay £100,000 for Curtis, Struel was once again prophetic with his choice of words. 'I very much hope that the time will come when Swansea City will be offering clubs that sort of money for players.'

The unbeaten run was ended at Roots Hall, where Southend, one of the sides above the Swans, won 2-1. When leaders Watford also won 2-1 at Vicarage Road the Swans slipped to seventh, five points behind the Hornets.

Young Charles tried to reassure the supporters, who were seeing their favourites falling way off the pace. 'We're not too worried. We haven't been playing badly but we are just not consistent enough. Once we tighten up a bit and stop giving away silly goals we will start climbing back up the table.'

Unfortunately, with only one victory in the next seven matches, something had to give. On 29 October it was announced that manager Griffiths and coach Roy Saunders were being relieved of their duties. Swansea had already lost their midfield dynamo, George Smith, who earlier in the month had been allowed to join Hartlepool.

Amidst the resulting confusion and poor results, attendances dipped back under the 5,000 mark, but Griffiths, showing what a true clubman he was, agreed to continue in the job until a successor was appointed. In what other walk of life could you be sacked, re-instated, and then have your job advertised while you were still doing it to the best of your ability? That was the situation confronted by the popular Griffiths, who tried manfully to steer the club back in amongst the Division Four promotion pace-setters.

In mid-November a 5-0 thrashing of Crewe, which included a Curtis hat-trick in the last six minutes, was a welcome result and a boost for the club and its supporters. The next game saw a 2-0 success at Brentford, which also notched a first away victory of the season. It came despite the dismissal of Wyndham Evans on the hour. Swansea's resurgence resulted in Griffiths becoming manager of the month, though behind the scenes, an attempt to prise Colin Addison away from Newport to take over at the Vetch failed, leaving Griffiths to continue to toil away.

When Roy Saunders was released, Eddie May took over to become player-coach and for a time results improved: 'It was a joint thing really.

Harry and I changed a few things and added a bit of variety into the training. I had always intended to go into coaching when I packed in playing and to be given the chance so early was marvellous.'

For once, the FA Cup hoodoo was banished, though only just. Non-league Leatherhead were beaten 2-1 at the Vetch in a replay after the Swans were held 0-0 at their place. With the Cup success came more good League results. The side moved up to sixth, only to suffer a disastrous 2-4 home defeat by Northampton.

Portsmouth were beaten in round two, again after a replay, but the Cup journey ended at Fellowes Park where Walsall won 4-1. Wales manager Mike Smith was at the game to run the rule over some of Swansea's players and he was baffled by the scoreline. 'Swansea created more and had better quality chances than Walsall but they couldn't finish,' was his assessment of the game.

With just over half the season completed the promotion pendulum had swung back Swansea's way. They lay third, one place behind Barnsley but nine points adrift of runaway leaders Watford, who also had a game in hand.

The manager's position came to the fore again in February when Struel came close to appointing Eddie McCreadie. The former Chelsea and Scotland defender even attended the match against Newport on 17 February. In the event, he turned down the offer and instead jetted off to Memphis to coach in America. He was the third man in four months to turn the job down, following Addison – who decided to stay with Newport – and Bill McGarry, who not surprisingly opted instead for the manager's job at First Division Newcastle United on his return from the Middle East.

Struel felt it necessary to go public about the problems he was having in filling the post so ably covered by Griffiths: 'As far as I was concerned, Colin Addison had agreed to join us in October. As I recall, we had shaken hands on it. Then Frank O'Farrell decided to stay at Torquay instead of moving to Newcastle, leaving that post vacant for McGarry. It's the same with McCreadie. If Malcolm Allison hadn't left Memphis, there would have been no vacancy there and he would have joined us.'

Griffiths was now working under intolerable circumstances, but Struel assured him that when the new appointment was made he would be given the task of controlling the club's youth policy. Struel then began talks with a fourth candidate and this time he would prove successful. So began the most remarkable rise to the top in Football League history.

2

TOSHACK MAKES HIS MARK

(March 1978 – May 1981)

On 26 February 1978, Swansea chairman Malcolm Struel began negotiations with John Smith, his opposite number at Liverpool FC, regarding the possibility of John Toshack becoming the club's new player-manager. The Wales international striker had already turned down approaches from Newcastle, Norwich and Hereford, as well as from abroad, so Struel was well aware that he had to sell the club hard, along with its future prospects and potential. The following day he attended a meeting of all the interested parties at Anfield, taking with him none other than Harry Griffiths, who now found himself in the strange position of persuading a friend to take over his job.

Toshack had been in South Wales a week or so earlier, calling into Ninian Park to meet Cardiff City manager Jimmy Andrews. Talks on a position with the Bluebirds proved fruitless. 'I had a chat with Jimmy and it became clear to me after a very short time that the Cardiff City I knew and loved had long since gone.'

Toshack accepted the terms offered by Swansea before seeing his new charges in action at Rochdale, who at that time were bottom of Division Four. His wisdom at taking on the Swans might have been quickly questioned: 'I walked into the directors box at Spotland, sat down, and the ball was in the back of the net,' he recalled. 'We were one down already. They weren't very good that night but Harry and the chairman convinced me that the 1-2 defeat was the worst they had played all season.'

News of the appointment was soon common knowledge. At 28 years old, the youngest manager in the Football League was bent on transforming the club. 'Only time would tell if we could win promotion,' he said. 'What I did know was that we had fifteen games left, so we went hell-for-leather to get out of that Fourth Division.' The Swans were in fifth spot, four points behind third-placed Barnsley, six behind Southend, and twelve short of leaders Watford.

At around this time, Bob Latchford became the first £300,000 footballer, when he moved from Birmingham City to Everton.

Four days after taking over, Toshack picked himself to start against visiting Watford. A creditable 3-3 draw was obtained with the new manager opening his account with one of Swansea's goals. There was a setback at York with a 1-2 defeat before the club went on a six-game winning run. This included an historic encounter on April Fools Day against

Hartlepool, who were thrashed at the Vetch 8-0. The 'eight' equalled the club's scoring record against Bristol Rovers (8-1 in 1922) and Bradford City (8-1 in 1926). There were pools of water on the pitch when the match started but it didn't seem to affect the Swans. Robbie James and Alan Curtis both netted hat-tricks, Pat Lally struck one, and another, the fifth, came from the player-manager himself. By now Curtis had built up a sizeable reputation and the club had already turned down a bid of £170,000 for him from Sunderland.

The Swans were now fourth but lowly Crewe knocked the wind out of their sails with a 2-1 win at Gresty Road, big Eddie May netting a rare goal for the losers. Wins against Barnsley and promotion rivals Brentford were offset by defeats in the next two matches, against Grimsby and Northampton, but that left them with a simple equation. Two home matches to complete the season and two victories required.

On 25 April, the day of the visit of Scunthorpe, tragedy struck when Harry Griffiths collapsed and died whilst working in the treatment room. The crowd, which had been in high spirits, were suddenly silenced at the news that someone who had given over thirty years unstinting service to the club should pass away just as promotion was in sight. The team just had to win the match for him and they didn't let him down. Two goals from Curtis and one from Dave Bruton gave them a 3-1 victory. Now all rested on the final day, when Halifax were the visitors.

The fans packed into the Vetch, hoping to see their idols clinch promotion. The 16,130 present was the second largest attendance of the season, only exceeded a fortnight earlier against Brentford. The Shaymen kept the Swans at bay for more than an hour. Swansea were then awarded a free-kick and the boss himself shaped up to take it. Toshack bent the ball around the wall and into the net to give his side the lead. Four minutes from time Curtis added a second to spark a promotion party.

The first phase of the Toshack revolution had been completed. The lowest attendance during the 1977-78 promotion-winning season was 4,253 for the visit of Crewe Alexandra, while the season's average had shot up to 8,052.

During the close season there was plenty of player-movement in and out of the Vetch. Toshack persuaded Curtis to stay with the club despite the striker having earlier sought a transfer. He then signed Leicester striker Alan Waddle for £24,000 and persuaded Terry Medwin into returning to the club as his assistant manager.

But the most intriguing signing of all came when Toshack went back to Anfield and talked legendary 'Iron Man' Tommy Smith into finishing his career with the Swans. The fans could hardly believe what they were witnessing, when another £30,000 went to Crewe for their capable goal-keeper Geoff Crudgington.

Of course, the traffic was not all one way. Pat Lally left for Doncaster, while Dave Bruton joined Newport and Eddie May went to Leicester as player-coach. Chairman Struel was delighted with the upturn in the club's fortunes because season ticket sales had increased to 2,360, the highest sold for more than twenty years. The commercial department remained strong. As well as providing the manager funds for new players, £150,000 was invested in ground improvements.

In early August, Everton came for a pre-season friendly, with the proceeds going to the widow of the much-missed Griffiths.

Tommy Smith made his debut in the 3-0 home win over Lincoln on 22 August 1978 in front of a crowd of 17,000. He had been at Anfield for thirteen years, the highest point of which must surely have been scoring in his 600th game for the club against Borussia Monchengladbach in the 1976-77 European Cup final in Rome. 'There are some very good young players here,' he said. 'If we can get the right blend of youth and experience I am sure we will be alright.'

Swansea came out of the League Cup hat with Tottenham, and a near full house of 24,335 saw goals by Robbie James and Jeremy Charles give them a 2-2 draw. The replay at White Hart Lane went even better as Spurs crumbled to a 3-1 defeat, Toshack netting one of the goals despite playing at centre-half. Watching in the stands that night was a former team-mate of Toshack and Smith. His name was Ian Callaghan and he was impressed by what he saw.

Toshack then broke the club's transfer record by paying Luton Town £35,000 for Phil Boersma, another ex-Liverpool man, while 36-year-old Callaghan was finally persuaded to join the Anfield clan, making his debut on 16 September in a 4-3 victory over Tranmere. Cally could have thrown his lot in with Stan Bowles, Gerry Francis and John Hollins at Queens Park Rangers, but instead decided to sign for Swansea. The arrival of Smith and Callaghan boosted season ticket sales to a peak of around £60,000, and the Swans responded by going top of Division Three after six games.

As ever, something always comes along to spoil the party. Not only did Swansea lose their unbeaten tag at Chester, they also lost Smith, who was dismissed eight minutes from the final whistle after being booked for a second time. Strangely enough for a man of Smith's reputation, both bookings were for dissent.

After the high of winning at Spurs, Swans lost 0-2 to QPR in the next round of the League Cup. The manager accepted full responsibility for the defeat, after once again playing in the back four. 'I was a liability there. When I moved up front we improved, but that was because I was out of the way at the back.' The one bright spot came from a superb performance by Robbie James. It earned him, along with Charles and Curtis, a call-up to the Wales squad for the European Championship match against Malta.

A 10,957 crowd saw a Toshack free-kick seal the points against Exeter to move back up to third, behind leaders Shrewsbury and old foes Watford. In late October Swansea thrashed Peterborough 4-1 for their best win of the season. Attendances stayed around the 10-11,000 mark as the Swans took root amongst the pacesetters.

The FA Cup threw up another potential banana skin when Hillingdon Borough came out of the hat, but they were dispatched 4-1. Woking held on for a replay before going the same way in the next round, but Bristol Rovers put an end to any hopes of Cup glory by winning 1-0 at the Vetch in round three.

By now Leighton Phillips had joined the club from Aston Villa for another sizeable fee. 'The style and standard of play was obviously very different and adjusting was a problem, but the move to Swansea was the right one for me,' said the Wales international who had started his career with Cardiff City.

Christmas came early for Phil Boersma. On 2 December he returned to first-team action after a three-week lay-off to hammer the first goal against Sheffield Wednesday after just fifty seconds. Swansea went on to win 4-2, with a Toshack double and another from Charles helping them to slip into second place, two points behind Watford.

By early 1979 the club's fortunes had improved so much that they were looking for a return to the Combination League in order to give the reserves a higher standard of football. At the same time, Toshack was in talks with Richie Morgan, his counterpart at Cardiff, over the £20,000 transfer of defender Brian Attley, a player the Swansea chief had trailed for several months.

On the field, however, a shortage of goals was causing concern. One seven-match run realised only four goals and five points. Boersma's absence through yet another injury gave the manager selection headaches and he pulled no punches when stating that some players were not pulling their weight. The net result was that Toshack moved himself back into the attack.

There was no lack of success on the commercial side, the club making a £100,000 profit on its Cashcade lottery. Chairman Struel stressed that the money would be used for the benefit of the club and not kept in the coffers. Team strengthening was a priority, but the West Stand would also be renovated at a cost of £35,000, and another large sum would be used to upgrade the floodlighting.

There had been a wholesale transformation at the club since Toshack sat in the stand at Rochdale twelve months previously. On the evidence of his first year, supporters had every reason to be optimistic. When run-away leaders Watford came to the Vetch on 20 March, 19,850 came out to witness a 3-2 victory. The management believed that with continued success that figure could be reached, or exceeded, regularly.

Three further League wins had fans talking once again of promotion, only for the side to slip up 1-2 against basement dwellers Lincoln. But that was to be their final defeat in 1978-79. Boersma fractured an ankle in a 1-0 win at Swindon on 14 April when Crudgington kept the Robins at bay. This left Swansea with six matches remaining.

With just two games left, Swansea were at the top with Watford, Gillingham, and Shrewsbury in close attendance. It was back into the melting pot after Plymouth forced a 2-2 draw at Home Park in the last away game, broadcast by the *Match of the Day* cameras.

The situation was now clear. Swansea had to beat Chesterfield in their final match and hope that some of their rivals slipped up. Fans clutched at omens, believing that because Chesterfield had also been their final opponents in a previous promotion-winning season, the result would once again be in the Swans' favour.

However, when the Spireites opened the scoring after fifteen minutes you could hear a pin drop inside the Vetch Field. Waddle equalised but the Derbyshire side held firm. Toshack needed to change the pattern of play so he put himself on in place of Attley with 22 minutes left. It was not until eight minutes from the end that Toshack met a Danny Bartley free-kick and thundered a header into the net.

After fourteen years in the wilderness, the Swans were back in Division Two. The lowest attendance during 1978-79 was the 7,983 recorded for the visit of Chester, while the average had now leapt up to 13,633. Toshack celebrated promotion in style eight days later by smashing a hat-trick playing for Wales against Scotland.

Life in the higher division was going to be harder without Alan Curtis, who was granted his wish to leave. He joined Division One Leeds for a fee said to be £400,000. Toshack used some of that money to buy Dave Rushbery from Sheffield Wednesday. That deal made history, for his fee – £60,000 – was set by the Transfer Appeals Commission at their very first meeting. Tommy Craig arrived from Aston Villa for a club record fee of £150,000, while John Mahoney cost £100,000 from Middlesbrough.

Not surprisingly there were departures. Tommy Smith's knees finally told him to call it a day, Geoff Crudgington left for Plymouth, and Danny Bartley threw in his lot with Hereford.

Curtis showed he was good enough for top-flight football by scoring for Leeds after just nine minutes in their opening First Division match against Bristol City.

Swansea started the new 1979-80 season with a 2-0 home win over Shrewsbury, in which the highlight was a shot from an acute angle by Robbie James. In some quarters the Swans were being tipped for a third successive promotion, but Toshack was more circumspect: 'People kept coming up and saying "First Division next year" – but that was dangerous talk. We had just come into the Second and to start talking about the First Division was putting on unfair pressure.'

However, with 13,500 turning up for a League Cup-tie against lower class opposition, it was an indication of what could be expected with a winning side. With Curtis gone, Robbie James was the centre of attention, with Leeds and Arsenal monitoring his progress. Away support was also building up. Eight coaches were regularly used for away games, while for the Cup-tie at Stoke, the club chartered a train. A Friends of Swansea City travel club was formed on the basis of the increased support.

Briton Ferry-born Glen Letheran signed from Chesterfield and kept a clean sheet on his debut against Notts County. But Chairman Struel announced the kitty was now empty, and rumours spread of a clear-out to recoup the £50,000 paid for Letheran.

A crowd of 15,104 saw Leicester beat Swansea 2-0 on 29 September. That made it just one point from four games, but suddenly the Swans were facing a greater problem. The Safety of Sports Ground Act would mean massive expenditure in upgrading the Vetch Field.

On the field, Toshack admitted that life in Division Two was so much harder than in the lower divisions. 'It had become abundantly clear that unless we strengthened our staff we were going to have problems.'

In October the club announced profits of £320,000, the biggest in its history. Compare this to a £30,000 profit in 1976-77 and £15,000 the following year. Gate receipts and season tickets soared from £125,000 to £290,000 and the club reported net profits of £179,500 in transfer fees.

The board duly made about £350,000 available for the purchase of new players. With the money burning a hole in Chairman Struel's pocket, Toshack went to Everton and bought full-back Neil Robinson. Plans were also announced for a new-look Vetch Field, which would cost the club £700,000 by providing a new cantilever centre stand and a new grandstand on the east bank.

Hooliganism was also raising its head, not just in Swansea, but across Britain. Struel defended his board's record, saying that £500 per match was being spent on police assistance at home games.

After twelve matches the Swans lay twelfth, but in late November Toshack signed the player he had been seeking – Wrexham's 23-year-old David Giles for £70,000. Giles had been at odds with Robins manager Arfon Griffiths after being dropped following a shock defeat by Bristol Rovers. 'I thought I had played well enough in that match but the boss dropped me and when I asked for an explanation he blew his top,' said the Cardiff-born winger.

New Year's Day 1980 promised to be busy for Swansea, as well as the South Wales Constabulary, as Cardiff City would be the visitors. In the event there was little trouble. The Swans won 2-1 with goals from the former Bluebirds pairing of Toshack and Giles.

Ian Callaghan reached a milestone in the second FA Cup replay against Crystal Palace when he equalled Stanley Matthews' record of playing in 85 FA Cup-ties. He would post a new record at West Ham in the next round.

With Swansea drifting off the pace, Toshack squeezed another £55,000 from Struel and signed the experienced West Brom keeper Dave Stewart. Toshack admitted that of all the players he had signed since he arrived at the club, he knew the least about Stewart. 'If someone had said to me when I started the job that I would sign a player without seeing him play I would have said they were talking rubbish. However, with Stewart I took a calculated gamble but it was one I was sure would take off.'

Stewart kept goal for the last fifteen games. He was joined in the final game by a new signing from Burnley, Leighton James, who came off the bench to score in a 2-1 defeat of Charlton. James was allowed to play because neither side was involved in promotion or relegation.

Twelfth in the League was not what many supporters had been hoping for, but it was a season of consolidation and the Swans ended up only ten points behind the third promoted club. The lowest attendance for a League match during 1979-80 was the 10,352 for the visit of Orient, while the average attendance was up yet again to 14,315.

As a build-up to the 1980-81 season Swansea toured Scotland, but there were no new players in the party. The opening League game was lost 1-2 at Watford, who included Kenny Jackett, but it was their only defeat from the first seven matches.

In the League Cup, Swansea were paired with Arsenal. A Robbie James goal earned a 1-1 draw at the Vetch in front of 17,036, but the Swans were beaten 1-3 in the second leg. Making his debut at Highbury was Yugoslav international Dzemal Hadziabdic. Although 'Jimmy', as he was known, had been at the club for weeks, there had been a delay in obtaining a work permit. He had come to the Vetch from the Velez Mostar club.

A shortage of goals also brought about the re-instatement of Waddle, who was now transfer-listed. The results were only average but Toshack wanted the side to become more consistent. He expected it to take eight to ten games to sort themselves out.

When the Wales squad was named for training at Lilleshall, five Swans were included, proving the huge strides the club had made over recent seasons. Jeremy Charles, Leighton Phillips, David Giles, and Leighton and Robbie James were the players selected.

After seven League matches Swansea were up to fourth, three points behind Blackburn and one adrift of West Ham and Notts County. All three home games had seen crowds topping 11,000. Success on the field was put to one side when the club's balance sheet revealed that in the last financial year they had incurred a huge loss of £400,000.

'No cause for alarm,' said Struel. 'As we had a good profit the previous year, our working loss over two years was only £71,000 and in that time we have built a team worth £3 million.' The manager had spent £591,000 more than he received in the transfer market but he was satisfied that if necessary he could recoup that sum by selling a player.

Having completed twenty League matches the Swans were still fourth, seven points behind West Ham, five behind Chelsea and four back from Notts County.

In the next game, on 13 December 1980, the Swans blitzed Newcastle 4-0. Watching from the stands was old favourite Alan Curtis, who had returned to his first club from Leeds for a £175,000 fee. Before the teams took to the field, Toshack and Curtis walked out to the centre circle to rapturous applause. It had been eighteen months since he left for Elland Road. 'When I left Swansea it was something I had to do but I only played in thirty first-team games for Leeds and in that respect the move was a disaster.' It did, indeed, seem that Toshack would be forced to sell a player or two to help finance the deal, but that wasn't on Curtis's mind when he came off the bench to net from the spot against Watford to give the club a much-needed 1-0 win.

By the turn of the year the Swans were up to second, four points behind West Ham but two ahead of Chelsea and Notts County.

The FA Cup was quickly forgotten as the Swans were given a footballing lesson in round three by Middlesbrough, who won 5-0, handing them their worst defeat of the season.

Waddle turned out to be the fall guy following Curtis's return. He joined Newport for a record fee of £80,000, a staggering sum from an outfit already deep in the red. He started repaying County by scoring on his debut as Newport beat Sheffield United 4-0, with another former Swan, Kevin Moore, also on the scoresheet.

Table-toppers West Ham extended their lead when they came to the Vetch and won 3-1. That sparked a run of five successive defeats and promotion began to look a long way off. But Leighton James bagged his first hat-trick for the club, including two penalties, when they beat Bolton 3-0 and suddenly the corner was turned. Swansea would lose only one of their last eleven games. On Easter Saturday, and with three matches left to play, 16,063 packed into the Vetch for the visit of promotion rivals Chelsea. Robinson and Hadziabdic, his first goal for the club, gave the Swans a 2-0 interval lead, and Robbie James completed the scoring. Two days later, Tommy Craig and Leighton James had the Swans leading Luton 2-0, but Ricky Hill pounced twice to level the match.

Once again it was down to the final match, at Preston. A win would be enough to bring First Division football to Swansea for the first time. Once again they made hard work of it, after seemingly having the game sewn up in the first half, but a late strike by Charles was enough for the celebrations to begin.

'Of course I wanted to play, but it was fitting that the side contained so many Swansea-born players,' said substitute on the day, David Giles. 'I never got on the field, but then I was luckier than John Mahoney who had to be content with a seat in the stand.'

The following week the players and management toured Swansea in an open-topped bus and were greeted by thousands who came out to support their idols. The tour finished outside the Guild Hall, where Chairman Struel and the manager addressed the throng. 'This is just a rehearsal,' said Toshack. 'We are not going into the First Division just to make the numbers up.' Nevertheless, before the new season had even started, London bookmakers had installed Swansea City as favourites for relegation straight back to Division Two.

During the close season Wales played Iceland in a World Cup qualifier in Reykjavik. Swansea were represented by Leighton Phillips, David Giles and Leighton James. Giles scored one of the goals in a 4-0 victory but the return match at the Vetch Field sixteen months later would turn out to be entirely different for a number of reasons.

3

REACHING THE TOP

(August-October 1981)

John Toshack knew he would have to strengthen the side if they were to succeed in the First Division. His first foray in the transfer market took him to Goodison Park to pay £125,000 for England international striker Bob Latchford. Birmingham-born Latchford started his career as an apprentice at his home-town club in August 1968, and after 160 League games and 68 goals he joined Everton in February 1974. He had recorded almost a goal every two games with the Toffeemen, hitting 106 League goals in 236 appearances over seven years. Toshack had seen the burly striker at close quarters when he was at Anfield.

When Toshack signed Latchford it gave the 29-year-old the chance to revive a career that had ground to a halt. Hamstring injuries had dogged him in Everton colours. Not surprisingly, he had to pass a rigorous medical before signing the forms that made him a Swansea player. Latchford, who won the last of his twelve England caps in a 3-4 defeat in Austria in June 1979, made it clear that he had not abandoned hope of a recall to the international scene. 'I knew that if I could score goals they wouldn't be able to overlook me,' he said after joining the Swans.

With Latchford in the bag, Toshack went for his second purchase, but his offer of £25,000 to Wrexham for the current Wales international keeper Dai Davies was rejected by Robins manager Mel Sutton, a former team-mate of Toshack at Cardiff. Wrexham wanted a massive £150,000 for the keeper who had started his career at the Vetch before moving to Everton in December 1970. He had played six games on loan for the Swans in 1973-74, while with the Goodison Park club, before transferring to Wrexham. Davies had earned 44 caps with Everton (16) and Wrexham (28), so while the North Walians' valuation seemed high, the Swansea chief was definitely trying to get him cheap by offering just £20,000. As it happened, a Football League tribunal decided that Swansea should pay £45,000, which made Toshack far happier than Sutton. 'We must all abide by the decisions that are made in this respect,' said the delighted Swansea boss, who had expected to shell out at least £75,000 for his man.

After completing the signatures of the two internationals, Toshack made it clear that he was still looking to improve his squad, even hinting that he could blitz the transfer fee record of £175,000 which he set when bringing Alan Curtis back to the Vetch. 'I was quite happy to start the season off in the First Division with the staff of 26 that I already had at the club, but I wouldn't have hesitated to smash the record if the opportunity for the right player materialised.'

Record pre-season ticket sales had strengthened the Swans' ability to compete in the transfer market. Nearly 4,000 stand seasons and 5,000 field tickets had been sold. However, the figures being touted for transfer targets were higher than even the most ardent fan had expected.

Said Toshack: 'My assistant Phil Boersma, coach Doug Livermore and myself were all in the deep end together, as none of us had managed or coached at the top level. We knew how difficult it was going to be but the whole place was buzzing with expectation and we knew we had to enjoy the experience.' Boersma had replaced the unwell Terry Medwin, who had become chief scout, while Livermore was well known to many of the Swansea players as he was also the Wales international team trainer.

On a pre-season tour of Lancashire, Swansea beat Wigan 3-2 and Blackpool 4-2. There were no places for David Giles, John Mahoney or Brian Attley, who played for the reserves against Cardiff to boost their fitness, but they were included for the trip to Yugoslavia. Giles had injured an ankle playing for Wales against Czechoslovakia the previous November and had taken a long time to fully recover.

Before leaving for Sarajevo, Toshack had a £320,000 bid for defender Colin Irwin turned down by Liverpool. The Merseysiders were already on their pre-season tour in Zurich and it was from there that manager Bob Paisley blocked the sale, at any price. He regarded Irwin as a valuable squad member in Liverpool's attempt to retain their crown. Irwin had played just 27 first-team games for the Reds, as cover for Phil Thompson and Alan Hansen, though he appeared against West Ham in the 1981 Wembley League Cup final and the semi-final of the European Cup against Bayern Munich. He had been a junior at the club during Toshack's early days there. Toshack believed that Irwin partnering Ante Rajkovic would keep out most First Division attacks.

In the meanwhile, a move by the City Council to close the grandstand caused Chairman Struel, in Yugoslavia with the squad, a degree of bother. The row had blown up because the club had refused to pay compensation to residents in the Sandfields area of the city, who complained that the new grandstand blocked out the sun and allowed spectators climbing the steps to see into their houses.

On 16 August 1981, Toshack finally got his man. Liverpool agreed to an increased bid of £350,000 for Irwin who flew straight to Yugoslavia to join the touring party. He was allowed to leave Anfield, along with Ray Clemence and Jimmy Case, in order to help fund the £900,000 purchase of Mark Lawrenson from Brighton.

Irwin was pencilled in for the game against Velez Mostar. Swansea did not win a game on their short tour but it was a useful experience. There was just one friendly left – against Luton. Irwin signed his transfer form on the pitch, leaving the 6,500 crowd aghast that their club's record out-going transfer fee had been doubled in one fell swoop.

Leaving the Vetch was Dave Rushberry, who joined Bob Stokoe at Carlisle for £40,000 – £20,000 less than the Swans paid for him two years previously. Rushberry had made 71 appearances, but only twelve of them in the past season. Also off was Leighton Phillips, who joined Charlton for £25,000. The small fee reflected the service given by Phillips at the Vetch in over 100 first-team matches.

As the 29 August curtain-raiser against Leeds approached, the club and Post Office produced a special commemorative cover to mark the Swans' debut in the First Division. Toshack was upbeat about his side's chances: 'We were going into the unknown but we were ready for it. We had a strong squad containing no less than twelve internationals so we weren't afraid of anyone. We were an attacking side but we just needed to be a little more aware of the fact that we would be up against players better equipped to expose any weaknesses.'

Two days before the Leeds game Toshack swooped for yet another player with a Liverpool connection – 24-year-old Blackpool defender Max Thompson. Blackpool had been amongst the Division Two leaders when Thompson signed for them from the Merseysiders, but when they nose-dived down into Division Four he was understandably keen to get a new start elsewhere. He had been at Anfield at the same time as Toshack and Boersma and they held him in high regard. Thompson had played his only game in the Liverpool first team when he was just seventeen. The Swans paid £20,000 for the player, who signed a one-year deal, but there was a clause giving Blackpool an extra £20,000 when he had appeared in twenty first-team matches. At least Thompson was cheap by comparison to some of the other purchases.

The draw for the Cup-Winners' Cup paired Swansea with Locomotiv Leipzig, after the East Germans had beaten Politechnica Timisoara of Romania 5-2 on aggregate in a preliminary round. After losing the first leg 0-2, Locomotiv won 5-0 at home to progress.

Dai Davies would face Leeds, having passed a fitness test the previous evening in the reserves at Cardiff. This meant no place for the popular Dave Stewart, who had not missed a first-team game since joining the Swans in February 1980 from West Brom. Included in the Leeds line-up were two Welsh internationals, Brian Flynn, later to manage the Swans, and Neath-born Carl Harris.

Pinned up on the the Swans' dressing room notice board was a good-luck telegram from Toshack's mentor and former manager, Bill Shankly. The teams emerged onto the lush Vetch Field turf to a tumultuous welcome from 23,489 spectators. They didn't have long to wait, as Jeremy Charles netted Swansea's first goal in the First Division after just five minutes. Latchford dummied a cross and the ball ran to Charles, who wrong-footed Leeds keeper John Lukic. Leeds were level midway through the first period when Scottish international Derek Parlane headed home a Harris centre.

Immediately after the break, Swansea took over, with Latchford striking a hat-trick inside ten minutes. Charles nodded down a Robbie James centre for the former Everton man to lash in the first. He then tapped in at the near post, and claimed the match ball with an unstoppable header from a free-kick by Leighton James. But the best was yet to come. Curtis ghosted past Trevor Cherry before uncorking a fierce shot that swerved high into the net at the near post. Flynn had worked hard for the losers, as had Harris, but little was seen of £930,000 signing Peter Barnes, who was making his Leeds debut.

'That 5-1 scoreline was beyond our wildest dreams,' said Curtis, looking back at a staggering result that launched Swansea into the First Division. Toshack was proud of the way his side had disposed of their visitors, who had finished the previous season ninth: 'We were unstoppable in the second half. Two saves by Dai Davies probably won us the game but after that hat-trick it was goodnight and the game was over.'

Leeds boss Allan Clarke was lost for words and could only blurt out 'I have nothing to say – the result speaks for itself.' For Leeds it was the start of a hard season that would end in relegation.

Struel was calculating in his assessment. He still expected it to take a couple of months before settling down in this 'highly exalted' division. He considered it a nice start, but amid all the euphoria an air of realism was still required.

The afternoon was somewhat marred when visiting fans hurled missiles onto the pitch in their disgust. A bottle smashed just behind Lukic's goal and a cordon of thirty policemen formed a barrier between the goalkeeper and his own supporters. Handlers moved into the offending area with their dogs to bring the disturbance under control. The Swansea City club had done everything possible to ensure supporters' safety and no blame was attached to them. The incident was not reported to the Football League and no further action was taken.

That opening game in the top flight produced record club receipts of £32,181, not including season tickets, which then stood at £650,000.

Not surprisingly, Toshack kept the same side for the visit two days later to Brighton, who had just drawn at West Ham. Two goals in the first quarter of an hour set the Swans on their way. Thereafter the defence was given a severe examination by the home side in a 'no-holds barred' meeting, but the Swans held on to win 2-1. The luck had been with them when Curtis cut inside and his shot was deflected by Brighton centre-half Steve Foster to Leighton James, who shot into the corner of the net. Four minutes later Charles headed on Leighton James's corner to Latchford at the far post. The Swansea defence were caught square before the interval, allowing Andy Ritchie to reduce the deficit from Irish international Gerard Ryan's free-kick. In the second half, Robinson and Rajkovic were booked, along with Brighton's Tony Grealish, Mick Robinson and Ryan. Leighton James was taken off and an extra defender, Brian Attley, went on to help out the defence.

Two days later the Wales squad to visit Czechoslovakia in a World Cup qualifier was announced. Although four Swans were included, there was no place for David Giles. 'Obviously I was very disappointed to miss out, particularly as I scored the winner the last time we played the Czechs. Not being in the Swansea side had cost me my place. Every player dreams about playing in the First Division and I was no different so I just had to get my head down and work even harder. If you are not in your club side it is always very difficult to be considered for international duty.' Giles's performances for club and country had seen him hailed as another Kevin Keegan, and this was the first time he had failed to make the squad of sixteen since Mike England had become manager.

After light training at home, the Swans travelled to West Brom. With four players in the Welsh party for Prague – Davies, Leighton James, Charles and Curtis – Toshack was anxious that thoughts of international duty would be put to one side. He made it clear that the best boost for Welsh chances would be a Swansea victory over Albion. Such a result was sure to lift confidence in Prague.

For the third match running the same starting eleven was named, with former Cardiff full-back Attley once again the single substitute. Toshack had watched Albion's 0-2 home loss to Arsenal, but he was aware that they would play better this time. They boasted Cyrille Regis, Gary Owen and David Mills up front, and in midfield was young Bryan Robson, who would soon sign for Manchester United for £1.5 million.

Albion boss Ronnie Allen reckoned the Arsenal defeat was the worst performance in his thirty years at the Hawthorns, but they were delighted with the news that Regis had been pronounced fit to make his first appearance of the season.

The Swans never knew what hit them, although it turned out to be a man called Regis. His hat-trick gave Swansea and manager Toshack a stern reminder of how mistakes are punished at the highest level. It was only 0-1 at half-time after Remi Moses slipped a pass into the path of the unmarked Regis. Midway through the second half Regis outjumped Irwin, scampered after the loose ball, and fired in a second. Within a further five minutes Steve Mackenzie had scored the third and Regis completed his hat-trick. Robinson's thirty-yard piledriver was too late to mount a recovery.

The unfortunate Charles was injured and had been replaced at half-time by Robinson, who switched to midfield, allowing Attley to take over at full-back. The injury would cost Charles his place in the Wales squad. The Swansea defence would also be without him for some time after he was diagnosed with a torn thigh muscle.

The home midweek reserve game against Nottingham Forest suddenly took on a new meaning as a number of defenders looked to stake their claims. Although the Swans were the highest scorers in the division with eight goals from three matches, the defence would have to be sorted before Notts County arrived.

In Prague, a freak own-goal by Davies helped switch out the lights on Welsh hopes of qualification. After keeping a clean sheet in four successive internationals, the Swansea keeper let in an unusual goal. From Panenka's free-kick, Byron Stevenson diverted the ball against a post and the luckless Davies knocked the rebound into his own net. Later, Robbie James replaced Mickey Thomas, to make it four Swans on the field, but the Czechs scored again for a 2-0 win.

Back at the Vetch, Max Thompson received the call to strengthen the rearguard. All four Swans in action at the Rosicky Stadium reported back unscathed, but their week-long absence had done little to help preparation for a match against a side joint top of the table.

The match against County saw a section of home supporters jeer Davies every time he touched the ball. Whether it was because of his performance in Prague, or a couple of mistakes against County, he was given a hard time. Fortunately a late error did not cost any points. He came out of his area to head the ball clear but missed it completely. Iain McCulloch walked the loose ball into the net. With the Swans leading 3-1 at the time, it didn't prove costly.

'The crowd never bothered me,' said Davies. 'When I made my debut against Leeds there was some jeering but they pay their money and make their choice.' Toshack was disgusted with the small minority that picked on Davies. 'You don't barrack your own players. Some of the shouts out there made me sick. I wouldn't want to think what they would be like if we were bottom of the League.'

County had been outclassed for much of the game. Curtis gave the Swans the lead with a close-range shot, and Leighton James added a second before the interval. Latchford made it three with his fifth strike of the season before Ray O'Brien pulled one back. Davies' error then made it a tense last five minutes.

Following a 0-1 home defeat in the Cup-Winners' Cup by Leipzig, the Swans were on their way to Old Trafford for one of those fixtures that make playing in the top division so worthwhile. Toshack gave Davies a vote of confidence for this first visit to United in 44 years, but the Welsh speaker who hailed from Glanamman was having a hard time trying to convince fans that he was as reliable as Dave Stewart. Nigel Stevenson and David Giles also travelled, along with Max Thompson, but Charles was still out with his damaged thigh muscle and Leighton James was also now on the treatment table after being injured against Leipzig.

United's £1.2 million striker Gary Birtles had yet to start repaying that massive outlay, failing to score in his first 29 games. They had started the season poorly and were bottom of the division, without a win and with just two points.

Toshack knew his team was being stretched and was keen to see how they would react to the pressure. 'By the end of October the new players would have had enough time to settle in and we would have found out just how good our squad really was. We knew that we wouldn't keep any players we felt were not good enough to play at this level.'

In the event, the game brought United's first win and Birtles his first goal. Frank Stapleton chested a pass from Ray Wilkins into Birtles' path and he flashed a 25-yard shot inside the post. Swansea felt hard done by, as only a superb stop by Gary Bailey denied Robbie James a second-half equaliser. Giles, on as a replacement for Latchford, might also have won a penalty when brought down by Arthur Albiston as he was about to slide home a pass from Hadziabdic. Later on, Giles headed wide from Ante Rajkovic's cross: 'I knew straight away that I should have scored,' said Giles, 'and deep down I knew my days at the Vetch were probably numbered. Tosh had a saying – "the posts don't move" – and that is all he said to me when we reached the dressing room after the match.'

It was a surprise that United had made such a poor start because they still had players of the calibre of Steve Coppell, Martin Buchan, Gordon McQueen, Sammy McIlroy and Lou Macari, who were all in the eleven that played against the Swans. The Reds would eventually pick themselves up to finish in third place.

(19 September '81)	P	W	D	L	F	A	Pts
1 Ipswich	5	3	2	0	12	6	11
2 West Ham	5	3	2	0	10	3	11
3 Southampton	5	3	1	1	9	4	10
4 SWANSEA	5	3	0	2	11	9	9
5 Tottenham	5	3	0	2	8	8	9

Ugo Valerio was a prime mover in forming the 'Friends of Swansea City' when the club reached the top divisions. They organised trips to away matches and Ugo remembers that defeat: 'We ran trips to every match but the visit to Old Trafford was somehow very special. There were 5,000 Swans fans behind the goal and we out-sang the home supporters all afternoon. Unfortunately, the Birtles goal did spoil it a little but the knowledge that we were up there playing sides like that on a regular basis meant that we quickly put the result to one side and started looking forward to the next match.'

FA Cup holders Spurs were due in midweek. They weren't the force of a few years earlier but could still boast Argentinian World Cup stars Ardiles and Villa, plus Glenn Hoddle and Steve Archibald. It was Hoddle's penalty against QPR which won the Cup after a replay in May, and eight of the Wembley winners would be in the starting line-up at the Vetch. Spurs had just won 3-1 in a first-leg Cup-Winners' Cup-tie at Ajax of Amsterdam and were no strangers to the Swans, who had beaten them in two of their last three meetings. As these were in a two-leg League Cup-tie and a pre-season friendly, it counted for little.

Charles, Leighton James and Latchford all needed late fitness tests. A thigh strain worried Robbie James and John Mahoney had a sore Achilles. In the event, all were passed fit, and the only change from Old Trafford was Leighton James back in place of Attley.

The West Terrace was made available for home supporters, while Tottenham's were accommodated in the enclosure. Spurs arrived with a 100 per cent away record, but Robbie James broke the deadlock on the hour, volleying in Latchford's cross. Hoddle levelled from the spot three minutes later, after Robinson had brought down Tony Galvin, but Curtis scored a vintage winner, secured by Davies' thrilling late tip-over from Falco.

Toshack was still anxious to sign Gary Stanley from Everton for a fee of £150,000. The player travelled down to watch the Tottenham game and look around the area but asked for time to think things over: 'I had lived in big cities such as London and Liverpool all my life so I wasn't sure how I would take a move to a smaller place like Swansea.'

On 28 September, Stanley signed, taking Swansea's spending spree to a staggering £650,000. He was born in Burton in March 1954 and became an apprentice at Chelsea in 1971 on his seventeenth birthday. After playing in 109 League matches and scoring fifteen goals, he joined Everton in August 1979 and spent two seasons at Goodison, appearing in another 52 League matches.

Chairman Struel stressed there was no danger of the club over-reaching themselves. 'Ever since we climbed out of the Fourth Division people have been saying that the bubble is going to burst. Well it hasn't burst yet and it's not going to.' He also confirmed the club had spent £2 million during 1980 and 1981. £1 million had gone on the ground and another £1 million on players. 'We have assembled a talented squad of players and the public are prepared to support what we are doing at this club. We are very careful to ensure that we operate within a financial orbit that we can afford.' Those words would come to haunt Struel in the coming months, because Stanley's fee would have a profound effect on Swansea's place in the First Division.

Keen to preserve their 100 per cent home record, Swansea entertained lowly Sunderland. Charles in place of Thompson was the only change from the side that beat Spurs. Charles was celebrating his 22nd birthday and almost crowned it with a goal, but Sunderland keeper Barry Siddall dived to save his firm header. After a poor first half Toshack gave his side a dressing-down during the interval.

The Swans took the lead ten minutes after the re-start. Shaun Elliott cleared a Latchford header to Curtis, who nodded the ball beyond the keeper. The fifth straight home win of the season was settled by a late Leighton James penalty.

A midweek trip to Leipzig followed, but despite a Charles goal, the Swans bowed out of the Cup-Winners' Cup 1-3 on aggregate.

It was an emotional week for football, as Bill Shankly, founder of the great Liverpool side and mentor to John Toshack, passed away. Toshack had been in touch with Shankly continually since taking over at the Vetch Field, and sought advice from the great man whenever he looked to sign a new player. As fate would have it, Anfield's first match after Shankly's death would be the visit of Swansea on 3 October 1981.

Grown men were reduced to tears as the stadium filled for what had almost become a memorial. The teams lined up for a minute's silence and Toshack even wore a Liverpool shirt out of respect for the man who had taught him so much.

The television cameras and Anfield's second largest crowd of the season (it was only surpassed by the Merseyside derby against Everton) were present for a game worthy of the great man. Toshack made one change in the starting line-up, preferring the defensive qualities of Thompson to the all-round play of Charles. Liverpool fielded an all-international eleven and, with Eire international Kevin Sheedy on the bench, that made a full set of capped players for Bob Paisley's side. However, he was without the influential but suspended Ray Kennedy.

It was a match full of tension, with five players booked, the last of which was Davies, who bizarrely barged Terry McDermott into the net after the second Liverpool penalty, and home fans bayed for him to be sent off.

The Swans shocked the Kop by taking a fifteenth-minute lead. Phil Thompson brought down Robinson and referee Challinor pointed to the spot. The Kop tried, and failed, to put Leighton James off. In the second half the First Division upstarts went further ahead. Thompson dallied and Latchford nipped in to beat Grobbelaar.

Just as Swansea were scenting victory they had it snatched away with two penalty decisions inside four minutes. Robinson brought down McDermott for the first, and Davies upended McDermott for the second, despite the Liverpool player running away from goal. On both occasions McDermott rifled his spot-kicks into the net. The Swans had to be content with a point from a 2-2 draw. It felt like two points dropped (this was the first season when three points were awarded for a win), especially as Liverpool at that time were down in thirteenth, although they would recover with a vengeance.

It was an emotional day for Toshack, who strolled over to the Kop at the end to receive a rousing ovation from fans who remembered the contribution he had made to their club.

Two days later Toshack slapped five players on the transfer list – Tommy Craig and David Giles, who between them had cost £220,000, Brian Attley, Nigel Stevenson and Wyndham Evans. According to the manager, it was one of the hardest and most difficult parts of the job to make decisions like that. 'But you cannot let sentiment and loyalty stand in the way of progress. Some of these players had helped get us up to the First Division but they had gone as far as they could go.'

Swansea then went to Oakwell for the first leg of their Milk Cup-tie against mid-table Second Division Barnsley, who were not thought likely to prevent the Swans' march to the next round. Toshack brought in eighteen-year-old Dudley Lewis and young full-back Chris Marustik for their first starts of the season. Stanley replaced Robbie James in midfield.

The rain-soaked turf proved a leveller. Two minutes after the interval, Glyn Riley, a real handful in the first half, beat Davies with a header from a Derrick Parker cross. Marustik was booked for throwing the ball at the referee after a decision went against him, and from the ensuing free-kick Swansea fell further behind – to centre-half Ian Evans' firm header (Evans would briefly become Swansea's manager during 1989-90.)

There were three League games before the second leg on 27 October. Injuries denied Toshack the use of Thompson, Charles and Hadziabdic, so transfer-listed Stevenson was pulled from the reserves at Swindon, along with Marustik. There was an explosive start. Robbie James was booked in the third minute for a foul on Ray McHale, who presumably held no grudges because he joined the Swans a few seasons later. A linesman was then struck by a firework thrown from the terraces. After treatment for a chest burn, the official was able to continue. Barnsley manager Norman Hunter, the former Leeds and England wing-half, appealed to his fans for calm, as the missile had come from the away section.

Swansea took the lead against the run of play. Evans tripped Curtis, and Leighton James converted the penalty. The Tykes equalised straight after half-time, when Parker's low drive was parried into the net by Davies. Irwin scored his first goal for Swansea to restore the lead, and Curtis levelled the tie at 3-3 on aggregate when heading in Stanley's cross. Seven minutes from the end of extra-time Neil Cooper restored Barnsley's advantage. There was still time for Robinson and Barnsley's Winston Campbell to be dismissed for fighting, to round off an explosive encounter that had also seen eight bookings.

The Swansea players were summoned to a crisis meeting at the Vetch the following day. 'Some unacceptable stuff went on in that match that didn't impress me at all,' said a concerned Toshack. 'It's all very well for my players to say they were frustrated but if anyone was entitled to feel frustrated it was me. I did not want to be associated with what I had seen in the second period of extra-time. It's no good for my players to say they didn't think – they are paid to think.'

Swansea were out of the Milk Cup, but being in the First Division meant playing big games almost every week. Having faced Manchester United, Tottenham and Liverpool in three of their previous four League encounters, another giant, Arsenal, were next up.

The Gunners had had an indifferent start and were well down the table, yet they boasted a number of top quality players. These included Irishmen Pat Jennings in goal and David O'Leary at centre-half, Brian Talbot and John Hollins (later to become Swansea manager) in midfield, and Alan Sunderland and Charlie Nicholas up front. Toshack reverted to the side that performed so well at Anfield for Arsenal's first ever visit to the Vetch Field on 10 October 1981.

The visitors might have had an early penalty when Thompson tangled with Willie Young after an Arsenal corner. Fortunately for Swansea, the decision went against Young. The opening goal came when Leighton James half-volleyed past Jennings. Arsenal thought they had equalised through young John Hawley, but the referee had spotted a handball. Charles replaced Latchford as Swansea looked to close the game down, which became easier when Thompson met a Hadziabdic free-kick on the volley to send a screamer into the Arsenal net. The win sent Swansea up to second place.

Wales manager Mike England was an interested onlooker, as no fewer than seven Swans had been included in the Wales squad to meet Iceland the following week. A surprise inclusion amongst the seven was midfield battler John Mahoney who had won the last of his 47 caps against Turkey in Izmir back in 1979.

A week later the Swans turned out at Stoke, who languished near the bottom of the table. Teenager Paul Bracewell was the home side's playmaker, while up front they had the hard-running Lee Chapman. It was understandable that Toshack kept the same side. Gary Stanley – unused in the League since his arrival from Everton – was selected at last, albeit at No 12.

The Potters, with only three wins under their belts, shocked the visiting fans by taking a first-half lead via Peter Griffiths, after a corner was headed on by Irish international Brendan O'Callaghan. It was not until midway through the second half that Swansea levelled, courtesy of substitute Stanley, on for Leighton James. Stanley then sent over a free-kick that was headed in by Latchford. The 2-1 victory sent the Swans to the top of the League. It was the first occasion any Welsh club had topped the First Division for almost sixty years.

(17 October '81)	P	W	D	L	F	A	Pts
1 SWANSEA	10	7	1	2	21	13	22
2 Tottenham	10	7	0	3	17	10	21
3 Man United	12	5	5	2	14	6	20
4 Ipswich	10	6	2	2	20	13	20
5 Nott'm For	10	5	3	2	14	12	18
6 West Ham	10	4	5	1	20	12	17

Just six years after finishing in 90th position, third from bottom of Division Four, Swansea City were in first place, having reached the very top of the tree. Whether they had the resources and ability to stay there was another matter entirely.

Swansea's position looking down on everyone else lasted just seven days, because they failed to do themselves justice at mid-table Coventry in their next match. Stanley slotted in at full-back in place of the injured Hadziabdic, and it was he who gifted the Sky Blues a goal in the 36th minute. Steve Whitton sneaked behind him at Brian Roberts' free-kick to whip over a cross to Mark Hateley. Two minutes later another free-kick wrought havoc in the Swans' defence, and Rudi Kaiser's downward header just had enough to beat Davies' attempt to push it away. Hateley made it 3-0 in the 52nd minute, although the Swans grabbed a goal when Curtis netted from a Leighton James cross.

Toshack put a positive gloss on the result: 'There were no shock waves in Swansea just because we had gone from first to third place.' Stoke boss Richie Barker, on the other hand, believed the Swans could give the top sides a run for their money and even emulate Brian Clough's Nottingham Forest team that won the 1977-78 title in their first season after winning promotion: 'Forest didn't blow up when they were in a similar position and there was no reason to believe that Swansea's start was just a flash in the pan,' he said.

There was good news for Toshack when Charles was discharged from hospital after an exploratory operation disclosed nothing seriously wrong with the knee that had troubled him all summer. At least it wasn't the cartilage trouble he had been dreading. He was cleared to resume training, but would not be fit for the next couple of games. It also meant that he missed out on selection for the Wales squad travelling to Tbilisi to play the Soviet Union. Charles joined the other casualties, hamstring-victim Hadziabdic, and Thompson – who damaged knee ligaments in the defeat at Coventry – in a run-out for the reserves.

The Highfield Road setback was followed by Barnsley knocking the Swans out of the Milk Cup, but the usual platitudes of 'concentrating on the League' seemed to appease most supporters.

Next up at the Vetch, on 31 October, were Wolverhampton, who were having a terrible time in the League and occupied 21st place. They had only managed two wins in their eleven starts and had failed to score in seven of those games, including the last four. Toshack omitted Robinson from the starting eleven, using Stanley and Brian Attley as the full-backs, while Giles earned a seat on the bench.

Wolves defended stoutly, with George Berry keen to show watching Wales manager Mike England that he deserved a place against the Soviet Union. There were few glimpses of the form that had taken Swansea to the top. Berry had a fine game, making one acrobatic clearance following a Stanley corner. For Swansea it was another two points dropped.

4

PUTTING DOWN A MARKER

(November 1981 – May 1982)

Entering November 1981 in fourth place, Swansea were still surprising all the pundits who had reckoned that they were heading for the drop.

Brian Attley was the only one to lose his place for the trip to Ipswich. Bobby Robson's side were up to second, and had young central defenders Russell Osman and Terry Butcher hoping for international honours. England manager Ron Greenwood was in the crowd to see Alan Curtis net from a Bob Latchford cut-back after seven minutes. Paul Mariner equalised when he headed in a cross from Arnold Muhren. Back came the Swans with a solo effort from Latchford, only for Dutch international Muhren to make it 2-2. Two minutes from the final whistle Gary Stanley restored Swansea's lead.

Lifelong Swansea fan Ugo Valerio reckons that victory was one of the Swans' best all season, though he remembers the occasion for other reasons as well: 'Even the home supporters said that we were the best side they had seen. We had arranged for two "Friends of Swansea City" coaches to travel to Ipswich overnight, and of course a lot of fans made their own way by car. One of the coaches stopped in Colchester early on the Saturday morning and we all got off to have a look around the shops and local hostelries. The people were very friendly but we hadn't been off the bus very long when the police arrived and told us that we couldn't stay in Colchester. We had to quickly round up everyone and move on, even though we were just the one coachload. The other bus went direct to Ipswich and stopped at a plush hotel. Some of them staged a mock wedding for fans travelling to the game. Everyone dressed up and a good time was had by all. That weekend we were on television as ITV showed brief highlights of our win. In those days we travelled away expecting to win every game no matter who our opponents were.'

The visit to Manchester City brought the heaviest defeat of the season – 0-4. A fit Dzemal Hadziabdic was preferred to Neil Robinson, but that was the only change. Kevin Reeves (later to be assistant manager under Brian Flynn at the Vetch) almost netted straight from the kick-off. John Bond's side went ahead from the spot when Bobby McDonald went down in the area. £1.25-million man Reeves grabbed two goals, and Tueart added to his penalty with five minutes left.

Brighton were due at the Vetch on the Tuesday. Max Thompson came in for Nigel Stevenson as the only change, while Jeremy Charles was fit

enough to resume on the bench. He replaced Ante Rajkovic but made little difference and for the second match running the Swans failed to score.
One disappointment to Toshack was the low turnout, with only 14,459 in
the ground when play started. However, the point earned did move the
Swans back up to third.

(24 November '81)	P	W	D	L	F	A	Pts
1 Man United	16	8	5	3	24	12	29
2 Tottenham	14	9	0	5	23	15	27
3 SWANSEA	15	8	3	4	25	22	27
4 Ipswich	14	8	2	4	25	19	26

Long-serving defender Wyndham Evans was offered the chance of
joining Newport but his ambition to play at the top level persuaded him
to stay: 'I still had hopes of playing in Division One and if I had gone to
County, even on loan, it would have been the beginning of the end for
me.' His contract had until July 1982 to run, so there was plenty of time
to impress the manager and earn an extension. Evans was one of four
Swans to have appeared during each of the four seasons in which the
club had leapt from the Fourth to the First Division. The others were
Robbie James, Charles, and Toshack.

Tommy Craig also rejected offers to rekindle his career back in
Scotland, at Dundee or Partick Thistle, but while Evans and Craig decid-
ed to stay, David Giles agreed to a loan move to Orient. Brian Attley and
Stevenson remained on the transfer list.

A 1-0 home win over a Birmingham side including Alan Curbishley,
Wales international Pat van den Hauwe, Frank Worthington and Archie
Gemmill was earned by Robbie James's second-half strike. The game had
been put back to the evening, as Swansea RFC were entertaining the touring Australians at St Helen's on the Saturday afternoon. They were beat-
en 3-12 by the Wallabies.

Round two of the Welsh Cup was next on the agenda. Toshack dear-
ly wanted another crack at European football and it was a strong side that
travelled to Stafford Rangers on 2 December, winning 4-0 in front of
3,077 spectators, thanks to goals from Latchford, Curtis, Thompson and
an own-goal.

Back in the League, the Swans lost 1-3 at Everton, with Latchford netting against his former club. It then became two defeats in a row when
Nottingham Forest won 2-1 at the Vetch. The previous day had seen the
coldest night in Britain since 1881 and the Arctic air brought snow to
much of the country. Swansea's game was one of the few to survive.

Robbie James's first-half goal had given his side a great chance to take advantage of so many postponements and move back to the top of the division. With twelve minutes remaining, debutant Willie Young headed a corner inside the near post. Young had recently joined Brian Clough's men after a £170,000 move from Arsenal, and had been in the Gunners' side beaten at the Vetch in October. The game was lost in the dying seconds when Robinson needlessly handled and John Robertson lashed in the spot-kick. With hindsight, home fans probably wished that their game, too, had been postponed.

Aston Villa arrived in south-west Wales on the back of two defeats. Toshack restored Stanley and Stevenson in place of Robinson and the injured Colin Irwin. The attendance was almost 2,500 down on the Forest game, but those who came saw Robbie James fire a twelfth-minute goal which was immediately cancelled out when Thompson sliced the ball past Dai Davies into his own net. Fortunately, James cracked in his second to complete the scoring and Jimmy Rimmer made some fine saves on the ground he would one day call his own. The result put the Swans on top of the First Division for a second time.

(15 December '81)		W	D	L	F	A	Pts
1 SWANSEA	19	10	3	6	30	28	33
2 Man United	18	9	5	4	28	15	32
3 Ipswich	16	10	2	4	28	19	32
4 Southampton	18	9	3	6	32	27	30
5 Tottenham	17	9	2	6	26	19	29
6 Nott'm For	18	8	5	5	23	23	29

There was some light relief with the tie against Worcester City in the Welsh Cup. In 1978-79 Worcester beat Cardiff 3-2 before losing 0-2 in the semi-final to Shrewsbury. In the quest for European football the non-leaguers were blitzed 6-0, with Robbie James claiming a hat-trick. Stanley, Attley, and Leighton James netted the others in front of nearly 5,000 spectators.

Over the Christmas period, Giles was recalled from his loan spell with Orient and was eager to press his first-team claims: 'I had enjoyed my spell at Brisbane Road and scored a couple of goals and it certainly helped me get my confidence back.' As Giles returned, Tommy Craig joined Carlisle on a free transfer, helping them win promotion from the Third Division that same season.

The final League match of 1981 was at the Dell. Southampton were bristling with star players. England internationals Kevin Keegan, Mick

Channon and Alan Ball all plied their trade for Lawrie McMenemy's team, and average home crowds were 22,000.

Hadziabdic and Irwin came back in place of Chris Marustik and Stevenson. David Armstrong, also an England international, quickly put the Saints ahead but Rajkovic squared it with his first Swans goal. Keegan struck twice early in the second period so it was a sad way to end a year in which Swansea City FC had achieved so much.

Following their 2-2 draw at Anfield in the League, Swans supporters keenly awaited taking on the Reds at the Vetch Field in the FA Cup third round on 2 January 1982. Hadziabdic was dropped for the first time since signing eighteen months earlier and Thompson was relegated to the substitutes' bench. Stevenson and Marustik lined up from the start. Swans were 'favourites' as they were nine points better off than opponents who Toshack had modelled his side upon. Curiously, both teams changed their skipper, with Rajkovic taking over from Irwin and Graeme Souness replacing Phil Thompson.

Before kick-off Toshack was presented with a crystal decanter from Struel. The gift, on behalf of the club directors, was in recognition of the manager's award of an MBE in the New Year's Honours.

Sadly, the match itself was a 'no contest'. Liverpool were in command throughout, despite the waterlogged conditions. Goals from Ian Rush (two) and future *Match of the Day* pundits Alan Hansen and Mark Lawrenson gave the Merseysiders a 4-0 victory to knock Swansea out of the Cup at the first stage for the second year running. The danger signs were flashing, as that Cup defeat made it four losses from the last five games, excluding the Welsh Cup-tie, and that was a recipe for disaster.

Leeds had a score to settle with the Swans after being humiliated on the opening day. The match at Elland Road was in doubt because snow covered the country, putting training at the Vetch on stop. It was the difficult travelling conditions that caused the uncertainty, not Leeds' pitch, which had undersoil heating. The Swansea travelling party did not receive the go-ahead until late morning on the Friday. Because of the blanketed roads, the players faced an eight-hour train journey via Paddington and Kings Cross, arriving in Leeds at 7.15pm. Robinson and Hadziabdic were added to the twelve on duty against Liverpool in the Cup.

Only 18,709, Leeds' lowest crowd of the season to date, saw the home side win 2-0. Wales international Byron Stevenson scored one as Leeds maintained the only unbeaten home record in the division. After the match Toshack slammed the dreadful conditions: 'I knew they spent £2,000 operating the undersoil heating but it didn't seem to have any effect on the pitch.'

Absent from the Leeds line-up that day was Brian Flynn, transfer listed by Allan Clarke. There was talk that Flynn would join Swansea for £200,000, but assistant manager Phil Boersma rebuffed that idea: 'We just haven't got the money at the moment,' he said. Toshack's only glint of a change in fortune came with the news that the versatile Charles was nearing match fitness.

On 19 January, Toshack was presented with the *Western Mail* Sports Personality of the Year award on behalf of the club. None other than Ivor Allchurch – at that time Wales' most capped player – made the presentation. It was only the fourth time in 28 years that association football had scooped Welsh sports top accolade, which had also been won by Allchurch himself back in 1962.

The Swans were offered a few days in Malta to celebrate the opening of a new £4 million national stadium, which boasted the only grass pitch on the island. They were to play top Dutch side Twente Enschede. The schedule meant travelling out on 21 January and returning five days later. It was an honour to be invited, even though it was mainly a PR exercise. Unfortunately, the clearance and guarantees requested from the Maltese FA never materialised and the trip was called off.

Irrespective of that offer, Toshack had already arranged a five-day break in Spain for the end of January. He had always insisted on a mid-winter sun-break for the players. Before heading off, however, there was the small matter of hosting Manchester United on 30 January. Toshack demanded more effort from his players, in particular front-runners Curtis and Leighton James. Swansea had one of the best home records in the division but in the previous five matches at the Vetch they had only scored four goals – all by Robbie James.

While the weather prevented any training or playing, Toshack took the opportunity of assessing his staff and concluded that some of them were not up to First Division standard. This was a fair assumption because when five players went on the list earlier in the season there had been few enquiries from other clubs. He also knew that his team had to get back on the rails against the star-studded outfit managed by Ron Atkinson. As the players had been fairly inactive, three reserve games were arranged to give everyone much-needed match practice.

But Toshack had another trick up his sleeve. Just a few days before meeting United he signed Ray Kennedy from Liverpool for £160,000. The former Arsenal and England midfielder's arrival gave everyone a boost and Toshack was delighted that he had persuaded him to join the club. Kennedy made his debut in place of Mahoney as the only change from the side beaten by Leeds.

More than 200 police officers were drafted in to help cope with the influx of United fans. A 'special' train and between 20-30 coaches were expected to boost the crowd to near capacity. Shopkeepers in the area continued their policy of closing their doors during the time that spectators were exiting the ground.

Kennedy gave a masterful performance to convince the 23,900 crowd – Swansea's biggest of the season – that he was worth the huge layout. United had been top of the League when they arrived at the Vetch but they left well beaten. Two quick-fire second-half goals from Curtis and Robbie James sealed the victory, although Atkinson thought the Swans were lucky. 'The first goal was so offside that my players were staggered when it was awarded,' he moaned.

That strike, by Curtis, saw him chase Thompson's long ball before firing past Gary Bailey. The second was made by substitute Leighton James, whose low cross was pounced upon by Robbie James.

Following the short trip to Spain, Brian Attley became the first of the 'unwanted' players to go. He joined Second Division Derby for £25,000, having been at the Vetch for three years since signing from Cardiff.

The first-team players flew straight to Nottingham from Spain to prepare to take on high-flying Notts County and secure their first away win in three months. The hero at Meadow Lane was the much-maligned Dai Davies. Many fans still blamed him for ousting the popular Dave Stewart and he had found it hard to be accepted by the rank and file supporter. Against County, however, he was unbeatable, particularly in the second half when the home side piled forward. Swansea had taken an early lead when Curtis was brought down in the box. Leighton James, a late replacement for Latchford – who had a slight Achilles tendon strain – netted the penalty.

The Swans next took on Colwyn Bay for a fifth-round Welsh Cup-tie. It was the first time in thirty years that a non-league club from north Wales had met a First Division giant in a competitive game. The Welsh League (North) champions caused embarrassment by holding Swansea to a 2-2 draw. Schoolteacher Paul Phillips scored twice for Bay, with Stanley equalising the first, and Irwin saving home blushes.

Bottom club Middlesbrough were finding life in the First Division very difficult. In fact they hadn't scored a goal in the last four matches. One of Boro's lowest League gates of the season, 11,209, were treated to a dire match in which both sides were abysmally poor. Toshack was scathing about his side's performance. 'We had never played that badly in any of the other matches in the First Division and we were lucky to come away from Middlesbrough with a point,' he reckoned.

Swansea had gone ahead through Ray Kennedy's header, but Tony McAndrew levelled from the penalty spot after Stanley had hauled down David Hodgson.

There was a buzz around Swansea preceding the visit of Liverpool in midweek. After treatment Rajkovic was pronounced fit to start but Latchford and Mahoney were still out injured. Thompson for Hadziabdic was the only change from the side on duty at Ayresome Park. Swansea had taken a battering from Liverpool just six weeks previously in the Cup but memories of that defeat were soon put aside.

Leighton James celebrated his 29th birthday with a super show, climaxed by a brilliant strike against the European champions. With just sixteen minutes left, Alan Hansen fouled Curtis thirty yards out. James took a long run and hammered the free-kick through the 'wall' and beyond Bruce Grobbelaar. Curtis clinched the points with one of his speciality swerving runs that took him beyond four defenders before shooting low and hard. It was his 100th goal for the Swans in 323 outings.

The result proved to any remaining doubters that Swansea's lofty position in the First Division was justified.

(16 February '82)	P	W	D	L	F	A	Pts
1 Southampton	26	14	5	7	47	37	47
2 Man United	24	13	6	5	38	19	45
3 Arsenal	24	13	5	6	22	16	44
4 SWANSEA	25	13	4	8	37	34	43
5 Man City	25	12	6	7	40	28	42
6 Ipswich	21	13	2	6	41	32	41

Thompson had received a two-match ban for reaching twenty penalty points and his replacement at Sunderland was Stevenson, who had come off the transfer list. It was yet another match against a side fighting for their lives at the wrong end of the table. The Swans should have won by a greater margin than 1-0 but they had to rely on yet another Leighton James rocket to secure all three points. Little was seen of Ally McCoist, who was leading the Sunderland attack. James also hit a post in front of a poor Roker Park crowd, but that didn't prevent two home fans from running onto the pitch just before half-time to protest in front of the directors' box. The game was delayed for three minutes while they were escorted off.

Four days later David Giles signed for Crystal Palace, with Ian Walsh coming to the Vetch in straight exchange. Walsh hailed from St David's in Dyfed. The current Wales international, with seven goals in his twelve appearances, said: 'I had known David well from our times in the Wales side but it was a strange deal with two current Wales internationals swapping clubs. I was very happy at coming back to Wales and to be back in the First Division made it even better.'

Giles had given good service to Swansea City but, having found himself with few opportunities, he jumped at the chance of regular first-team football with Palace in the Second Division.

The Swansea injured list was still causing concern because four internationals – Mahoney, Latchford, Charles and Hadziabdic – were all unfit for the trip to Highbury. Despite that, the Swans could still field a side with seven full and two Under-21 internationals. Walsh was substitute, while former team-mates from his Palace days – Peter Nicholas and Kenny Sansom – lined up for Arsenal.

It was a fairytale return for former Gunner Kennedy, eight years since he last played in Arsenal colours. Nicholas slipped up at the near post and Kennedy pounced. Walsh joined the action at half-time in place of the injured Leighton James. Curtis struck a post and was then brought down on the edge of the area by David O'Leary. Despite Arsenal protests, a penalty was awarded and Robbie James sent George Wood the wrong way to complete a famous Swans double over Arsenal.

Colin Jones has been a Swansea supporter ever since making his way to the Vetch in 1961-62 from his Burry Port home. Now living in Sketty, he was Swansea's programme editor for four years from 2000-04: 'During the rise up the divisions I would usually go to matches with my father-in-law Eddie Hawkes. We would make our way to the Sandfields for a drink before the game and then take up our places standing in the lower section of the double-decker. After the match it was back to the Sandfields for a refresher and chat about the game with the other fans who used to gather there. I went to away matches as well, and remember standing in the cold in Alexandra Road by the Reference Library waiting for the coach to take us to Highbury for the first time. On that occasion I went with my twelve-year-old nephew Carl Yates, and although he went to home matches, it was his first trip away so I had a good reason for going. We were all looking forward to the game as we had given the Gunners a bit of a pasting when they came to the Vetch. The trip was very well organised and only cost us about £3 each and to make it an even better day out we beat the Arsenal again.'

From Arsenal to Colwyn Bay, who had decided to stage the Welsh Cup replay at the Vetch. Walsh was ineligible, having not been signed in time, and Leighton James had joined the injury list, but under rain-lashed skies 5,000 spectators saw a near full-strength Swansea make no mistake.

Two goals from Robbie James and one from Curtis settled the fifth-round replay 3-0, but it was all over after just six minutes, when the Swans were two up. Davies did not have a save to make.

The visit of mid-table Stoke on 6 March saw the long-awaited return of Charles who celebrated his comeback by netting his first goal in over six months as the Potters were slain 3-0 on a paddy field of a pitch. This was Swans' sixth victory in seven League matches, four of them away from home. It also signalled their fourth double of the season.

The conditions were so bad that Toshack was undecided whether the match should start. Relentless rain, added to the televising of the rugby international between England and Wales, dipped the crowd to 11,811, the lowest turnout at the Vetch all season. The rain-soaked crowd saw a brace from Robbie James either side of Charles' strike.

Now it was Coventry's turn to try and stop the Swansea bandwagon. It was the Sky Blues who had knocked the Swans off the top of the table the first time they reached the summit. But Dave Sexton's side were on a depressing run without a win in twelve matches.

Toshack sensed it was one of those days when Charles damaged knee ligaments just before the interval after a challenge on Coventry keeper Les Sealey. Charles needed surgery and his season was over. To add to Toshack's woes, Rajkovic was booked for a fifth time, leaving him facing a suspension. On the credit side, the 0-0 draw at least allowed Swansea to maintain their unbeaten run although Coventry's Steve Whitton hit the crossbar twice.

In the two-legged semi-final of the Welsh Cup, Bangor City of the Northern Premier League surrendered home advantage at Farrar Road to play the first leg at the Vetch Field. The non-leaguers took the lead mid-way through the first half through Bruce Urquhart. Bangor manager Dave Elliott thought his team were good value for the lead but they couldn't hold on and Ray Kennedy set up Leighton James to level from 25 yards. Swansea made it 2-1 when Curtis slid the ball home from close range twelve minutes from time.

The Swans' eight-match undefeated League run would be put to the test at Molineux. Although Wolves had only managed two victories from their last fourteen games, they had beaten Leeds last time out. Toshack jiggled the side held 0-0 by Coventry. Stanley and Hadziabdic replaced full-backs Robinson and Marustik, while Walsh took over from Leighton James in attack. Relegation-threatened Wolves dragged the high-flying Swans down to their wretched standards in a low-quality encounter. The home side had more clear-cut scoring opportunities but they squandered them, while Swansea took one of their only two chances.

Andy Gray and Wayne Clarke, brother of Leeds boss Allan, missed open goals, but when Curtis broke down the right, Gray made the mistake of signalling to the linesman that he had been fouled instead of blocking the Swansea forward's run. The referee waved play on and Curtis's cross was headed into the net by Walsh, despite Wolves keeper Paul Bradshaw getting a hand to the ball. In the second half Swansea's defence played keep-ball, which provoked the home crowd into boos and jeers. Kenny Hibbitt put Clarke through late on but the striker shot tamely at Davies. The 1-0 win sent Swansea back to the top.

(20 March '82)	P	W	D	L	F	A	Pts
1 SWANSEA	30	17	5	8	44	34	56
2 Southampton	32	16	7	9	55	45	55
3 Man United	29	15	8	6	43	22	53
4 Liverpool	28	15	6	7	52	24	51
5 Ipswich	28	16	3	9	51	39	51
6 Tottenham	26	15	5	6	45	25	50

Three days later Toshack, watched by his family, was presented with the MBE by the Queen at a ceremony in Buckingham Palace.

These were heady days for the Swans because no fewer than five were capped as Wales drew 1-1 with Spain in Valencia. Earning his first, at full-back, was Marustik, who was Swansea-born but the son of a chef from Czechoslovakia. He joined Davies, Walsh, Curtis and Robbie James – who scored Wales' goal.

The only one of the five missing against Ipswich was Walsh, who had taken a knock in Valencia. Crucially, Rajkovic was also absent, serving a one-match suspension. Ipswich were only five points behind the Swans, but had two games in hand. Manager Bobby Robson was without a host of star players, with Paul Mariner, Franz Thijssen, Terry Butcher and Paul Cooper all on the injured list.

The new multi-purpose gymnasium under Vetch Field's East Stand was officially opened before kick-off. The Swansea City vice-presidents had raised all the money for the new facility.

A tough game was settled by Eric Gates' volley two minutes from time, consigning the Swans to a first defeat in nine League matches and knocking them off the top of the table. There was a lack of adventure about the home side's play. Alan Brazil put Ipswich ahead and it took a penalty, after John Wark handled, to level the score. Gates' brilliant late strike lifted his side up to fifth place and back in with a shout of the League Championship.

Swansea had now topped the First Division on three separate occasions, only to lose their next match each time. Just when consolidation was required, the pressure seemed to be too much and the Swans were always knocked off their perch.

Ipswich's first goal also ended Davies' run of clean sheets, which extended to six matches, breaking the club's previous record of clean sheets shared by Jack Parry and Tony Millington.

The midweek visit of West Ham would be a crucial test of the Swans' staying power. The two clubs had been promoted together after spending two years in the Second Division, where the Hammers had won four out their five meetings – one of which was in the FA Cup at Upton Park. Those five games had yielded only three goals for the Swans, while their opponents had found the net on ten occasions.

Having served his suspension, Rajkovic replaced Thompson and once again the full-backs were changed. The combination of Robinson and Hadziabdic was preferred to Stanley and Marustik.

A second successive home defeat sent the Swans plummeting down to fourth. The Hammers bogey struck early when Belgian international Francois van der Elst let fly from thirty yards. The result was a devastating blow to Swansea's title aspirations. With just ten games left they had squandered six home points in four days.

The Swans had a score to settle with West Brom. It was the Midlands outfit who had inflicted their first ever Division One defeat. Since then Albion had been inconsistent, hovering around the mid-table. Marustik came in for Robinson, and Stanley replaced Leighton James, who was relegated to the bench. Kennedy had been suffering from a stomach complaint but he passed himself fit.

It looked like the same old story when the visitors led 1-0 at half-time, thanks to a strike from Steve Mackenzie moments earlier. Leighton James came on for Stanley and set out to prove that he should have started. Marustik netted his first senior League goal to equalise and in the last ten minutes goals by Curtis and Latchford put the Swans back on the winning trail.

The games were now coming thick and fast, and the Swans were off to London for a quick return meeting with West Ham. The Hammers had won 1-0 at Manchester City and beaten Wolves 3-1 at home since winning at the Vetch, and Paul Goddard had scored three of those four goals. They were unchanged from the eleven which did duty at the Vetch, while there were two changes from the Swansea line-up that day, with Marustik resuming from Robinson at full-back and Stanley replacing Leighton James out on the flanks.

A spectacular shot from Robbie James looked like laying the West Ham bogey, but the Swans failed to clear Alan Devonshire's 87th-minute corner and the unmarked Goddard hammered in a low shot to equalise. Nevertheless, the draw took Swansea back up to third.

Just three days later, 13 April 1982, came the visit of Southampton. Lawrie McMenemy's side were in the top six, but England internationals Keegan and Channon were well-shackled by Rajkovic and Stevenson. Saints' best chances fell to debut-making Keith Cassells, from Division Three Oxford, but he spurned every opportunity. Curtis's first-half goal settled the match, which also gave Davies his first clean sheet in four games.

More good news for Swansea City came when the Wales squad to meet England at Cardiff on 27 April was announced. Five Swans were included – Davies, Marustik, Curtis, Robbie James and Leighton James.

Swansea's fifth home game out of six saw the visit of John Bond's Manchester City. The Light Blues were on a depressing run, having lost their three previous games and conceding ten goals in the process. In fact they had only won one of their last ten matches. Despite this, their early season form – which had brought them a 4-0 win over Swansea – meant they were still in the top half of the table.

The visitors were struck a blow before kick-off when experienced keeper Joe Corrigan felt unwell and had to pull out. His place was taken by Alex Williams who made a nervous start in only his fourth first-team appearance. He was at fault with the Swans' first goal, scored by Stanley, and his lack of confidence spread to his defenders. Latchford doubled the lead late in the first half with his eleventh goal in 27 appearances.

City boss Bond reckoned that Toshack should be given at least a ten-year contract for what he had already achieved at Swansea.

(17 April '82)	P	W	D	L	F	A	Pts
1 Liverpool	35	22	6	7	68	26	72
2 Ipswich	35	21	4	10	63	45	67
3 SWANSEA	36	20	6	10	52	39	66
4 Man United	35	17	11	7	49	26	62
5 Southampton	37	18	8	11	63	54	62
6 Tottenham	32	17	7	8	53	33	58

The Swans wrapped up a place in the Welsh Cup final when they drew 0-0 with Bangor City, having won the first leg 2-1.

Stevenson's topsy-turvy career at Swansea City hit a new high on 22 April when he was selected to represent Wales against England in the

Home Championship in Cardiff. Seven months previously he had been one of five players put up for transfer by the Swans, but Toshack took him off the list eight weeks later. The player had forced his way back into contention to become a regular member of the team.

Stevenson became the sixth Swan recognised by Wales manager Mike England when he took the place of namesake Byron Stevenson, who was needed by relegation-threatened Birmingham for a vital League match against Spurs 24 hours after the international.

That same week, Marustik received his Young Player of the Month award from Mike England at a special ceremony in Newport. It had only been six months since Marustik made his First Division debut as a second-half substitute at Coventry.

Irwin was fit again after missing the Manchester City victory with a leg injury. He joined the squad travelling to Birmingham, which also included Robinson, Mahoney, Walsh and Wyndham Evans. Latchford's Achilles problem ruled him out.

Ten points from three victories and a draw had Swans fans dreaming of another spell on top but they were brought back down to earth at St Andrews. The Blues seemed more focused, possibly because they were fighting for survival, and Swansea spluttered to their first away defeat in more than three months.

Only when Walsh replaced Irwin for the second half and equalised in the 55th minute did Swansea look like salvaging anything. Birmingham keeper Tony Coton only had to deal with a wayward back-pass during a one-sided first half, while at the other end Kevin Dillon's shot rebounded to Kevan Broadhurst, who slammed a 25-yard drive past Davies. Walsh's equaliser, a lob, was his second goal in three appearances since joining from Palace. Mick Harford scored Birmingham's winner with a diving header from Dillon's cross. It was Harford's third goal in three games since signing from Bristol City.

In the Home Championship at Cardiff, England defeated Wales 1-0 with a goal from Trevor Francis. Five Swans started the match and Leighton James came on as a sixth when he replaced Mickey Thomas for the second half.

Latchford was back in the Swansea side for the May Day visit of his former club Everton. The Toffees had won 3-1 at Goodison, and now claimed a double with a repeat score in Swansea. Adrian Heath set the visitors on their way and, when Marustik pulled down Steve McMahon early in the second half, Graeme Sharp netted from the spot. A second Sharp goal ten minutes later put the result beyond doubt, but Robbie James headed home a Leighton James cross to ease the pain a little.

Something was needed to spark Swansea's run-in. It came from a surprising source when Toshack called up long-serving Wyndham Evans for the game at Tottenham.

Evans had recently pocketed £21,000 from his testimonial, having served the club for ten years, and now he found himself making his First Division debut against the Cup finalists. It realised a long-standing ambition for the full-back who must have thought many times that his opportunity of sampling League football at the highest level had passed him by. Toshack had called upon the resilient defender before, when the side was stumbling in the race for promotion from Division Two. He had been brought into the team in February and did so well that he kept his place to the end of that season.

With Irwin and Kennedy non-starters, Toshack was glad that Walsh, Robinson and Mahoney were fit and ready for duty against one of their rivals for a top placing.

Swansea were undone by a brace from young Gary Brooke, but the main topic of conversation was the ill-fortune that saw 31-year-old Evans carried off after only 22 minutes. His evening ended when he fell awkwardly and damaged knee ligaments after challenging Mark Falco in the air. Forced to re-organise, with Stanley taking over from Evans, Swansea were overrun by a Spurs side containing just four of the players likely to play at Wembley against Queens Park Rangers. The aggression of Steve Perryman and hard-man Graham Roberts was not matched by the Swans, and within four minutes of Evans' departure they were trailing to Brooke's goal from Archibald's pass. In the second half Stanley bowled over Brooke and the Spurs midfielder picked himself up to net from the spot.

Swansea set up a grandstand finish when Milija Aleksic dropped a Robbie James cross and Leighton James netted. Although Curtis went close to levelling, the Swans went down to a third defeat in a row.

Toshack made three changes for the trip to Nottingham Forest. Hadziabdic, Thompson and Latchford were recalled, and had an immediate effect on fortunes when Robbie James put the Swans ahead in the first minute. There was a worrying moment when Davies dropped the ball under pressure from Peter Davenport, but Player of the Year Rajkovic was outstanding in the Swansea rearguard. Robbie James struck another in the closing minutes when he out-ran Bryn Gunn before beating Peter Shilton with a low shot.

The attendance at the City Ground of 15,037 was the lowest recorded by Forest since their return to the First Division in 1977. For Swansea, it was a first victory at the ground since 1938.

(8 May '82)	P	W	D	L	F	A	Pts
1 Liverpool	39	25	7	7	76	30	82
2 Ipswich	40	25	5	10	72	49	80
3 Man United	40	20	12	8	54	29	72
4 Tottenham	38	20	10	8	63	39	70
5 SWANSEA	40	21	6	13	57	46	69
6 Arsenal	40	19	10	11	43	35	67

While the Swans hoped to improve on their fifth position with two League games remaining, the emphasis turned to the final of the Welsh Cup and the first leg against Cardiff City at Ninian Park. The rivals were meeting in the final for the first time since 1969 when Cardiff won 3-1 at the Vetch and 2-0 on their own ground. A certain John Toshack scored three of the Bluebirds' goals.

It was a night for the defences, with Cardiff's seventeen-year-old keeper Andy Dibble performing well for the Bluebirds, while Davies helped keep the scoresheet blank with a superb reflex save from Tarki Micallef. Robbie James thought he had snatched a late winner but his effort was ruled out for offside. The first leg ended goalless.

Doomed Middlesbrough were the visitors for the last home match of the season on 15 May. Tempers frayed as both teams let the tension get the better of them during a frantic first half. It even spilled over to the dug-out. Toshack was 'booked' for ungentlemanly conduct just before the interval when the referee – a police sergeant from Hampshire – raced straight towards the Swansea manager. 'I never paid a great deal of attention to what he said,' recalled Toshack. 'Everyone was tired at that stage of the season and when I looked at him he seemed more tired than anyone else.'

The Swans missed enough first-half chances to have wrapped up the game but it was not until thirteen minutes from time that Latchford touched home a Stevenson cross. With everyone expecting further Swans goals, Boro's Heine Otto hooked in an equaliser, and with one minute left substitute Stanley sliced a clearance into his own net. Boro had snatched an unlikely 2-1 victory.

The attendance for that final home game was 12,961, compared to the 23,489 who watched the opening match against Leeds United.

Swansea were now presented with two games in two days to conclude the season. The second leg of the Welsh Cup at the Vetch Field was scheduled for Thursday, 20 May, while the following evening Aston Villa would bring the curtain down on Swansea's first season in the First Division.

The lure of European football made it necessary to pick the strongest side for the Welsh Cup final, but when Gary Bennett gave the Bluebirds a shock lead the 15,828 crowd fell silent. It was a messy goal as skipper Rajkovic's sliced clearance went straight to Bennett who bundled the ball into the net off chest and knee. The lead only lasted a few minutes before Latchford hit an unstoppable volley past Dibble. The young keeper had no chance with Swansea's second, as a mistake by Tim Gilbert allowed Latchford with a clear strike on goal. There was time for Rajkovic to be red-carded for tripping Phil Lythgoe, but the Yugoslav returned at the end to receive the trophy that ensured participation in the 1982-83 Cup-Winners' Cup.

As most of his regulars had played in the 2-1 win over the Bluebirds, Toshack blooded a few younger players against Villa. Four teenagers – Chris Sander, Gary Richards, Dudley Lewis and Jimmy Loveridge – were in from the start and another, Darren Gale, would come off the bench as as substitute.

It was a difficult task against the European Cup finalists – who in a few days would defeat Bayern Munich to claim European football's richest prize. Tony Morley and Des Bremner had Villa 2-0 up by half-time. Peter Withe later scored a third with a shot deflected by Irwin. Latchford hit the woodwork twice but Swansea ended their season with a comprehensive 0-3 defeat.

They finished sixth in the League but had done more than enough to show that in 1982-83 they might be a major force in the division.

The season wasn't over for Swansea's large contingent of Welsh internationals. Six of them started the game against Scotland in Glasgow on 24 May, which ended in a 0-1 reverse, and Ian Walsh went on during the second half to lift the Swans' representation up to seven.

5

THE EUROPEAN ADVENTURE

The prize for beating Hereford in the 1979-80 Welsh Cup final was a place in the following season's European Cup-Winners' Cup. But that was not the first time the Swans had taken part in UEFA's second most prestigious tournament. Swansea Town, as they were then known, had the honour of being the first Welsh participants back in 1961 when they were among 22 other national cup winners taking part after defeating Bangor City 3-1 in the Welsh Cup final in Cardiff. The Swans' reward was to be paired with SC Motor Jena of East Germany. This was at the height of the Cold War and there was a ban on all East German nationals from entering NATO countries, so the Motor Jena staff and players were barred from travelling to Wales.

Nevertheless, the first leg was still advertised as being at the Vetch Field and tickets were on sale less than fourteen days before the scheduled first round. The club tried to switch the home leg to 'neutral' Dublin. Although their opponents agreed, the Republic of Ireland Government did not.

UEFA intervened, instructing the Swans to play their 'home' leg in Sweden, Switzerland or Austria. Both ties also had to be completed by 18 October. Unless a 'home' venue could be found, Swansea could have suffered the same fate that befell Northern Irish club Glenavon in 1960-61. Paired in the European Cup against East German opponents, they failed to agree on a home venue and Wismut K-M-S went through on a technical walkover.

UEFA advised that if Swansea agreed to play in the Austrian town of Linz they would reimburse the club if it failed to recover expenses from the gate receipts. All travelling expenses from Linz to Jena for the second leg, two days later, would be met by SC Motor Jena. While all this was going on, the clubs already knew their future opponents in round two – Alliance Dudelange of Luxembourg.

Swansea's fourteen-man squad included Graham Williams, who had scored for Wales in the 1-1 draw with England the day before departure.

After being delayed by fog at Heathrow the Swans flew to Munich, arriving in Linz just a few hours before the scheduled kick-off time. With no preparation, they shrugged off their weariness and Colin Webster shot straight at Jena keeper, Harald Fritsche. Cardiff-born Webster had been in the Manchester United side beaten by AC Milan in the semi-final of the 1958 European Cup, shortly after the Munich air disaster.

The game ended 2-2 with Brayley Reynolds and a Mel Nurse penalty making up their score. The Swans survived the last eleven minutes a man short after Webster was sent off for exacting retribution on Egelmeyer after he had already been cautioned.

The Swansea party were then escorted into East Germany through numerous border controls until they reached the small town of Jena. On the pitch the captains exchanged bouquets. This – and the playing of the national anthems – delayed the kick-off by fifteen minutes. Hopes were high when Reynolds volleyed the Swans ahead but from then on they were outclassed and beaten 1-5 on the day and 3-7 on aggregate. The East Germans went on to reach the semi-final, where they were beaten 0-5 over the two legs to eventual winners Atletico Madrid.

It would be another five years before Swansea earned the right to a second tilt at European opposition. A 2-1 Welsh Cup final victory over Chester in a play-off at Sealand Road saw them paired with the Bulgarian club Slavia Sofia. Although struggling for points in Division Three, the Swans were keen to eradicate memories of their first foray into Europe. Once again lack of co-ordination caused problems and it was not until four days before the first leg at the Vetch, on 21 September 1966, that Slavia confirmed their travel arrangements. After a gruelling trip by plane, coach and train, they arrived in Swansea four hours late. No one in their party spoke English, so an interpreter from the Russian Department of Swansea University was recruited to assist.

The Bulgarians contained three players from their country's 1966 World Cup side yet they could only draw 1-1 with the Swans – playing in their second strip of tangerine shirts – in front of a crowd of 12,107. The gate receipts of £2,262 just about covered the costs of the trip to Bulgaria. The squad flew from London to Sofia two days before the second leg scheduled for 5 October, but the whole trip lasted a tiring fourteen hours. The Swans showed just one change, Herbie Williams coming in for Brian Hughes, both players being survivors from the Motor Jena tie. Manager Glyn Davies decided on all-out attack but the plan misfired and Slavia romped to a 4-0 win. Ivor Allchurch played in both legs for Swansea to become the first Welsh player to appear for two different Welsh clubs in Europe. He had also been in the Cardiff City side that played in Esbjerg in 1964.

When Swansea defeated Hereford 2-1 on aggregate in the 1980 Welsh Cup final their place in Europe had already been assured because an English club could not represent Wales in Europe. This was the first time a Welsh entry had come from the First Division and hopes were high that at last the Swans would be able to make some progress.

East German opponents Lokomotiv Leipzig had been forced to play a preliminary round tie against Politechnica Timisoara of Romania, over-turning a 0-2 first-leg deficit by scoring five goals in the 39,000-capacity Zentralstadion in Leipzig.

The Swans went into the match four days after beating Notts County 3-2 in the First Division, a result that had taken them up to second place. Unfortunately, changes had to be made. Colin Irwin and Max Thompson were ineligible as they had not been signed in time according to UEFA rules, while Jeremy Charles was absent through injury.

Lokomotiv had experience of playing Football League sides. In reach-ing the 1974 UEFA Cup semi-final they knocked out two English clubs – Wolves on the away-goals rule after a 4-4 aggregate in the second round, then after beating Fortuna Dusseldorf, Ipswich in a quarter-final which they won on penalties. In 1978, however, they were soundly defeat-ed 1-7 on aggregate in the Cup-Winners' Cup by Arsenal.

Reserve keeper Dave Stewart was the only Swan with European expe-rience. He had actually played in a European Cup final, being in goal for Leeds when they lost to Bayern Munich in the 1975 final at the Parc des Princes in Paris. Stewart would have to be content with a place in the six-teen permitted under UEFA rules.

The squad from the German Democratic Republic arrived on the Tuesday. Manager Harro Muller and club president Peter Glessner had come over earlier to watch the Swans beat Notts County.

Straight from the kick-off in driving rain the East Germans funnelled back on defence allowing the Swans to camp in their half. Leighton James was hurt in a crude tackle by Joachim Fritzsche midway through the opening period and David Giles replaced him. The former Cardiff City, Wrexham and Wales star thereby became the first player to appear for three Welsh sides in European competition.

Alan Curtis came closest to breaking the deadlock in front of the 10,295 crowd when his shot whistled past the Lokomotiv post. Wyndham Evans was sent on for Brian Attley but Lokomotiv continued to stifle the Swans' attacks. The only goal of the game came in the 70th minute and stemmed from an error by Dai Davies. The former Wrexham keeper spilled a shot from Lutz Moldt, and Jurgen Kinne raced in to poke the loose ball over the line.

Swansea fan Colin Jones remembers the match for a different reason. 'It was a filthy night with rain pouring down most of the game and we were all depressed enough without the antics of the East Germans. They fell over looking for free-kicks if any Swansea player came within a few yards of them. This went on for most of the game, with their players dropping like flies until one went down, without being touched, right in front of us. Quick as a flash, a crutch was hurled over the perimeter fence, accompanied by a few choice words telling the Leipzig man where he could put it. It gave us all a laugh but I suppose if that happened now the police and stewards would be in like a shot.'

While it was a disappointing result it was a deserved victory for the visitors. They had upped the pace in the second period and forced more chances on goal than the Swans.

The task in Leipzig fourteen days later was formidable. Toshack had never been on a winning side in East Germany despite playing there three times for Liverpool and once for Wales. The squad flew to Leipzig the day before the game and were granted use of all the facilities at the Zentralstadion. Swansea players and staff were in subdued mood following the death of former Liverpool manager Bill Shankly, particularly as there was a strong Merseyside contingent in the club.

Straight from the kick-off Andreas Bornschein, who had received the ball out wide, was injured swinging a pass into the goalmouth. He had to be replaced by Peter Schoene with less than a minute on the clock.

The Swans fell behind when Jurgen Kinne stole in on the blind-side of skipper John Mahoney to head in Schoene's cross. It was all over midway through the first half when Kuhn set up another, brushing off Nigel Stevenson and Ante Rajkovic before crossing into the Swans danger area. Dai Davies failed to gather cleanly and Moldt had an easy tap-in from close range.

Any hopes Swansea had of salvaging the tie disappeared just before the interval when Alan Curtis was sent off by the Italian referee. After an ugly scuffle with Stefan Fritzsche, Curtis was seen to elbow and then slap his opponent.

Evans replaced Stevenson at the interval and Jeremy Charles made it 2-1 on the night thanks to an error by keeper Muller who dropped a Leighton James cross at his feet. After such an ill-tempered game both sides dispensed with the customary after-match handshakes. Swansea had been in Europe on three different occasions, played six matches, and were still looking for their first victory.

A win over Cardiff City in the Welsh Cup of 1982 gave the Swans an immediate opportunity to redress that situation. Cardiff manager Len Ashurst had signed Phil Lythgoe and Stan McEwan for the sole purpose of playing them in the final. The sides drew 0-0 at Ninian Park but at a volatile Vetch eight days later the Swans won 2-1.

Our story now jumps ahead to the 1982-83 European Cup-Winners' Cup, even though we have not reached that season in our League narrative. When the draw was made, luck seemed to pass the Swans by again, as they were one of just four of the 34 participants to have to go through a preliminary round. The other three were Sporting Braga, Aberdeen and Sion of Switzerland. The Swans were matched with Portuguese cup finalists Braga, with the first leg at home on 17 August 1982, eleven days before the home football season commenced.

Braga had been beaten 0-4 in their domestic final by Sporting Lisbon, but as Sporting were also league champions, the losing finalists took their place in the Cup-Winners' Cup. Braga had appeared in the UEFA Cup in 1978-79, when they lost 0-3 on aggregate to West Brom in the second round after beating Hibernians of Malta 7-3 over two legs.

Toshack gained some insight into Braga's style of play when Swansea City's secretary Tony Howard travelled to Portugal to watch them draw 3-3 in a friendly with Amadora.

The Swansea line-up in front of their own fans contained ten internationals with Colin Irwin, Swansea's record purchase, the odd one out. Curtis was ruled out as he was suspended for three European matches following his sending off in Leipzig.

After six unsuccessful attempts the Swans achieved their first victory in Europe by winning 3-0 in front of 10,614 spectators. It was a triumphant return for Jeremy Charles after two cartilage operations had forced him to miss most of the previous season. He scored twice, while Braga skipper Cardoso contributed an own-goal. Charles had scored the Swans' first goal in the First Division and now their first in Swansea's maiden victory in European competition. There was an element of luck about it. Ray Kennedy sliced a shot to Irwin who fired against a post, the ball falling to Charles. In the second half, Leighton James's corner was flicked into his own net by the Braga captain. The third and tie-killing score arrived after a Robbie James shot had rebounded back from a Portuguese defender. Quick as a flash, Charles drove it in. Toshack would have been happy with a two-goal advantage and knew that the extra goal had almost guaranteed passage through to the next round.

Kennedy stayed behind on the treatment table, along with Stevenson, when the squad travelled to Oporto for the second leg. Toshack and secretary Tony Howard flew out early to make another form check on Braga in a pre-season cup competition against Guimaraes. Like Swansea, their domestic season had not yet started.

Braga was about thirty miles from Oporto in northern Portugal. The main party travelled out on the Monday beforehand, unaware of the drama that was unfolding. As the players patiently waited for permission to use the facilities at the nearby ground of Varzim, Swansea officials were compiling evidence to lodge a complaint with UEFA about the conduct of the Braga club.

The problems had started when Toshack and Howard went to watch them in action on the Sunday, only to miss out because the kick-off had been brought forward by four hours. Then the Swans were refused permission to train under floodlights at their Primeiro de Maio ground, which was against UEFA rules. Braga counterclaimed that as the ground was owned and controlled by the municipal authority it was not their fault that the gates were locked at 6.30pm.

To make matters worse, Toshack was unhappy with the hotel in Oporto allocated to the club. According to the Swansea chief it was ideal for the businessman's overnight stop but totally unsuitable for a football club. He spent a whole day arranging to change from that hotel to one more acceptable about eighteen miles from Braga.

As Swansea never received permission to use the facilities at Varzim, they were forced to move further out to Famalicao, where they were warmly received and given use of a training ground. The other obstacle in Swansea's path was the 80 degree heat in Braga but as the match was scheduled for a 9.30pm kick-off it was expected to be much cooler by then.

Toshack's side took the field on their own as yet another row blew up with the Braga officials. When the teams lined up in the tunnel it was noticed that three Braga players omitted from the team-sheet were kitted out and ready to play. This was pointed out to the referee, who sent the Portuguese players to the dressing room. The Swans waited almost ten minutes out on the pitch. Just as they were about to go back inside, the Braga players began trooping out in twos and threes. Eventually the game commenced fifteen minutes late.

John Mahoney and Gary Stanley started in place of the injured Stevenson and Kennedy. Predictably the Swans slowed the game down and played defensively, leaving only Leighton James up front. Braga forced ten corners in the first half alone. Latchford might have snatched the lead in the thirteenth minute when a snapshot shaved the home crossbar during a rare breakaway.

The Portuguese side's only goal came two minutes from time when Fontes shot through a crowded goalmouth. Chris Marustik stuck out a leg and diverted the ball past Davies and into the net, but it was the Swans who went through to the next round with a 3-1 aggregate victory.

Swiss referee Jacob Baumann sent a critical report to UEFA regarding Braga's breach of the rules, but it was understood they were only disciplined for a late start.

Next up for Toshack's men, in the first round proper, were Sliema Wanderers of Malta. It would not be their first trip to Wales as in 1963 they had been knocked out in the first round by Borough United, a Welsh League (North) side who therefore became the first Welsh club to make progress in a European competition.

The first leg was scheduled for 15 September. When the Sliema party arrived in Swansea they immediately requested permission to train on the Vetch Field. All their players were amateurs and unused to playing on grass, or even under floodlights, so Swansea already held all the aces. They were also without competitive matches as the start of their season was still some weeks away. The day after their first training session they decided to go sight-seeing round the Gower, after which they completed their final work-out at the Swansea University College playing fields at Fairwood.

Sliema were well used to European competition but had rarely survived for long. They had twice advanced to the second round but both times it was a result of weak opposition from Iceland and Luxembourg. In the 1980-81 UEFA Cup however they caused a stir by only losing 0-2 at home to mighty Barcelona, before losing 0-1 (a penalty) in the second leg in Spain. The current Sliema side contained six survivors from the Barcelona tie.

Toshack paid Sliema the compliment of sending out his best available starting eleven except for Curtis, who was sitting out the third game of his three-match suspension. Poor Sliema were massacred 12-0 with Swansea registering a new club goalscoring record in the process. Sadly, only 5,130 spectators turned up to see the slaughter, which included an eleven-minute hat-trick from substitute Ian Walsh. The low turn-out was put down to increased ticket prices, though it was claimed by the Swansea management that cheaper tickets would have made little difference to the gate.

The final scoreline eclipsed the previous club best of 8-0 which had been registered against Hartlepool in the Fourth Division on April Fools Day, 1978. Swansea led Sliema 4-0 at the interval but Sliema keeper Alan Zammitt, a hotel receptionist, was even busier in the second half. He had a reputation for being quick about his box, not surprising as he was the Maltese record holder over 100 and 200 metres. In fact, he missed out on selection for the European athletics championships in order to play for his club in Swansea.

A scoring European debut for nineteen-year-old Jimmy Loveridge was the main feature of that first half. Three goals came in a six-minute period. Latchford struck the fourth three minutes before the interval.

The one-way traffic continued after the break with Jimmy Hadziabdic and a second for Loveridge counting by the 65th minute. Playing a lone role up front for the Maltese was Simon Tortell who had relinquished the chance of a career with Manchester United to study law.

Seven minutes after replacing Latchford, Walsh struck his first with a ferocious drive. Two minutes later Charles was on target, and then Walsh completed his amazing hat-trick in the 79th and 86th minutes to take his side into double figures. 'I scored with a left foot shot, one with my right, and a header,' recalled Walsh. 'I don't have a photograph of any of my goals but I do have the match ball in my trophy cabinet at home and you can still just about make out all the signatures of the lads who played that night.' There was still time for Stevenson and Rajkovic to put their names on the scoresheet as the Swans re-wrote the record book.

The Sliema party didn't let the trouncing spoil their trip because the next day they travelled to London to spend three days sightseeing before returning home. Their players had each received two Maltese pounds as appearance money but that wouldn't have lasted very long in Oxford Street.

All talk about the second leg on 29 September centred on the possibility of Toshack's side creating a new UEFA aggregate record score. Chelsea held that honour after overwhelming Luxembourg's Jeunesse Hautcharage in the Cup-Winners' Cup of 1971. They won the first leg 13-0 at Stamford Bridge and 8-0 in the return, making the overall aggregate 21-0 in their favour. It was a record that had scarcely been threatened – until now.

The Swans already held the biggest victory for a Welsh club in Europe after eclipsing the 8-0 win by Cardiff City over PO Larnaca of Cyprus in September 1970. Toshack himself had scored two of the goals for the Bluebirds in that first-leg romp.

Swansea's main worry as they journeyed to the George Cross Island was that their 1982-83 League form was poor. Four successive League defeats had left them seventeenth in the First Division. Toshack rested Davies, Mahoney, Robbie James and Latchford, and named himself as one of the two substitutes allowed. Irwin was missing after suffering knee ligament damage at Villa Park. By coincidence, the Swans would play the second leg in the Ta Qali Stadium which they had been invited to officially open the previous year. Only red tape had stopped them from making that trip. After looking over the stadium, Swans skipper Ray Kennedy was dismissive. 'They must have spent a few million on the building work but only about £500 on the pitch. The surrounds were marvellous but the playing surface was rubbish.'

The new ground had been built on an old airfield near the ancient city of Mdina. It was the only ground in Malta with grass, so every Maltese team used it, hence the well-worn state of the pitch.

The Swans treated the game like a training exercise and won 5-0, though they never really looked like attacking Chelsea's aggregate record. Highlight of the evening was a last-minute goal from Toshack himself, who replaced two-goal Curtis in the attack. Toshack's appearance was strictly a one-off, however. At 33, not having played for almost two years, he promptly went back into retirement.

The Maltese rarely looked like scoring even one goal. Their only opportunity came in the first minute when Chris Sander failed to hold a free-kick by Joe Aquilina, and Dudley Lewis cleared behind for a corner.

Talk was now of the next round, as there were plenty of top clubs still involved – Real Madrid, Barcelona, Bayern Munich, Inter Milan – while Aberdeen, like Swansea, had only conceded a single goal in getting past the preliminary and first-round stages.

Diplomatically, no preference was expressed from the Vetch but there was quiet satisfaction when Swansea were linked with Paris St Germain who had beaten Lokomotiv Sofia 5-2 on aggregate in the first round. The French club had made a poor start to their domestic season but with Ossie Ardiles (who was officially still a Tottenham player), Dutch international Kees Kist and French winger Dominique Rochetau to call on, they could guarantee the Swans a good crowd for the home leg scheduled for 20 October.

When viewing a video of the Paris side in action, Toshack described them as the best Continental opposition ever to visit the Vetch Field. He had also watched them play Sochaux at the Parc des Princes. As he sat in the directors box in the world-renowned stadium, he felt proud of the fact that his club would soon be performing in such surroundings. The last time he had been there was to see his old club Liverpool beat Real Madrid 1-0 in the 1981 European Cup final.

Paris St Germain relied on bursts of individual brilliance, and they had a few players in their line-up capable of achieving that. The French party flew in to Cardiff Airport without Rochetau who stayed behind because of a knee injury suffered against Northern Ireland in the summer's World Cup. The players trained under the Vetch Field lights before embarking on a sight-seeing trip the following day.

Because of a glut of injuries, Toshack called up all his available senior professionals. He even included himself to make up a squad of seventeen although he had no intention of taking any part. He was without four centre-backs: Thompson, Rajkovic, Irwin and Stevenson were all injured, so Toshack named Wyndham Evans in his starting eleven after Charles failed a late fitness test.

Having given his players a verbal lashing at the weekend following their poor League form, Toshack was unrepentant. 'I had said my piece and got a lot off my chest and felt much the better for it.'

Swansea played in a change strip of blue as Paris St Germain's colours were also white. Unlike domestic regulations, UEFA's stated that home clubs should always change if there is a clash of colours.

It was an emotional evening for Ardiles, setting foot on British soil for the first time since the Falklands War. He had left Spurs on a one-year loan to avoid any possible hostility on account of his nationality.

The Swans lost 0-1 when their defence was opened up by a through ball from Pascal Zaremba and Chad international Nambatingue Toko hit a right-foot shot under Davies for a priceless away goal. The Swans could have clawed something back but Curtis ballooned the ball over the bar from two yards. Another disappointment was the meagre attendance of 9,505 to watch such attractive opposition.

Swansea were mystified by the low attendance as there had been a bigger gate for the visit of Braga. Unceasing rain for a day and a half might have dampened enthusiasm, yet the rain had stopped when play commenced and the pitch was in remarkably good condition. It was quickly decided not to pursue the cut-price ticket experiment unless more fans turned up for the next cup match.

In the League, the Swans beat Southampton at home but lost at Manchester City before the second leg in Paris on 3 November. Those League games hadn't been without cost, as now Toshack was definitely without Thompson, Kennedy and Irwin. Charles, Rajkovic, and Stevenson all needed lengthy treatment before making themselves available for the trip. Kennedy's thigh strain was still causing concern and when he was forced to pull out of the game at Maine Road it was felt that he needed rest to improve his condition.

Neil Robinson, now recovered from his knee operation, was drafted into the squad. He had established his fitness in two reserve games and flew out with the rest on the Monday. Also travelling for a rare outing with the squad was nineteen-year-old Gary Richards who had made his League debut in the final match of the 1981-82 season, at Villa Park.

The Swans made their headquarters in Versailles. Toshack made four changes to the side beaten at the Vetch. Rajkovic, Stevenson, Leighton James and Charles all took up their positions on a foggy night at the Parc des Princes. Toshack had a seat on the bench in order to circumvent an FA of Wales touchline ban which was in force until 1 March 1983.

David Giles beats Wrexham keeper Dai Davies for Swansea's goal in
the 1-1 draw at the Racecourse (October 1980)

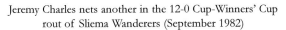

Jeremy Charles nets another in the 12-0 Cup-Winners' Cup
rout of Sliema Wanderers (September 1982)

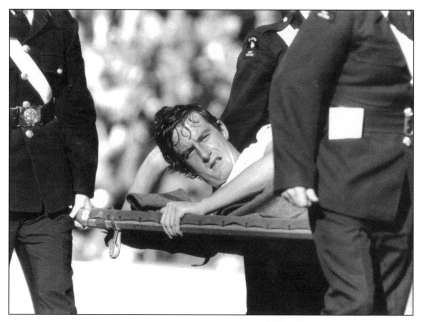

Colin Irwin is stretchered off in a 0-2 defeat at Aston Villa with a knee injury that would end his career (September 1982)

Match programme for Cup-Winners' Cup-tie lost 0-1 to FC Magdeburg of East Germany (August 1983)

David Giles heads home a pass from John Toshack in a 4-1 victory over
Reading in the FA Cup (January 1980)

Jeremy Charles connects with ball and teammate Alan Curtis as the Swans
attack the Coventry goal in this 0-0 draw (March 1982)

Match programme for Cup-Winners'
Cup-tie lost 0-1 to Paris St Germain
(October 1982)

Swans keeper Jimmy Rimmer deflects a shot from Sheffield Wednesday's John Pearson, with Nigel Stevenson in attendance. Swansea lost 0-1 (August 1983)

John Bond gathers an armful of suits when leaving the club as the liquidators moved in (December 1985)

Dai Davies dives at the feet of Liverpool's Alan Kennedy during the
0-3 defeat by Liverpool. Colin Irwin is in the background (September 1982)

David Giles and Alan Waddle attack the Crystal Palace goal during
their 2-2 draw in the FA Cup (January 1980)

Jeremy Charles slots home in the 3-0 Cup-Winners' Cup victory over
Sporting Braga of Portugal (August 1982)

Eight Swansea City internationals in 1981. Top: Leighton James (Wales), Dave Stewart (Scotland), Leighton Phillips (Wales), David Giles (Wales). Bottom: Ian Callaghan (England), Tommy Craig (Scotland), John Mahoney (Wales), Robbie James (Wales)

Match programme for Cup-Winners Cup-tie against FC Magdeburg which ended 1-1 (August 1983)

A diving header from David Giles during the 1-1 draw with Notts County
(September 1980)

Darren Gale wrong-foots Ipswich defenders George Burley and Terry Butcher
during this 1-1 draw (April 1983)

Max Thompson shields Stoke's Lee Chapman at a corner. Swansea won 3-0 (March 1982)

Swansea's new chairman, Doug Sharpe, says farewell after John Toshack's first resignation. Vice-Chairman Bobby Jones is between them (October 1983)

Dean Saunders is pressured by Derby's Bobby Davison.
Swansea lost 1-5 (December 1984)

Mel Nurse scored from the spot in Swans'
2-2 Cup-Winners' Cup draw against SC
Motor Jena of Linz (October 1961)

Frank Lampard and Robbie James jump for a cross during the 0-1 defeat to West Ham
(March 1982)

Andy Legg beats Jean-Luc Ettori for the Swans' goal in their 1-2 Cup-Winners' Cup
defeat by Monaco (September 1991)

Ante Rajkovic tries to intercept Tottenham's Mark Falco at White Hart Lane.
Swansea lost 1-2 (May 1982)

Alan Curtis lifts the ball over Notts County keeper Raddy Avramovic and over the bar.
Swansea won 3-2 (September 1981)

Willie Young and Jurgen Rober of Nottingham Forest clear their lines, watched by
Robbie James and Max Thompson. Swansea lost 1-2 (December 1981)

Alan Curtis shows a clean pair of heels to Manchester United's Gordon McQueen and Arthur Albiston in Swansea's 2-0 victory (January 1982)

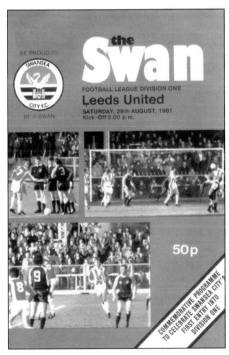

Match programme from Swansea's opening game in Division One, against Leeds. Swansea won 5-1 (August 1981)

Kenny Dalglish's shirt is shown-off by 9-year-old Cameron, a present from dad, John Toshack. Sally Ann (7), Craig (5) and wife Sue are with them at home (1979)

Ante Rajkovic tackles Liverpool's Craig Johnston during Swansea's 0-3 defeat (September 1982)

Brayley Reynolds in action for Swansea. He scored the Swans' first goal in Europe, against SC Motor Jena (October 1961)

Chairman Doug Sharpe shows the press a cheque for £1,000 from the departing John Toshack (October 1983)

Jeremy Charles' teammates admire his new car in the shadow of the prison wall (1980)

Colin Webster, who scored 65 Swansea goals in 159 League appearances between 1958-62

Tottenham's Gary Mabbutt is helpless as Jeremy Charles powers in
a header in Swansea's 2-0 win (October 1982)

Gary Richards heads clear from Manchester City's Bobby McDonald and David Cross.
Swansea won 4-1 (March 1983)

Match programme for Cup-Winners'
Cup-tie against Lokomotiv Leipzig.
Swansea lost 1-2 (September 1981)

Colin Irwin slides in to tackle Manchester United's Bryan Robson during
Swansea's 2-0 victory (January 1982)

Nigel Stevenson and Dzemal Hadziabdic combine to stop Notts County's
Justin Fashanu during Swansea's 2-0 win (January 1983)

Bob Latchford is brought down by Leeds' Eddie Gray during Swansea's first ever
Division One game, which they won 5-1 (August 1981)

Brian Attley fires Swansea into the lead against Sunderland, despite the close attention
of Shaun Elliott. Swansea won 3-1 (November 1979)

David Giles holds his Player of the Year award and Tommy Craig receives the
Vice-Presidents award. John Toshack is far left, Chairman Malcolm Struel is far right

Ray Kennedy in action for the Swans.
He scored two League goals in 42
appearances between January 1982 and
November 1983

Jeremy Charles tries to block Watford's John Barnes during Swansea's 1-3 defeat
(February 1983)

Dai Davies played 86 League games for
Swansea in three different spells at the
club. He also won 52 caps for Wales

Alan Curtis follows his shot into the net for Swansea's first goal in
their 2-0 win over Sunderland (September 1981)

Leighton James lifts the
ball over Notts County's
Raddy Avramovic during
the Swans' 3-2 victory
(September 1981)

Max Thompson clears as Arsenal's Alan Sunderland rushes in during Swansea's 2-0 win
(October 1981)

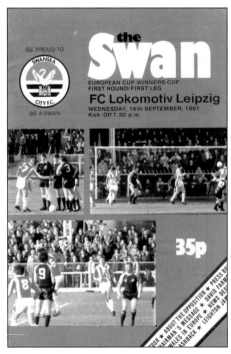

Programme for the Cup-Winners'
Cup-tie against Lokomotiv Leipzig.
Swansea lost 0-1 (September 1981)

Player-manager John Toshack in action during the 1-0 victory over Preston
(December 1979)

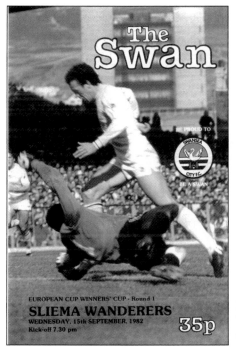

Match programme for visit of Sliema
Wanderers when Swansea rewrote the
record books (September 1982)

Worried looks from the dug-out as John Toshack, Doug Livermore and Phil Boersma watch the Swans against Cambridge United (September 1983)

Seeing double. David Giles and Kevin Keegan before the Swans beat Southampton 1-0
(April 1982)

Newspaper advertisement for a game that never took place. UEFA forced the Swans to
travel to Linz in Austria to play their 'home' leg on 16 October 1961

EUROPEAN CUP WINNERS CUP
Swansea Town v. S.C. Motor Jena
VETCH FIELD, SWANSEA
TUESDAY, SEPTEMBER 26, 1961

ADMISSION BY TICKET ONLY   **Kick-off 7.15 p.m.**

Prices: Centre Stand 10/-; Wing West 9/-; Enclosure 5/-
Field 4/-   Boys 2/-

Postal application from season ticket holders giving row and seat number
enclosing coupon "C" with stamped addressed envelope addressed to -

SECRETARY, VETCH FIELD, SWANSEA

Field Tickets on sale Thursday, September 14. 8.0 a.m. - 8.0 p.m.
Friday, September 15th from 10 a.m.

Cardiff's Peter Kitchen heads a late equaliser past Dave Stewart (April 1981)

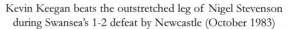

Kevin Keegan beats the outstretched leg of Nigel Stevenson
during Swansea's 1-2 defeat by Newcastle (October 1983)

Watford's Luther Blissett heads for goal in Swansea's 1-3 defeat.
Kenny Jackett watches from behind Robbie James (February 1983)

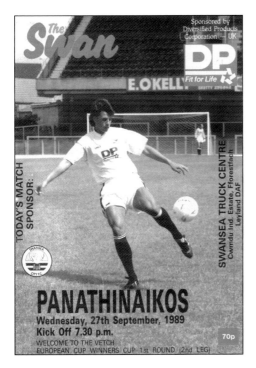

Chris Coleman featured on the programme for the 3-3 Cup-Winners' Cup draw against Panathinaikos (September 1989)

Ray Kennedy works his way past Ipswich's George Burley during Swansea's 1-2 defeat
(March 1982)

Ian Walsh beats David
Sutton of Huddersfield
when scoring both goals
in this 2-2 draw
(January 1984)

The second leg was expected to entice a full house to the Parc des Princes with receipts grossing at a staggering £380,000. This could be compared to Swansea's first-leg receipts of just £25,000. Welsh hopes were boosted with the news that Ardiles was out, injured in a French First Division game. Top player Saar Boubacar also failed a late fitness test and he joined the little Argentinian in the stand.

Michael Roberts, Welsh Office Minister with responsibility for Sport, was at the match on 'official business'. The Department of the Environment and the Football Association had been discussing ways of preventing crowd violence. They wanted to see at first hand the way clubs prepare for these matches and whether UEFA regulations were strictly adhered to.

As the French side had won both their League matches since the first leg, 4-1 to Strasbourg and 3-1 to Lyon, Toshack knew his team were in for a tough evening. In next to no time, Swansea's hold in the competition was broken as the French side took the lead in the fifth minute. First-leg scorer Toko slammed in a shot that Davies did well to block, but Kist was first to the loose ball and he hammered it into the back of the net. The Dutchman was a former Golden Boot winner having scored 34 goals for AZ 67 Alkmaar in 1978-79. For good measure he was also runner up in 1980-81.

Swansea might have scored even earlier but Charles' header was brilliantly saved by French international keeper Baratelli. Stevenson struck a post midway through the half as the Swans upped the tempo but Baratelli saved goalbound headers from Charles and Mahoney. The French side sealed the tie fifteen minutes from time when Luis Fernandez scored from inside the box after a cross from substitute Michel N'Gom.

The final whistle signalled the end of Swansea's European adventure for another season. Their flight from Paris was delayed by fog and it was a tired and subdued party that arrived back in Swansea. Paris St Germain went out at the next stage, the quarter-finals, where their 2-0 first-leg lead was overturned by the Belgian club Waterschei. Waterschei in turn fell to Alex Ferguson's Aberdeen who lifted the Cup after beating Real Madrid in Gothenberg.

Swansea would be back in the Cup-Winners' Cup the following year, 1983-84, only to suffer a first-round dismissal. They qualified by virtue of a 2-1 aggregate Welsh Cup victory over Wrexham, a strangely muted affair because both sides had suffered relegation. The Swans had dropped out of the First Division while Wrexham had fallen to the Fourth. At least the Swans were Welsh Cup-winners for the third successive season, so confirming their status as the top Welsh club side.

By the time of the first-leg tie against FC Magdeburg, yet another East German outfit, there had been a big change of personnel at the Vetch. Out went Robbie James and the two Yugoslavs, Rajkovic and Hadziabdic, while Jimmy Rimmer had replaced Davies in goal. Rimmer had been Aston Villa's nominated goalkeeper in their European Cup final of 1982, but an injury in the opening moments had seen him replaced by Nigel Spink. Youngster Huw Lake made his European bow as the sides met at the Vetch Field on 24 August 1983

There was a huge financial incentive to win this preliminary tie as the reward would be mighty Barcelona in the first round proper. The East Germans had accounted for Wrexham 7-5 on aggregate in 1979 and were top of their League this season. The game was goalless until the last ten minutes when Ian Walsh – on for Latchford – netted after a Kennedy shot had come off a defender. A minute from time a blunder by Marustik gifted the East Germans an equaliser. He passed back to Rimmer from 35 yards but the keeper was flat-footed on his line and Joachim Streich, holder of 93 caps, ran the ball into the net.

Seven days later the Swans turned out in the Ernst Gruber Stadion in Magdeburg for the second leg having endured a ten-hour journey before training on a pitch close to the stadium. Only one survivor of the East Germans' 1974 Cup-Winners' Cup-winning side remained – Jurgen Pommerenke – and he played in both legs.

First leg goalscorer Walsh started in place of young Lake. The Swans had to score to keep the tie alive but their task was made even more difficult when Pommerenke broke away to net on the half-hour. Gale replaced a tiring Latchford but the home defence was rarely troubled and the Swans bowed out 0-1 on the night and 1-2 on aggregate.

It would be another six years before Swansea City made their next European travel plans. In 1989 they were given another crack, routing Kidderminster Harriers 5-0 to set up a Cup-Winners' Cup clash with top Greek side Panathinaikos. Swans were then managed by former Welsh international Ian Evans but they had not enjoyed a bright start to the 1989-90 Division Three season. They were seventh from the bottom with only four points from the four games played. The tie in Athens took place in the Olympic Stadium to the north of the capital and not in the Greek club's normal 25,000 capacity stadium.

The Swansea party prepared in a luxury hotel on the outskirts of Athens, training in the evening because of the daytime heat. Veteran player-coach Tommy Hutchison was experiencing his first taste of European football approaching his 42nd birthday, while the Swans' skipper, twenty-year-old Andrew Melville, was one of the youngest captains in the

Football League. Chris Coleman was also in the starting line-up along with Robbie James and Crystal Palace loanee John Salako.

The young Swans – eight of them 23 years old or under – wilted in front of the 40,000 baying fans and after an hour found themselves trailing 0-3. Andy Legg went on for David D'Auria, Paul Raynor pulled one goal back, and Salako met a Hutchison corner to make it 2-3.

Four days before the second leg the Swans were humiliated 1-6 by Reading in the League at the Vetch. This affected the attendance because only 8,276 bothered to turn out to see if their favourites could pull back the deficit.

Star of the show for Swansea was skipper Melville whose two second-half goals had looked enough to take his club through. A Robbie James penalty had given them a half-time lead and Melville netted his first straight after the turnaround to put the Swans 4-3 up overall. A controversial goal for the Greeks, which came from an unseen handball, levelled the score but Melville struck again with an angled drive.

Then Terry Boyle pulled down Dimitris Saravakos in the box and it was 5-5 on aggregate. With both sides having scored twice away from home the tie was heading for extra-time but, with five minutes remaining, Saravakos netted his second goal to put the Greek side through.

Swansea had one last crack at the European carrot after they won the Welsh Cup in 1990, beating Wrexham 2-0 at the National Stadium. The Swans were in trouble at the bottom of Division Three and given little hope against Monaco, leaders of the French First Division. The French club were managed by Arsene Wenger and their line-up on 17 September 1991 included George Weah (future World Footballer of the Year), Rui Barros, Emmanuel Petit, and Yuri Djorkaeff.

By this time, Welsh clubs had fallen foul of UEFA's 'four foreigners' ruling. That meant no English-born players, as far as Welsh clubs were concerned, which made team selection very difficult for Frank Burrows, now Swansea manager. He was forced to include seven teenagers in his squad, five of whom had never appeared in a League match.

Prince Rainier and Prince Albert were at the Vetch for the first leg. They saw their side take an early lead from the penalty spot. Midway through the opening period they made it 2-0 but in the 71st minute Andy Legg seized on a poor back-pass to shoot past Jean-Luc Ettori.

Jimmy Gilligan was recalled for the second leg at the Stade Louis 11 Stadium. He had been out for five months with back trouble. Swansea's new keeper, Roger Freestone, was ineligible so Mark Kendall stayed between the posts. A five-goal first-half collapse saw Swansea chasing shadows and it was no better in the second period. Three more goals came after the interval and the Swans were humbled 0-8, still the biggest defeat for any Welsh club in Europe.

That was the last occasion Swansea played in Europe. Five years later Welsh clubs playing in a non-Welsh league were banned from entering any UEFA competition. It was a sad way to bow out, but the club must have rued the lost opportunities when they took their place amongst Europe's finest while they themselves were playing amongst the elite in the First Division of the Football League.

6

ON THE DOWNWARD SPIRAL

(August-December 1982)

John Toshack was expecting great things from the coming season and hoped the club would be well supported. Season ticket sales of £20,000 in 1977 had shot up to £480,000, a staggering rise. Despite the sudden increase in revenue, plans for the continued development of the Vetch Field were scrapped. £2 million had already been laid out on ground improvements and team-building in two years. Struel announced: 'We have no capital available to spend on the ground and we will just have to sit tight, hope we get a good season, and see where that takes us.'

Having built the East Stand and improved the North Terrace, it remained to replace the South and West Stands, originally planned to start in the close season. Struel noted that the club expected average gates of 24,000 last season but the real figure was nearer 18,000. As a sign of the times, on 30 July Wolves were saved from extinction by three minutes thanks to a consortium led by former player Derek Dougan.

The only departure from the Swans' playing staff was Dave Stewart, who reluctantly joined Hong Kong club Rhyoden on a free transfer. The new club skipper would be Ray Kennedy who would take over from Colin Irwin, who had shared the duties with Ante Rajkovic. Kennedy was one of the most successful players in the history of the game in terms of honours. Capped seventeen times by England, he had won five League Championships, three European Cups, one FA Cup and one UEFA Cup. To that total he could also add one Welsh Cup after being in the side that beat Cardiff City.

Swansea had to trim their pre-season schedule as they had been drawn to play in the preliminary round of the Cup-Winners' Cup. Their final friendly, on Friday, 20 August, was against Leicester but five defenders were injured and unavailable. Kennedy joined the walking wounded when he limped off with an ankle injury.

With the season just days away Toshack was forced to play down rumours that he was the man most likely to succeed Bob Paisley as the next boss of Liverpool. Paisley, 63, was to retire at the end of the season after an eight-year rein during which Liverpool had won eighteen trophies. Toshack was obviously a front-runner for one of the top jobs in British football, particularly with his close association with the club.

The Swansea boss had another battle on his hands as he faced disciplinary action from the Welsh FA following remarks made to the referee during the club's last home match of the season against Middlesbrough. He asked for a personal hearing but was still fined £150 and ordered to pay costs.

Seven players needed treatment following the European ties with Portuguese side Braga, and team selection for the visit to Notts County for the opening game was left to the last minute. The problems were compounded not only by the early involvement in the Cup-Winners' Cup, but also by eleven players being away at various times on international duty. With Ante Rajkovic suspended after being dismissed in the Welsh Cup final, the club had to call off the Football Combination game against Norwich at the Vetch on 28 August, the opening day of the season. The postponement was unfortunate as the Swans had worked hard to get back into the Combination having left for financial reasons almost eight years previously.

Despite their high casualty rate, Swansea had reasonable strength in depth and made the visit to Meadow Lane in good heart. Stand-in skipper Dai Davies set a shining example with a series of superb saves to help the Swans open the campaign with a 0-0 draw but he was lucky with a Rachid Harkouk free-kick in the last minute which struck a post. The midweek game in Portugal had taken a lot out of the players and everyone was thankful to come away with a point.

Three days later Coventry were the visitors to the Vetch. Rajkovic was back, but Kennedy was still out. Although in light training he had suffered a reaction, forcing him to miss his third match in a row. Swansea were ready for a tough game as they had failed to beat the Sky Blues in both matches last season. Steve Whitton scored early on for Coventry but Swansea were thrown a lifeline when Coventry full-back Danny Thomas was dismissed in the 52nd minute after two rapid fouls on Leighton James. Within eight minutes the Swans were level. Coventry goalscorer Whitton brought down Jeremy Charles in full flight and Robbie James beat sixteen-year-old keeper Perry Suckling from the spot. Four minutes later Rajkovic laid on an inch-perfect pass for Bob Latchford to make the final score 2-1. For the first home game of the season there was a pitifully low turnout of 11,712.

With a number of players nearing fitness, Toshack brought forward a reserve game against Cardiff to give them match practice and also to allow him to run the eye over some of his younger players.

Four points from the first two games meant hopes were already high that the new season could be even better than the last. Norwich were next up to visit the Vetch. They had started with a home defeat by Manchester City and a draw at Arsenal, having been promoted in third place behind

Luton and Watford. With Kennedy still out, Toshack brought Curtis back into the starting line-up.

The Swans reached heights against Norwich they would never match for the rest of the season. Latchford's twelfth hat-trick of his career, plus a goal by Robbie James, shot them up to an unrealistic second place after three matches. 'We have made a another bright and solid start,' said Latchford afterwards. 'If we carry on like this we will be well pleased.' The former Birmingham and Everton striker took his League tally to 190. His first two were typically powerful headers and a third goal near the end completed the rout. The 4-0 score would be the Swans biggest victory of the season.

Kennedy made his comeback at Watford in midweek but it was not a happy return as the Swans were edged out 1-2. Luther Blissett struck a post with a spot-kick on the stroke of half-time but the referee allowed him to take it again and this time he made no mistake. Nigel Callaghan and John Barnes, the Hornets teenage wingers, saw plenty of the ball, and Blissett set up Callaghan to increase the lead. Although Stevenson beat Steve Sherwood with a close-range header from a corner to make it 2-1, the Swans were unable to make further headway.

When the Wales squad to meet Norway at the Vetch on 22 September was announced, Charles was included in place of injured Arsenal strongman Peter Nicholas. Also named were Chris Marustik, Nigel Stevenson, Davies, Leighton and Robbie James, and Curtis. Added to the seven in the senior squad were four players called up to the Under-21s – Chris Sander, Jimmy Loveridge, Dudley Lewis and Ian Walsh. Included for the first time by Wales boss Mike England was Watford's twenty-year-old defender Kenny Jackett, in for the injured Byron Stevenson.

The trip to Stoke would be a harsh reminder of how tough life was in the First Division. Swansea were unlucky in a way to come up against Mickey Thomas at his magical best, and had the nerve to open the scoring with Latchford's fifth goal of the season. England's centre-half Dave Watson equalised, Davies pushed a shot into his own net for a bizarre own-goal, and thereafter the little Wales international took centre stage. Thomas made it 3-1 from the edge of the area, and when Kennedy pulled down Mark Chamberlain, Paul Maguire completed a hapless day for the Swans to leave them smarting with a 1-4 defeat.

The big news on the following Monday was that Swansea City had fallen behind in their payment instalments to Everton following the signings of Latchford and Stanley for a combined sum of £275,000. As a result of this failure, the Football League had banned Swansea City from signing any more players.

'We have had to re-schedule our payments with Everton and as part of that arrangement the Football League have directed that we are unable to buy other players until the payments are cleared,' said Struel. 'We are perfectly happy to comply with that ruling because we have no intention of buying any more players.'

It was obvious to everyone that with the Swans attracting just 12,000 paying customers, whereas last season it was 18,000, the consequent loss of revenue was already hitting hard.

The Maltese club Sliema Wanderers were put to the sword in the Cup-Winners' Cup before Swansea took on Liverpool at the Vetch Field on 18 September. The Merseysiders had notched up three wins and two draws in their five League matches to date so they were going to present a severe test for a Swansea side reeling from two straight League defeats. Furthermore, Paisley's side had not lost away from home since 16 February, a total of twelve games, when their opponents happened to be Swansea.

Toshack made one change, with Charles starting in place of Leighton James, but it had little effect. In fact it turned into one of Swansea's most disappointing performances in the manager's four-and-a-half-year reign. Liverpool strolled to an easy 3-0 victory to set the alarm bells ringing ever louder. The Swans failed to establish any pattern and their only goal attempt came near the end when a Kennedy shot had Bruce Grobbelaar diving to push away one-handed. Kenny Dalglish had a hand in all three goals, with two coming from Ian Rush in the first half and the third from Craig Johnston five minutes from the end.

Something had to be done to stop the rot but as no new signings were coming to the club it had to be put right from within.

Four days later Wales beat Norway 1-0 with Rush again on the score-sheet, but only 4,340 fans were at the Vetch to watch. Jackett was given his first cap although strangely he played in midfield: 'I had been playing at the back for Watford but I was just as happy in midfield. It was a fantastic experience playing for Wales for the very first time and one I will never forget.' Although he was born in Watford, Jackett's father Frank – who was also a professional footballer with Watford, and later Orient – was born in Pontardawe.

Chairman Struel felt obliged to have his say regarding the ridiculously low turn-out for an international match: 'The FA of Wales were charging £6 for a seat in the stand, which is dearer than our top price of £5, while Norway are a second class soccer nation and not much of an attraction. We warned them that we were disturbed about the prices they were charging but nothing was done. A low gate was inevitable.'

The next match, at Aston Villa, would provide another stern test as Villa were in the top half of the table but the Swans never expected to be dealt such a blow as losing Irwin for the remainder of the season. Swansea's most expensive signing was being tried as a sweeper when he snapped the tendon behind the kneecap after a mid-air collision with Gary Shaw and falling awkwardly. By then, Villa were already 2-0 ahead through Denis Mortimer and Scottish World Cup defender Allan Evans, though Latchford had had a goal ruled out for offside just before Irwin's departure. Villa were too strong and made it four League defeats in a row for Toshack's side.

(25 September '82)	P	W	D	L	F	A	Pts
17 SWANSEA	7	2	1	4	8	12	7
18 Sunderland	7	2	1	4	7	15	7
19 Ipswich	7	1	3	3	13	11	6
20 Norwich	7	1	3	3	10	13	6
21 Birmingham	7	1	1	5	3	18	4
22 Southampton	7	1	1	5	3	18	4

Tottenham were the attractive visitors to the Vetch Field on 2 October and Toshack caused a major surprise by selecting young Dudley Lewis in place of the experienced Dzemal Hadziabdic. After four straight league defeats he had to act somehow, but bringing in a teenager seemed to be a big gamble. Swansea played without a sweeper and pushed more men forward at every opportunity in order to keep Spurs penned back for long periods. The goal the Swans deserved came on the hour after they had forced a succession of corners. Leighton James swung over yet another, Robbie James glanced it on, and Max Thompson drove the ball in. The clincher came when Latchford fired in from a Curtis cross and the win lifted Swansea three places.

Three days after beating Spurs the struggle for league points took a back seat as it was time for the second round of the Milk Cup. Swans had to make the short trip to Bristol Rovers. The only change from the Spurs game was Jimmy Loveridge in for the injured Leighton James. James had to see a specialist after a recurrence of an Achilles tendon strain.

The Swans were given a scare by the Third Division club and were on the defensive for most of the game. Ian Holloway hit the bar with Davies beaten and Les Barrett almost forced his way through as Swansea wilted under the constant bombardment. Just as it looked as though Swansea had kept their goal intact, a Holloway cross was headed in by big centre-half Tim Parkin. The 1-0 victory was the least the Rovers deserved.

Still full of surprises, Toshack dropped his leading scorer Latchford for the weekend's League visit to mid-table Brighton. The team travelled more in hope than anticipation as they had only gained one point away from home in four matches. Swansea's cause wasn't helped when they fell behind after only 75 seconds. Jimmy Case's corner was hit goalwards by Steve Gatting, brother of cricketer Mike. Davies couldn't hold onto the ball and Steve Foster followed up. The south-coast side might have increased their lead but in the second half the Swans equalised when Lewis ghosted in to head a Leighton James corner over Brighton keeper Graham Moseley.

Everton had lost all four matches away from Goodison to date, so the Swans were in good heart as their meeting approached. Only one change from the starting line-up at the Goldstone Ground was made, Latchford replacing Mahoney. It took just thirty-seven seconds for that confidence to drain away. A hoof out of defence by John Bailey saw the ball fall to Graeme Sharp who miskicked in front of goal. In the confusion that followed Stevenson sliced the ball into his own net for probably the quickest own-goal on record. Walsh replaced the unfortunate Stevenson after the break as Swansea went searching for the much-needed equaliser but Everton went further ahead with a goal by Kevin Richardson. Home fans' misery was complete when full-back Bailey rounded Davies to give the Toffees a 3-0 victory.

Toshack threatened to hit his players 'in the pocket' in the aftermath of that defeat, which had made it five losses from the ten games played: 'We had been completely outclassed and maybe I should have cracked the whip a bit more. We had some players at the club who appeared to enjoy being injured. They did not deserve their wages and I was entitled to more from them.' Harsh words indeed, but were words enough to get the Swans back on the winning trail?

The club decided to cut admission prices for the next two cup matches. The games in question were the Cup-Winners' Cup-tie against Paris St Germain on 20 October and the second leg of the Milk Cup-tie against Bristol Rovers on 26 September. The reductions, in some cases by as much as £2.60, were an attempt to counteract falling gates. Admission to the terraces for those games would be £1.50 instead of £2.20. Normal prices had been in operation for the Sliema Wanderers match and the Swansea directors had reacted quickly to criticisms that spectators had been overcharged.

Despite this initiative the Swansea public failed to respond. There were only 9,505 inside the Vetch as Paris St Germain won 1-0 and as a result the club did not offer cut-price tickets for any more matches.

The visit of relegation-threatened Southampton would be a big pointer as to whether Toshack's post-Everton backlash had hit home. Charles, Thompson, Leighton James and Stevenson were all missing. When in trouble, call on Wyndham Evans, and that is exactly what Toshack did by installing him in the defence to add some steel. Evans responded as expected and by the ninth minute had earned himself a booking for bringing down Saints midfielder Steve Williams. Peter Wells, deputising in goal for the injured Peter Shilton, saved from Mahoney and Robbie James as Swans pressed but when the first goal came it was at the other end., Justin Fashanu lobbing over the advancing Davies.

Toshack must have issued more strong words in the dressing room because within six minutes of the change-round, a Dennis Rofe own-goal and a Robbie James strike had given Swansea a 2-1 lead. But the cheering had hardly died down when Fashanu made space down the right and his cross was hammered into the net by David Wallace. Not to be outdone, the Swans went back on the attack and two minutes from time Latchford scored the 193rd goal of his career to make it 3-2 and gain his club a priceless three points.

The Milk Cup second-leg against Bristol Rovers had to be fitted in between the Southampton match and a trip to Maine Road, and Toshack decided on his best available eleven in order to see off the Third Division outfit. Charles was recalled, but took up a place in the defence. Since the first leg the Swans had lost Thompson who was keeping Stevenson and Irwin company in the treatment room. The game became a showpiece for Latchford as the burly striker scored all three goals for his second hat-trick of the season to ease the Swans through to round three. The presence of Rajkovic in defence and the extra striker in Leighton James up front made all the difference and there was plenty of entertainment for the 9,755 crowd. Latchford's first was an angled drive from a Charles pass and in the second half he powered home two bullet headers. He had now reached 250 League and cup goals in his career while taking his season's tally to eleven, easily the Swans top scorer. Former England striker Mick Channon was a late substitute for Rovers.

On the eve of the Bristol Rovers game Toshack received a touchline ban and was fined £200 by the Welsh FA disciplinary committee. The fine took the total levied against him in the past four years to £725, and it was the fifth occasion that he had been called to appear before the Welsh FA. Toshack, who could not return to the touchline or dug-out until 1 March 1983, was handed the verdict after a two-and-a-half-hour meeting of the commission following a half-time incident during Swansea's match at Watford on 7 September. It was stated that Toshack's behaviour was likely to bring the game into disrepute and he was also ordered to pay costs. The Welsh FA president, Selwyn Jenkins, noted that if the Swansea manager were to name himself as a substitute then the ban would not be enforced.

It was off to Maine Road next, but at least after a win under their belts hopes were high that a first away success was just around the corner. Mahoney and Stevenson both passed late fitness tests to take their places in the starting eleven. Victory was there for the taking as Swansea had a number of good scoring opportunities yet spurned all but one. It was not until Asa Hartford's 65th-minute deflected goal, which made it 2-0 to the home side, that the Swans were finally stung into action. Straight from the restart Swansea won a free-kick and when Robbie James floated the ball into the danger area, Latchford headed powerfully past Joe Corrigan in the Blues goal. Denis Tueart had scored the opener, volleying home from a free-kick that Hartford clipped over the defensive wall. The net result was a 1-2 defeat.

Following elimination from the Cup-Winners' Cup in Paris, minds had to focus on a win-at-all-costs game against relegation-threatened Sunderland at the Vetch. Toshack was not helped by an injury situation that was getting worse, not better. He was forced to bring Marustik back into the team even though he had not played since the first leg against Paris St Germain. Kennedy, Latchford and Hadziabdic were all ruled out, and Kennedy in particular was upset about missing the opportunity of playing against the side he supported as a boy. He also had a score to settle with Sunderland, claiming that he had been ready to sign for them from Liverpool, only for Roker manager Alan Durban to keep him hanging around waiting while Durban discussed openly whether he really wanted to sign him or not.

Fortunately Curtis chose the afternoon to register his first goals of the season as Swansea destroyed a very poor Sunderland side 3-0. The victory showed that the players were capable of bouncing back after their European exit and the disruption caused by the lengthy injury list. Nine Welshman, a Yugoslav and an Englishman made up the home side and they quickly made Sunderland look vulnerable. Curtis nipped between the back four, rounded keeper Chris Turner, and slotted home after nine minutes. Robbie James scored the easiest goal of his career when he sidefooted in from point-blank range, and Curtis added his second midway through the second half when a Leighton James shot rebounded straight to him and he dived full length to beat Turner. Leighton James had been an early substitute for Marustik who joined the lengthy casualty list with a twisted ankle.

Preston showed interest in taking Max Thompson on loan as soon as he recovered from injury. He had been missing for three weeks with a tight hamstring but was nearing a return to action. Having only made three appearances in the current season, Toshack obviously felt that he could now do without the defender signed from Blackpool in September 1981.

The League Cup road now took Swansea to Third Division Brentford. The Bees had established a reputation as a high-scoring side with 34 League goals but on the two occasions that Swansea had them watched, at Plymouth and against Bradford City, they had failed to score. They had a couple of famous 'names' in their side, with Ron 'Chopper' Harris at the back and the diminutive Stan Bowles in midfield. There was also a place for Chris Kamara, now a television pundit. Toshack made three changes, with Hadziabdic, Kennedy and Latchford all starting to the exclusion of Marustik, Lewis and Walsh.

The first half was full of incident and three players were booked in the opening ten minutes. Latchford netted his thirteenth goal of the season after Brentford keeper Pat Roche, once of Manchester United, pushed out a Robbie James header and the big striker despatched the rebound. Bowles then put Rhyl-born Gary Roberts away down the right and Davies was beaten at his near post. It ended 1-1, forcing Swansea into an unwelcome replay.

Curtis was missing from the side that played at West Brom as league action resumed. After being examined by a specialist, the Welsh international was told that he had to rest. Leighton James took his place, eager to show the manager that he still had a future at the club rather than with Rotherham who were interested in taking him to Millmoor. James was still to open his goalscoring account after eighteen appearances.

When Swansea went 0-3 behind a minute into the second half they looked finished, yet they fought back to level and if the match had gone on any longer they would have surely won. Nicky Cross and Martin Jol had Albion ahead before the interval and the Swans were caught cold after the break when Peter Eastoe increased the lead. Suddenly the game changed and Swansea began playing confident and constructive football. Kennedy was now bossing midfield and Leighton James started tormenting the home defence. It was James who began the fight-back by chipping Tony Godden for his season's opener. Charles then headed in a James cross to pull another one back. Albion were now in disarray and it was no surprise when another James centre was turned in by Robbie James to complete a fantastic recovery. The Swans now lay twelfth, a healthy four points clear of the relegation positions.

(13 November '82)	P	W	D	L	F	A	Pts
11 Everton	14	5	3	6	25	24	18
12 SWANSEA	14	5	3	6	21	23	18
13 Coventry	14	5	3	6	13	19	18
14 Notts Co	14	5	3	6	17	24	18
15 Brighton	14	5	3	6	14	28	18
16 Ipswich	14	4	5	5	23	16	17
17 Arsenal	14	4	5	5	14	15	17
18 Luton	14	3	7	4	28	28	16
19 Southampton	14	4	3	7	14	27	15
20 Sunderland	14	3	5	6	18	28	14
21 Birmingham	14	2	6	6	9	24	12
22 Norwich	14	2	5	7	15	24	11

Leighton James had been put on the transfer list at a fee of £50,000 and Rotherham maintained their interest, but the player had done himself a power of good with his display against Albion. Coach Doug Livermore confirmed that James had been in talks with Millers' boss Emlyn Hughes but there were no new developments.

Because the Brentford League Cup replay was scheduled for 17 November, Toshack asked the Welsh FA to release his nine players from attending a three-day squad session in Cardiff. They were not due back in Swansea until the day before the game and some needed treatment, but Mike England agreed to let them back early with plenty of time to pre-pare for the cup-tie.

Brentford's preparation had received a setback when they were beat-en 0-2 at Huddersfield, but that had been without Stan Bowles. He was back for the replay at Swansea, along with 38-year-old Harris. The Swans were a goal down before many of the spectators had even taken their seats. Roberts began the move from the centre circle kick-off and had the ball in the Swansea net inside nineteen seconds. The Welshman, who had also hit the target at Griffin Park, swept home Francis Joseph's low cross without checking his stride.

The 6,674 crowd saw little to suggest that Swansea could get back into the game and in the 83rd minute the Londoners struck again when Tony Mahoney netted the rebound after Joseph's shot had cannoned off the foot of the upright. Although Loveridge, who had replaced Robinson, pulled one back a minute later, the visitors held out to book a place in the last sixteen where they would meet Nottingham Forest.

Curtis had missed the last couple of games and failed a fitness test on his troublesome knee that would now keep him out of the side to meet

Arsenal at the Vetch. Kennedy was also unfit after failing to recover from the knock he received against West Brom. Leighton James was left out and Lewis started along with Loveridge. George Wood was in the Arsenal goal, while David O'Leary had recovered from concussion to take his place at the centre of defence.

When a brilliant strike by Latchford gave the Swans a priceless lead on the hour it was expected that they would go on to beat the Gunners yet dogged persistence saw Arsenal hit back to win 2-1. Woodcock levelled and then, with time running out, substitute Lee Chapman was on hand to snatch a late winner.

It was a bitter pill to swallow although the home players could not be faulted for lack of effort. Somehow the spark that had been evident throughout the previous season was missing, and at this level more than just honest endeavour was needed. A small section of the crowd showed their disapproval of the evening's events and six people later appeared at Swansea magistrates for breach of the peace offences.

Curtis and Kennedy both had to sit out the trip to Ipswich. The only change in the Swans starting eleven was a surprise as Toshack included attacker Leighton James while dispensing with Lewis, a defender. This was Swansea's eighth away match of the season and they were still seeking their first victory.

Two moments of madness at corners cost Swansea the points. Rajkovic left Russell Osman free at a corner and he headed in off the crossbar. At another Steve McCall flag-kick Stanley allowed John Wark the freedom to hit his tenth goal of the season. Full-back George Burley added another goal in between, his first since November 1978. It might have been worse as Paul Mariner missed three glorious opportunities and Alan Brazil struck a post. Leighton James scored a late consolation when his shot was deflected over Paul Cooper's head by Terry Butcher.

At least Curtis and Kennedy would be fit for the visit of Luton on the first Saturday in December. With only Irwin and Thompson now on the treatment table, Toshack could set his mind solely on lifting his side clear of the drop zone. Three successive defeats, two in the League and one in the Milk Cup, had seen the confidence drain out of the squad but the return of Curtis and Kennedy was a real boost to players and fans alike. Loveridge and Leighton James dropped out to accommodate the two internationals, with James being given the substitute's spot. The Swans' defence had been a major cause for concern, with eight goals conceded in the last three League games. Rajkovic had not yet reached his best form following his injury but Toshack continued to persevere with the Yugoslav.

With only three victories to date, the Hatters were in an even worse position than Swansea. The catalyst for the Swans' precious victory was Latchford who hit his fifteenth goal of the season in the 2-0 result. He was now top of the First Division goal chart, having taken over from previous leader Ian Rush. The only disappointment of the afternoon came when Curtis's knee trouble flared up after an hour and he was replaced by Leighton James. It was Curtis who had put his side ahead soon after half-time. He latched onto a Stanley cross and found the corner of the net with a close-range header. When Latchford made it 2-0 there was no way back for David Pleat's side. The victory lifted the Swans up to fourteenth, while Luton slipped further into the mire.

Morale was lifted even higher when the Wales party to meet Yugoslavia in Titograd was announced. Included in the squad were Robbie James, Mahoney, Leighton James and Curtis, although he would be pulled out by Toshack and replaced by Charles. Lewis, Marustik and Loveridge were all part of the Under-21 squad named at the same time. Charles, Stevenson and Marustik were all omitted from the senior squad but tried not to let their heads drop as they realised they had all come a long way in a very short time. They had been Fourth Division players when Toshack arrived and they had had to readjust almost every season since then.

The Welsh Cup came round once again and the Swans were keen to keep hold of the trophy and, with it, entry into European competition. Welsh League side Spencer Works would provide the first opposition but, as in the previously successful campaigns, Toshack refused to field a weakened side. Nevertheless, Stevenson was out with the calf muscle injury while Rajkovic and Kennedy also missed the first training session. Resources were stretched to the limit as there was also a Combination match to play at Millwall 24 hours later. Walsh and Robinson were both given an outing at the Den but reserve keeper Chris Sander was kept at home after having a wisdom tooth operation.

On the day of the Welsh Cup-tie Chairman Struel spoke publicly of his disappointment at the level of support the club was receiving. In what he described as a bitter-sweet season he reckoned that he had been let down by the public: 'I was very disappointed that last season's average was only just over 18,000 when we had such a successful season. It is also a surprise that we remain one of the few First Division clubs yet to attract a major shirt sponsor, particularly as the commercial potential for a sponsor allied to this club is tremendous.'

Although the Swans had finished the 1981-82 season sixth from the top, they actually finished sixth from the bottom in terms of gates: 'The fortunes of the club will depend on the quantity and quality of the support it receives,' Struel added, ominously. His insisted he was unhappy with the level of support, coming as it does from a potential catchment area of 600,000 people.

Following that broadside the Swans took the field against their Welsh League opponents in defence of the cup they had won for the last two years and they strolled to a 3-0 success. First-half goals in the space of three minutes from Robbie James and Latchford put the game beyond the minnows and James added his second late in the match. He was prevented from recording a hat-trick when the Spencer keeper saved his spot-kick in the last minute.

For the trip to high-flying Nottingham Forest, Robinson was summoned for his first game of the season as Toshack looked for a hardman to make his presence felt in the centre of the field. Curtis also made a surprise appearance, considering his withdrawal from the Wales squad. That would lead to an inquest by the Welsh FA as they sought to clarify Curtis's situation. The reason ultimately given, and accepted, was that the player was not fit enough to play two games in a week.

Swansea's victory over Forest back in May was their last success on their travels. In a bid to emulate that result, Davies showed why he was the holder of so many Welsh caps. He made tremendous saves throughout the match to keep Forest at bay and without him Swansea would have been sunk without trace. Kennedy was hobbling for much of the match, leaving Mahoney with twice the work to do. Eventually the strain on the side told.

Brian Clough's side went ahead midway through the first half after a goalmouth scramble. The ball fell kindly to Colin Walsh and he rifled it in despite a brave attempt by Davies to block. They increased their advantage on the hour when Ian Wallace poked the ball through to Mark Proctor. Davies saved his first shot on goal but the young midfielder made no mistake with the rebound. Swansea were somehow back in the match when Robbie James hit a twenty-yarder past Steve Sutton but it made no difference to the outcome.

On 15 December, Wales drew 4-4 against Yugoslavia in Titograd, with Robbie James claiming a late but deserved equaliser.

Toshack realised that he had to stiffen his defence but as the club were banned from signing any new players he knew the answer had to come from within. For the visit of second-placed Manchester United he turned to the club's senior professional Wyndham Evans. Evans had only made one full appearance in the First Division in his twelve years at the club after being carried off early on during his debut in the top flight against

Tottenham in 1981-82. The manager had turned to Evans a number of times, especially when he needed a touch of steel added to the side, but Manchester United had the best defensive record in the division and would be a hard nut to crack.

Kennedy was a non-starter and Stevenson and Marustik were in London with the reserves at Arsenal but Mahoney passed a late fitness test after incurring an ankle injury on Wales duty in Yugoslavia.

United's five-match winning run was halted by the Swans who ground out a 0-0 draw. The introduction of an additional man in midfield shackled the United side who were unable to play an expansive game. Frank Stapleton looked to have scored when his header appeared to be over the line before Latchford hacked it clear but the referee waved play on. The visitors never really threatened the home goal after that early scare and in fact Robbie James might almost have sneaked all three points for his side, only for Gary Bailey to deny him with a superb reflex save. James had been a model of consistency ever since the Swans arrived in the First Division as he had never missed a game in the top flight for his hometown club.

There was no time for the players to enjoy the festive season. They trained on Christmas morning and again on Sunday before leaving for London in the search for that elusive away victory. West Ham had been a bit of a bogey side to the Swans ever since they both challenged for promotion from the Second Division. Robbie James was given the captaincy in the absence of the injured Kennedy while Stevenson, Marustik and reserve keeper Chris Sander were all added to the travelling squad.

At half-time it looked as though fans' Christmas wishes were being answered as the team led 2-0 after a brace of goals from leading marksman Latchford. Yet it all conspired to go wrong when play resumed in the second half. The Swans had been well worth that lead after Latchford ran on to a pass from Rajkovic in the 26th minute, swerved past Alvin Martin and wrong-footed Hammers keeper Phil Parkes. With Charles outstanding at the heart of the defence, the Hammers couldn't get started and in the 38th minute Swansea doubled their lead. A cross from Leighton James was dummied by Robbie James and Latchford was on hand to slide the ball in.

The second half was a different story. Ray Stewart pulled one back from the spot after Stanley had brought down Alan Devonshire. Francois van der Elst equalised from close in after a Devonshire run had opened up the defence, and just when it seemed that both sides would leave with a point apiece, Paul Goddard's volley was deflected by Rajkovic. It wrong-footed Davies and the Hammers had stolen a 3-2 victory.

North Bank regular Tony Gilbert had been following the Swans way back in 1964 when they reached the FA Cup semi-final: 'I went to Liverpool for the quarter-final because a pal of mine got me a ticket. The only drawback was that I ended up on the Kop and had to keep my mouth shut all through the game. I'll never forget Noel Dwyer's performance that day.

'During the good days when we were on the way up to Division One I went to quite a few away matches including a long train journey up to Newcastle. I also recall the coach trips to and from London for the West Ham game. We always seemed to stop in strange places for a breather on the way back and I remember that on the long trip home from Upton Park we stopped off at a Darby and Joan club and had a really good time there.

'Supporting the Swans, especially in that first season, was no hardship as we genuinely felt we could beat anyone. It's a shame it ended the way it did.'

There was no time for the players to feel sorry for themselves as two days later, 29 December, Birmingham City were at the Vetch in the last game of a very eventful 1982. Toshack decided on all-out attack, with fit again Curtis replacing Stanley. It was a shade early for Kennedy's return but he did play for the reserves at Oxford.

With the Blues in even more trouble than the Swans, plenty of goals were expected, but in a tension-packed match where both sides were desperate for points it was defences who came out on top. To make matters worse the injury jinx struck again and Charles was forced off at half-time. When Robbie James also went off injured there was the prospect of the Swans finishing the game with ten men but fortunately he was able to return after lengthy treatment.

Swansea needed the three points while Birmingham were still without an away win in the League, and this put the emphasis for both sides on commitment rather than skill. The point gained from a 0-0 draw saw the Swans end 1982 in seventeenth place, four above their opponents.

(29 December '82)	P	W	D	L	F	A	Pts
16 Arsenal	21	7	6	8	25	28	27
17 SWANSEA	21	6	5	10	28	33	23
18 Luton	21	5	8	8	37	44	23
19 Norwich	21	6	5	10	24	35	23
20 Brighton	21	6	4	11	19	40	22
21 Birmingham	21	4	9	8	15	29	21
22 Sunderland	21	4	7	10	24	37	19

With Charles likely to miss the New Year opening matches it was not looking good for the Swansea chief. The ongoing injury list was proving to be too tough to overcome, and with the ban on signing new players help had to come from within the club. It was with much apprehension that Swans fans viewed the second half of the season.

7

THE END OF THE DREAM

(January-May 1983)

New Year celebrations were few and far between as far as the Swansea City FC players, staff and supporters were concerned. Having been down amongst the bottom clubs for most of the first half of the season, the Swans knew that a big improvement was necessary to haul themselves away from trouble.

On New Year's Eve the players travelled to London in readiness for a crucial game against Arsenal who rather surprisingly were also having a poor season just one place above Swansea. The loss of Robbie James and Jeremy Charles through injury was a bitter blow that John Toshack's side would find hard to overcome. Dudley Lewis and Nigel Stevenson were brought into the side and Gary Stanley named on the bench. The absence of James meant that he had lost his record of appearing in every First Division match played by the Swans.

It turned out to be a disastrous afternoon at Highbury as within six minutes the Gunners had raced into a two-goal lead. Alan Sunderland's half-hit shot was deflected into the net and two minutes later the debut-making Yugoslav, Vladimir Petrovic, set up a second. He sent Woodcock racing through the middle to slam the ball past Davies. Swansea hit back in the second half when Alan Curtis headed past Pat Jennings and might even have snatched an undeserved equaliser when John Mahoney drilled a thirty-yard shot that Pat Jennings palmed away.

The results of the other clubs in the basement didn't go Swansea's way. Three of the five clubs fighting it out at the bottom picked up points while Swansea were falling to their eighth away defeat of the season. Only three points now separated them from bottom-of-the-table Sunderland.

Two days later Swansea suffered an even bigger blow as Norwich, one of the few clubs below them, won 1-0 at Carrow Road to leave the Swans level bottom along with three other clubs. A goal from veteran Mick Channon in the second half sank the Swans. The former England international, signed from Bristol Rovers on a free transfer before Christmas, pounced in the 58th minute when Davies couldn't hold onto a shot from John Deehan. The result was hardly ideal preparation for the third round of the FA Cup as the Swans had to travel back to Carrow Road on 8 January.

Tensions were running high at the Vetch Field. On 6 January Toshack stripped Kennedy of the captaincy and suspended him for two weeks. He described his actions as in the best interests of the club. Kennedy had not played first-team football since being taken off in the second half of the 1-2 defeat at Nottingham Forest on 18 December. Appointed captain at the start of the season, the former Liverpool midfielder had been in miserable form while constantly troubled by injury. He had played two reserve games as he attempted a come-back and was due to play another one but withdrew an hour before kick-off. His suspension meant that he would not be training with the club although he would still receive his full salary. Robbie James would be the new skipper and his high level of commitment made him an ideal choice.

Toshack also revealed that Leighton James, who had joined the club from Burnley in a £120,000 deal, had been given a free transfer. The Swansea chief called a press conference to announce the decisions he had taken regarding two of his senior players. He also accepted full responsibility for Swansea's decline to joint bottom place in the First Division and reckoned that he had somehow to recreate the spirit of the previous season and put some life back into a jaded team. Toshack made the point that everything that could go wrong had done so and the injury to Colin Irwin had been the biggest problem. More crucially, he felt that some of the players were still not contributing enough to the cause.

Darren Gale was called up to make his FA Cup debut as the Swans made a quick return to East Anglia. Gale's only two League appearances had been as a substitute against Aston Villa and Brighton but he had bagged four goals for the reserves in their last two outings. Toshack also found a place for nineteen-year-old full-back Gary Richards who was making his first appearance of the season. Nigel Stevenson came in to strengthen the defence. The three players missing from the League defeat five days previously were the injured Neil Robinson along with Wyndham Evans and John Mahoney.

Before leaving for Norwich, Toshack learned that his appeal against his fine and suspension had been rejected by the Welsh FA executive at a meeting in Birmingham.

Toshack was obviously looking to the future, as his side named to face Norwich contained eight local discoveries. The two Yugoslavs and Bob Latchford were the only non-Welshmen in the team. Leighton James was not considered as he was involved in talks with Sunderland manager Alan Durban about a move to Roker Park.

Striker Keith Bertschin foiled Toshack's gamble by scoring twice in the Canaries' 2-1 victory. Gale had stunned the home crowd by putting Swansea ahead with his first senior goal after fourteen minutes, sweeping home a loose ball.

Unfortunately Bertschin, without a goal in his previous eleven games, suddenly found his shooting boots. He scored twice in the first half and should have recorded a hat-trick after Lewis handled in the area. Davies came to Lewis's rescue by tipping away Bertschin's spot-kick. At the end, Toshack left the ground without talking to the press.

Leighton James asked to play for the reserves at Fulham on 11 January in order to keep match fit while talks with Sunderland proceeded. Joining him at Craven Cottage were Evans, Stevenson, Stanley, Robinson, Ian Walsh and Jimmy Loveridge. Interest in James also came from his former club Burnley, Rotherham and Third Division big spenders Portsmouth. In the event, he played his last game for Swansea in the reserves when they were beaten 0-1 at Fulham.

Still without that elusive away victory, the Swans had to maximize their home points to lift themselves out of the relegation zone. If only the players were fit it would give Toshack the opportunity of fielding a settled side, something that hadn't happened for most of the season.

Yet another blow came when Terry Medwin, youth development officer, resigned due to ill health. The fifty-year-old former Wales international, who began his career at the Vetch in 1950, returned to the club in July 1978 as assistant manager, but after his health deteriorated he accepted a less demanding role looking after the youth players.

In another unexpected development Manchester-based Harry Gregg, manager of the Swans 1972-75, was enlisted to strengthen the Vetch management team. Toshack reckoned that he needed an older, wiser man and as a former manager at the club, Gregg knew the set-up.

The Swans eased the pressure slightly when they beat Notts County 2-0, though it took two late goals to see off the Magpies. Gale came off the bench to score his first goal in League football and then made the other for Latchford. Gale had turned down the chance of Welsh Schools rugby trials to pursue a career with the round ball and the manner in which he was progressing suggested he had made the correct choice.

A swirling wind made play difficult but the home defence held firm for a rare clean sheet. On the debit side, the official attendance of 8,992 was Swansea's lowest for a Division One fixture.

With Shrewsbury next due at the Vetch for a Welsh Cup-tie the Swans were presented with a rare opportunity to post two home wins inside a week, but on the eve of the Shrews match Chairman Struel made an astonishing attack on the Welsh FA. He threatened that the club was seriously considering leaving the Welsh governing body to join the English FA. This came after a major row with the Welsh FA over four important issues which were outlined by Struel.

(1) Toshack's four-month ban.

(2) The difficulties of Football League clubs gaining representation on the Welsh FA.

(3) The Welsh FA's refusal to compensate League clubs for the use of international players.

(4) The Welsh FA's proposals towards staging international matches at Cardiff's National Stadium.

Welsh FA secretary Alun Evans responded by saying it would be impossible for Swansea to carry out their threat and even hinted that Struel's remarks bordered on bringing the game into disrepute. The Swansea match programme in which Struel vented his grievances would be carefully studied by the Welsh FA before they made a decision on what action, if any, would be taken.

Commenting on the possibility of international matches being played at the National Stadium, Struel wrote: 'I was astounded to read that it is seriously being contemplated. I think it is quite unbelievable that even a single Welsh FA member could think of playing soccer on a rugby ground, thereby putting money into rugby when we have perfectly good league grounds for the staging of matches.'

Clearly the Swansea chairman was under pressure both financially and on the field of play and no doubt that had much to do with his outburst.

Gale, the nineteen-year-old from Port Talbot, scored his third goal in three games as the Swans got back to playing football on 18 January. His goal helped Swansea beat Shrewsbury 2-1 to move on to the fifth round of the Welsh Cup. Gale set up a fifth-minute goal for Bob Latchford on his 32nd birthday and then scored himself with an angled shot that went under Shrewsbury keeper Steve Ogrizovic. Toshack was happy with his strike-force of Gale and Latchford as since they were paired together they had found the net five times in three games.

Coventry had climbed into the top six on the strength of only one home defeat, so winning at Highfield Road was a difficult task for the Swans. Nevertheless, they ground out a 0-0 draw. But the biggest talking point afterwards was the comments made by the Sky Blues public address announcer. As the teams were leaving the field he said over the tannoy system: 'That was a good point for Swansea but they won't have made any friends with a display like that.' It was a good thing Toshack didn't hear the outburst, particularly as he was still serving a touchline ban.

A rare piece of good news came when Jimmy Hadziabdic said he had changed his mind about leaving at the end of the season. Ante Rajkovic and Latchford also expressed their wish to stay for another year. Those three represented possibly the best investment during the Toshack era.

The Swans made a bit of history on 6 February when they played host to old rivals Watford. It was the first time that any First Division game had been played on a Sunday. Latchford scored the 200th goal of his career to give his side a first-half lead but Graham Taylor's Hornets hit back after the break to win 3-1. It was the first home loss in the League since Arsenal in November and it brought a swift end to the Swans' mini-revival. The one consolation was that the match attracted a crowd of 14,461, the fourth highest gate of the season, so the experiment of playing on a Sunday certainly worked in that respect. Latchford reached his milestone when forcing the ball home after a Curtis shot had been blocked. Luther Blissett's header and Stevenson's woefully short pass-back, intercepted by John Barnes, had turned the tables, and with one minute remaining, Jackett's cross was missed by Davies, leaving Blissett with a simple tap-in for his fourteenth strike of the season. Jeremy Charles had the dubious distinction of being the first Division One player ever booked on a Sunday when he was cautioned in the 61st minute.

Three days later the Swans welcomed Fourth Division Hereford in the fifth round of the Welsh Cup. Hadziabdic, who had been out of the team since helping the Swans beat Shrewsbury in the previous round, was added to the squad. The Bulls took the lead after just thirty seconds when Steve Phillips, a 21-year-old striker, got on the end of a free-kick from Jimmy Harvey. Latchford settled the nerves with an equaliser and put his side in front midway through the second half with a header from Chris Marustik's cross. Robbie James sealed a 3-1 victory in front of a sparse crowd totalling 2,688.

Swansea's poor run of form which had taken them deep into the relegation mire caused Toshack's new assistant Gregg to read the riot act. He was scathing about the attitude of the players and reckoned they had to roll up their sleeves and start believing in themselves. 'The Cinderella days of last season are over,' he ranted. 'The players were carried along on a tide of emotion but that should be forgotten and the real test is now. Let's see if they have got what it takes to come back from the dead.'

Gregg's harsh words seemed to have little effect on the players as they put in another lacklustre performance in losing 0-1 at Tottenham. The only reason it wasn't a heavier defeat was the lack of Spurs fire-power up front. Kennedy played at the heart of the Swansea defence and looked lost. Terry Gibson engineered the game's only goal when his deep first-half cross was met by Garth Crooks who couldn't fail to score from point-blank range. Rajkovic went off injured, to be replaced by Gale, and it was the youngster who produced Swansea's only serious threat on the Spurs goal in the dying seconds.

Such were the problems now facing Toshack that he stayed behind while the first-team squad enjoyed a four-day break in Spain. Ominously, he included himself in the reserves squad for the Combination home match against Norwich. By foregoing the annual winter break he had the opportunity of doing a bit of thinking on his own. Many supporters questioned the wisdom of sending the players on a costly winter trip abroad, particularly as there was little money left in the kitty. Toshack's answer was that although the club was skint, they had done it before and it had proved successful. Whether this trip would help the Swans move away from the relegation zone only time would tell.

On 18 February the Swans lost 0-1 in a friendly at Hibernian. Willie Irvine scored the goal. With Toshack again staying behind, Gregg was in charge of the squad at Easter Road. Five days later Mahoney and Robbie James started for Wales against England at Wembley but Wales lost 1-2 on a frozen pitch.

Curtis, Rajkovic and Charles were all non-starters for the trip to Everton when League football resumed on 26 February. The first two were unfit but Charles was starting a two-match suspension. A consequence of so many injuries and international call-ups meant the Swans were unable to make their usual pre-match preparations. Under the circumstances Toshack decided to give youth a fling and five graduates from the club's successful youth side were included in the thirteen-man squad. The Swansea chief publicly claimed that certain senior players had let him down. A hint to their identity came when Thompson and Stanley were placed on the transfer list. Stanley, who cost £150,000 from Everton, was available for just £30,000, while Thompson was given a free transfer.

The youngsters didn't let their manager down and Gale swept his side into a 2-1 lead with only nine minutes remaining. Sadly, a late Andy King strike, his second of the game, squared it at 2-2. It was King who opened the scoring in the first half but Robbie James replied from long range. Davies played well in the Swansea goal, particularly as the swirling wind made it difficult to judge crosses, and although King had the last word it was at least a point earned in a battling performance.

(26 February '83)	P	W	D	L	F	A	Pts
17 Sunderland	28	8	9	11	33	43	33
18 Luton	27	7	9	11	47	57	30
19 SWANSEA	28	7	7	14	34	42	28
20 Birmingham	27	5	12	10	23	36	27
21 Norwich	27	7	6	14	26	45	27
22 Brighton	28	6	7	15	25	53	25

Toshack was so delighted with the display at Everton that he named an unchanged side for the midweek visit of bottom club Brighton. The match was played on 1 March 1983, five years to the day that Toshack had taken charge, and with his touchline ban now completed he could once again sit in the dug-out.

Like Swansea, the Seagulls were without an away victory all season. In fact it was almost a year since they last triumphed on their travels. Yet Mike Robinson gave his side the lead when he chased a long ball from Steve Gatting. His first shot was blocked by Davies but he followed up to ram the rebound over the line. A 24th goal of the season for Latchford restored parity but the visitors snatched an unlikely win when Jimmy Case fired a twenty-yard rocket into the roof of the net. The result was catastrophic for Swansea's hopes of survival.

To make matters worse, Mahoney was hurt following a tackle with Tony Grealish and had to be replaced by the debut-making Colin Pascoe. Mahoney later underwent surgery at Singleton Hospital for a triple fracture of the ankle, which meant that he was out for the rest of the season. The hardworking midfielder had just celebrated his 51st international cap and his honest grafting in midfield would be sorely missed.

Supporters were shocked to read on 4 March that the club had agreed a fee of £100,000 with Chelsea for the sale of leading scorer Latchford. It was a move solely designed to ease their critical financial situation. The clubs had agreed the fee, now it was up to the player, who was finding it difficult to keep two houses going, one in Swansea and his old home in Southport. In view of the pending transfer Latchford would be omitted from the side to play Southampton. In the event, Latchford turned down the move to London as his wife wanted to stay in Swansea.

With only one win from the last twelve League games, the Swans had nose-dived into the bottom three and a 1-2 defeat at the Dell spelt even more trouble. For over an hour they looked capable of taking a point or even three from the game and they even took the lead when Loveridge collected a pass from Robbie James and steered his first League goal past Peter Shilton. Davies was powerless to stop Ian Baird from levelling soon afterwards. Swansea were then made to pay for slack defending when David Armstrong nipped in to prod home a Mick Mills cross.

Latchford celebrated his decision to stay in Wales by scoring the only goal of the Welsh Cup semi-final. The first leg against Colwyn Bay was played at Rhyl in front of 3,500 and although the Swans were on top for most of the match they failed to add to their tally.

The cash crisis and the fight against relegation were having a bad effect on morale, and Hadziabdic announced he was changing his mind once again and would be leaving at the end of the season when his contract terminated. He joined Davies and one or two others lining up on the departures list.

Harry Gregg's short-term contract turned out to be shorter than expected. He was sacked just two months after being recruited to strengthen the management team. Toshack admitted that he had made a mistake in bringing Gregg back to the club: 'I brought him back to help me but it wasn't working out so I dismissed him.'

Walsh was recalled to the squad for the visit of Manchester City after showing up well and scoring goals in the reserves. Toshack also included Chris Sander for the departing Davies. Latchford showed what the Swans would have been missing if they had allowed him to leave for Chelsea. He played a leading role in the club's first League win for eight weeks by scoring his 26th goal of the season and setting up Walsh for the first of his brace.

Robbie James was the architect of the first goal when his fierce drive was parried by Joe Corrigan, only for Latchford to hammer the loose ball into the net. The Swans notched their second when Walsh added the finishing touch after the Blues defence failed to clear. James earned a penalty on the stroke of half-time to make it 3-0 at the break. Walsh added his second early in the second half and would have claimed a hat-trick but for a superb stop by Corrigan. Bobby McDonald pulled one back for caretaker manager John Benson but the result extended his team's winless run to nine.

On 16 March it was reported that North American League club Tampa Bay Rowdies were interested in Kennedy. Swansea replied that they were willing to let him go and left it up to the player. Either Kennedy didn't fancy a move across the water or the Rowdies shelved their interest because nothing came of it. Ideally, Kennedy was looking for a move back to the North East but Newcastle hadn't pursued their early-season interest when they wanted him on loan.

More injury woes came with the news that Walsh was back on the treatment table, having turned an ankle in training. This was just a week after he had returned following a four-month absence. Toshack was not amused that a training accident had put the striker out of action.

Gale and Robinson came into the team to travel to Sunderland at the expense of the injured Charles and Walsh. The Swans played with five at the back, allowing Sunderland plenty of the ball, but young Sander was in cracking form. He flung himself to turn aside a powerful drive from former Swan Leighton James who was in action against his former teammates. He then pulled off another incredible stop from Gary Rowell.

Marustik gave the Swans the lead soon after the interval when the home defence made a mess of clearing from Stanley. There was some controversy about the Wearsiders' equaliser. Rowell headed towards goal but Sander scooped the ball away. The eagle-eyed linesman then flagged that the ball had crossed the line and the referee awarded the goal. There were few more goalmouth incidents and it ended 1-1.

On 23 March, Swansea put Colwyn Bay out of the Welsh Cup with a 3-0 victory on the night, 4-0 on aggregate. Stevenson made a good return to first-team duty by shooting his side ahead midway through the first period. It was not until the closing minutes that the result was settled when Curtis and Latchford took advantage of a tiring defence. Curtis only saw action for the last eighteen minutes when he replaced Walsh. It was his first appearance since the defeat at Spurs on 12 February.

The transfer deadline on 23 March passed with no British club coming in for Kennedy. Toshack would have liked to offload him and there were offers in from America and Sweden but surprisingly, none from the UK. It was a sign of the times that not even the country's most decorated player had clubs queuing up for his services. Stanley and Thompson also remained on the pay-roll although Stanley had buckled down to earn a regular spot in the first team.

Toshack was glad to have Rajkovic back in defence to help curb the threat of Cyrille Regis and Gary Thompson for West Brom's visit on 26 March. Rajkovic passed a late fitness test but Charles was not considered. Walsh was up front and Curtis had the place on the bench. Albion had recently paid Coventry £225,000 for Thompson and in the two games he and Regis had played together they had netted four times.

The Swans ended West Brom's seven-match unbeaten run with a superb performance which also totted up their seventh point from three games. Albion were pinned back in their own half for most of the match and their much-vaunted two-pronged strike threat was snuffed out by Stevenson and Rajkovic. Dudley Lewis, sweeping up behind them, was another key defender and it wasn't until the final minute that Thompson escaped to score his fourth goal in three matches.

The dressing room pre-match pep talk from welterweight champion Colin Jones and his manager Eddie Thomas seemed to have had the desired effect. They both appeared on the pitch with the Swansea players before kick-off and were given a great ovation by the 11,222 crowd. The Swans' first goal came when Stanley's free-kick was volleyed in by James. The second was another classic Swansea move. The ball was played to Marustik out on the right. The full-back crossed and in came Latchford to head into the net.

On the Sunday the Swans travelled to Glasgow to play Rangers in a testimonial for Tom Forsyth who had been forced to retire through injury. Rangers were 6-3 winners.

To Toshack's relief, the Welsh FA rejected an invitation for a senior Wales team to tour New Zealand during the summer. The Swansea chief reckoned that the prospect of his international players travelling to the other side of the world for a four or five-week period would have frightened him to death.

The bad news from the Vetch was that Curtis had broken down yet again and was unlikely to play over the crucial Easter period. He was to visit a specialist about the niggling knee trouble that had dogged him for most of the season.

Robinson was added to the squad travelling to Birmingham on Easter Saturday together with eighteen-year-old Huw Lake. The Blues were also in deep trouble down in the basement and the trip to St Andrews was seen as one of the best opportunities for the Swans to claim that elusive first away victory.

The win never materialised although Swansea did extend their unbeaten run to four matches by drawing 1-1. Blues defender Noel Blake somehow hooked away a goalbound shot from Loveridge but the hone team could do nothing about Latchford's goal ten minutes from time, even though it appeared to trickle ever so slowly over the line. Just as the final whistle was nearing, young Richards challenged Rob Hopkins in the area and when the striker went down the referee pointed to the spot. Up stepped Wales international Byron Stevenson to drive home the penalty that gave his side a draw they barely deserved.

The improved show of form had Toshack claiming that he was getting more job satisfaction now than at any other time during his tenure at the club. This was because lads who were still at school when Toshack first arrived on the scene in 1978 were now doing the business in the First Division. Since he called up Sander, Marustik, Richards, Lewis and Loveridge, the manager had regained his hopes that the team could survive in the top league.

(2 April '83)	P	W	D	L	F	A	Pts
17 Man City	35	11	8	16	43	59	41
18 SWANSEA	34	9	9	16	44	50	36
19 Norwich	33	9	9	15	36	52	36
20 Birmingham	33	7	13	13	31	45	34
21 Luton	32	8	10	14	50	65	34
22 Brighton	34	8	10	16	33	60	34

There was real hope that a great escape could be engineered, especially as the Swans were presently just outside the three relegation places. Eight games remained and with five of those at the Vetch Field the opportunity was there for a feat to rival the Great Houdini.

No rest over Easter however, for on Tuesday it was time for West Ham to visit the Vetch. Gale was brought back with a seat on the bench but the side that played at St Andrews started again. Even though the Swans had not enjoyed the best of results against the Hammers, few expected a 1-5 drubbing.

It was a bitterly disappointing result that certainly put a stop to their mini-revival. To make matters worse, relegation rivals Brighton earned a 0-0 draw at high-flying Southampton and the Swans could not afford to give away any more home points if they were to have a chance of beating the drop. Walsh had actually gave them the lead in the second minute but by half-time Geoff Pike and Alan Devonshire had made it 2-1 to the visitors. Gale replaced Walsh for the second half but the Swans conceded three more goals with Pike netting his second and Alan Dickens posting a six-minute double.

A glance at the fixture list made for grim reading as next on the horizon was a trip to Anfield. Pascoe and Robinson for Stevenson and Walsh were the only changes as Toshack gave his side a vote of confidence. Walsh was still suffering from concussion after a clash of heads with the Hammers' Alvin Martin. With no away wins in the league all season a visit to Anfield was a very daunting prospect.

The match was given a morning kick-off to avoid clashing with the Grand National at Aintree. Ian Rush led the Reds' front line after passing a fitness test for a groin strain. The champions-elect never played to their full potential but still did enough to claim a comfortable 3-0 victory. The Swans tried everything to avoid defeat and kept their hosts at bay for almost an hour. It was then that Rush popped up with his thirtieth goal of the season to set his side on their way. The match was ended as a contest by Sammy Lee's long-range drive from a Rush pass. Five minutes from time super-sub David Fairclough rifled in a shot from 25 yards.

An air of despondency now hung over Swansea City FC and the Vetch Field. Chairman Struel added to the gloom after attending a meeting of League chairman from the Wales and West region, at which freedom of contract for players was once again discussed: 'When contracts are renewed there will be cuts everywhere,' he prophesied. 'Not many clubs will have large wage increases next season. I am proud of the fact that Swansea City were the only club that went on record voting against freedom of contract.'

Virtually all 92 League clubs had opposed freedom of contract originally but gradually they had retreated from that position. If a vote were to be called now it was probable that there would be an entirely different response.

On the international scene, only James and Charles were included in the squad to play Bulgaria in Wrexham on 27 April in a European qualifier. Dai Davies had lost his place for the first time since making his debut in Hungary eight years earlier. He was replaced by Lincoln's Dave Felgate. It was a different story with the Under-21s, where seven Swansea starlets were included in the squad to play the Bulgarians a day earlier in Bangor – Sander, Lewis, Marustik, Loveridge, Gale, Pascoe and Richards.

Back in the manager's office at the Vetch, Toshack still refused to accept that the battle was lost. He believed the Swans were where they were because of unprecedented injuries and an overburdened fixture list. These were the prime causes of the club's predicament. That point was reinforced when it was revealed that Curtis had entered hospital for surgery to clear his long-standing knee problem.

Charles made a surprise return to first-team duty against Stoke where he claimed a place at the heart of the defence to the exclusion of Stanley. It was his first home outing since injuring stomach muscles in the 4-1 victory over Manchester City five weeks earlier.

A goal from Wales international Mickey Thomas did nothing to help Swansea's plight. He headed his twelfth goal of the season to equalise an earlier header from Charles. On balance of play Swansea deserved to win but yet again they had failed to preserve a lead. It was another frustrating day for James who was still looking for his 100th League goal. He thought he had it when he beat Peter Fox with a snap shot but the referee disallowed the goal because of a handling offence by Latchford.

Behind the scenes, a Swansea vice-president sought to claim assurances from the board that the club would not embark on a policy of selling their best players as had previously happened. Chairman Struel refused to give those assurances: 'The future depends on the quantity and quality of the support the club receives. It is not feasible to keep all the players on gates of 12,000.'

On top of that, the club were now facing the prospect of a 100 per dent rise in the rent payable to the local authority on the lease of the Vetch Field. The rental was fixed every five years and was coming up for renewal.

The visit to Luton was generally accepted as being the club's last chance of keeping survival hopes alive. A draw would give them hope but a win would be a great tonic to players and supporters alike. The Hatters were four points ahead of Swansea and a priceless first away win would close the gap to just one point. In four of the last five away matches the Swans had been leading until the closing stages. This time they knew they had to get in front – and stay there.

Kennedy for Walsh was the only change, but a depressing 1-3 defeat sent the Swans spinning to the bottom of the First Division. Toshack's plan of smothering Luton's free-scoring attack while trying to catch their defence on the break almost worked. Using a five-man defence, with Lewis the sweeper, Swansea frustrated the Hatters for almost an hour. The turning point came midway through the first half. Latchford challenged Luton keeper Tony Godden in the air, Marustik netted, but the referee penalised Latchford for the challenge.

Luton's England men, Ricky Hill and Paul Walsh, began forging openings and once Walsh had headed his side in front the result was really never in doubt. He went on to complete a fine hat-trick and although Latchford eventually pulled one back it failed to spark any revival.

(23 April '83)	P	W	D	L	F	A	Pts
17 Sunderland	38	11	12	15	43	56	45
18 Luton	37	11	11	15	61	74	44
19 Man City	39	12	8	19	45	67	44
20 Birmingham	38	9	13	16	34	53	40
21 Brighton	38	9	12	17	36	63	39
22 SWANSEA	38	9	10	19	47	62	37

Although relegation now looked odds-on, some good young players were coming into the side and the experience gained was sure to stand them in good stead for the coming seasons. The bleak outlook settled the minds of the two Yugoslavs who both confirmed that they would be returning home.

Wales beat Bulgaria 1-0 with a 78th-minute goal from substitute Charles. He had replaced Rush and when their keeper Velinov pushed out a Robbie James shot, Charles was on hand to prod into the net from close range for his first goal in senior international football.

Three games were now left at the Vetch and Swansea's tenuous hold on top-division status was to be tested by Ipswich. Toshack made just one change from the side put to the sword by the Hatters with Gale replacing the injured Robinson while Pascoe took up a place on the bench.

Marustik was soon in action at both ends as he fired in a thirty-yarder that Paul Cooper did well to gather, before being on hand in his own goal area to clear from Mitch D'Avray. Both sides stepped it up after the break but it was Bobby Ferguson's side who went ahead when Eire international Kevin O'Callaghan outwitted Charles before crossing to Mariner who sidefooted home. Swansea set up a grandstand finish and from a corner by Pascoe, Kennedy headed down and Rajkovic bundled in from close range to make the final score 1-1.

Swansea's financial plight was making it difficult to keep hold of their better players and Robbie James was attracting a lot of interest. The board had pledged to reduce their wage bill and they would find it hard to meet the demands of their longest-serving professional. Only three players, Herbie Williams, Ivor Allchurch and Harry Griffiths had bettered James's total of League appearances for the club.

The team that had done so well in its first season in the First Division was slowly breaking up. Leighton James had already gone, the two Yugoslavs and Davies were ready to leave at the end of the season, and Kennedy was probably about to follow. Losing Robbie James, however, would be a serious blow to the club's chances of making a swift return to the top flight.

European Cup-holders Aston Villa were the visitors on Monday, 2 May. Pascoe and Stanley were in for the injured Rajkovic and Loveridge. Villa were fourth in the table and fresh from a 4-0 trouncing of Stoke. They were seeking the win that would lift them up to second but the Swans lifted themselves off the bottom by winning 2-1 with two well-worked goals from teenagers Gale and Pascoe. Pascoe celebrated his first full home League appearance by giving his side a ninth-minute lead. Although Gary Shaw equalised, Gale restored Swansea's advantage early in the second half with a twenty-yard drive. James had yet another opportunity to notch his 100th League goal but Nigel Spink saved his 55th-minute spot-kick.

Having out-played the high-flying Villains, Swansea now had an even harder task ahead of them. Their final away trip of the season was to Old Trafford. Toshack decided to give the side that defeated Villa a chance to topple the Cup finalists in their home arena.

United missed early chances when Norman Whiteside's shot was saved by Sander and Bryan Robson drove wide when in the clear. Two minutes later though, Robson headed a cross from Whiteside into the corner of the net. Swansea's fate was sealed in the 77th minute when a glorious move involving Laurie Cunningham, Whiteside and Robson gave Frank Stapleton the time to drill home from just five yards.

In the final minute Latchford pulled a goal back but it was too late to change the course of events and Swansea City were finally and officially relegated.

Toshack wasted no time in letting his players know that their attitude had to be spot on for life in the Second Division. He told them that there was no way any of the players should be thinking it would be easier next season. He was disappointed that his side had not taken advantage of a below-strength United many of whose players had their eyes on the coming Wembley FA Cup final.

There was still time for the Swans to end the season with a trophy. In the final of the Welsh Cup they would play Wrexham over two legs. The first match was at the Racecourse and the Swans triumphed 2-1 with goals from Gale and Latchford. Swansea went behind to an early strike from Steve Dowman but Gale hit back with a shot that deceived Robins keeper Eddie Niedzwiecki. James assisted with the winner when his shot was pushed out by Niedzwiecki, only for Latchford to follow up.

Mike England was at the game casting an eye on possibles for the Wales side to play Scotland, while Ipswich manager Ferguson ran the rule over Swansea's James. But it couldn't have been easy for the players on a freezing cold night in Wrexham in front of only 2,296 fans.

As gate receipts only totalled £3,700 there were calls to reduce the finals to a one-off game in the future, even though it was expected that the second leg at the Vetch would draw a bigger and more enthusiastic crowd. With both sides having just suffered relegation however, this was by no means certain.

Supporters were invited to help the club by buying their 1983-84 season tickets early. To encourage more people to attend home games the club announced a discount system. Season tickets for the East Stand which would normally cost £112 were available for the discounted price of £90, providing they were purchased by the end of May. Season tickets for the terraces were available for £29.50, working out at just over a £1 for each of the 21 Second Division home matches. The main reason for these initiatives was that the running costs without matchday income needed to be met from other sources.

There was one final farewell match to play in the First Division. Charles failed a late fitness test but Pascoe came through to line up alongside Gale against Nottingham Forest. In a shock move Toshack left out James and Latchford and found a spot for Colin Irwin who had been absent for eight months.

It was a depressing finale as Swansea made a tame exit from the top division with a 0-3 defeat. Forest clinched a place in Europe far more easily than they should have expected and if Sander hadn't saved a penalty from John Robertson it would have been much worse as Brian Clough's side also had a Steve Hodge effort disallowed. Ian Wallace struck a first half brace and Viv Anderson completed an easy afternoon for the visitors with a 65th-minute header.

For Swansea's 60th and final match of the season, the second leg of the Welsh Cup final, James and Latchford were recalled but there was no place for Rajkovic. The Swans were bidding to win the cup for a third year in a row to match the feat achieved by Druids, Wrexham and Cardiff City. Playing in Europe once again would be a small crumb of comfort for the supporters.

The Swans won 2-0, 4-1 on aggregate, with both goals coming from Latchford. He therefore boasted the remarkable record of having scored in all seven ties for the club in the competition. He netted nine Welsh Cup goals and completed the season with 34 in all, a terrific return in a side that had struggled for most of the term. It was not surprising that the former Birmingham, Everton and England centre-forward had been voted Swansea's Player of the Year.

There were unconfirmed reports that a takeover of the club was under consideration. This was denied by vice-chairman Tom Phillips but he did admit to the possibility of two new directors joining the board. As the club was now more than £1 million in debt and still owing money for players purchased two years earlier, an injection of cash would be warmly welcomed.

At the end of the season Kennedy and Stanley were removed from the transfer list so that they could add their considerable experience to the push to regain top status at the first attempt. Their reinstatement was an acknowledgement of the effort they had made in the latter stages of the season.

Toshack listed five players he intended to release. They were Max Thompson, Davies, Evans and the two Yugoslavs. Robinson had been offered terms for 1983-84 and James was in negotiations for a new contract. Whether those talks would be fruitful remained to be seen. If money was slow in coming in from other sources then they would be forced to dispose of their saleable assets and top of that list was James.

8

BACK TO THE BEGINNING

(1983-86)

The summer of 1983 was not a happy one for Swansea City FC or its supporters. While the expected exodus of players never reached the mammoth proportions most fans expected, one Swansea icon did leave for pastures new. Robbie James joined Stoke in June for a knock-down £130,000. In view of the fact that his estimated value had been £350,000 it was plain to see that the club were on a rocky road leading in only one direction. The hard-working John Mahoney called it a day in the summer, when his ankle injury proved too serious to overcome at the age of 36 and Dai Davies left for Tranmere on a free transfer. That meant at least three stalwarts of the side that hit the top in 1981 would not be around to help the club bounce back.

The European Cup-Winners' Cup came and went with defeat to the East Germans of Magdeburg and not one pre-season friendly ended in victory so the start of the 1983-84 season and Second Division football was awaited with much trepidation. It was only when the Swans beat Cambridge 2-1 at the Vetch in the sixth match of the campaign that the first victory was in the bag. By then Swansea City were already at the bottom of the division.

The only bright spot was the form of Jimmy Rimmer, John Toshack's summer signing from Aston Villa. The 35-year-old England international stood tall as his defence stumbled through those early games. Toshack described him as one of the five best goalkeepers in the League, while blasting other players for falling below what they were capable of. Ray Kennedy had again been a disappointment in the opening three matches and was left out to give young Paul Maddy a chance. Gary Chivers was another newcomer, making his debut in the 3-1 home defeat by Brighton. The club's poor situation was reflected in the Wales senior squad selected for the European Championship qualifier against Norway. Gone were the days when Swansea players made up almost half the party. The seventeen players selected for Oslo included just two Swans – Jeremy Charles and Alan Curtis. Despite this, the future seemed to be in good hands as six Swansea youngsters were named in the Under-21s: Chris Sander, Dudley Lewis, Chris Marustik, Colin Pascoe, Darren Gale and Gary Richards. But were they worthy of Swansea's first team?

With the club languishing at the bottom of the Second Division, Kennedy was given a free transfer. His standing at the club had plunged to a new low and the Swans had written off his £160,000 fee. Toshack turned to another 'golden oldie' by persuading 36-year-old Emlyn Hughes to come out of retirement and help shore up the Swans leaky defence. Nigel Stevenson, Charles and Colin Irwin were all on the injured list and 'Crazy Horse' was signed on a three-month deal until the injury problems had abated. Hughes' home debut was the win over Cambridge but sadly that would be the only time in seven matches in a Swansea shirt that Hughes would be on the winning side. Only 7,197 were at the Vetch for that game, the lowest crowd since Hartlepool were dispatched 8-0 on 1 April 1978, but attendances would drop much lower than that in the coming months.

Toshack decided on an 'all out attack' policy using Bob Latchford, Curtis, Pascoe and Gale in the same side but that proved disastrous as Fulham won 5-0 at Craven Cottage with Wales international Gordon Davies grabbing a brace.

Curtis and Charles were banished to the reserves as the troubled manager tried in vain to stem the downward spiral by giving youth a fling. Sunderland immediately stepped in with an enquiry for Curtis but when told the asking price was £150,000 they quickly lost interest.

In the last week of October the bank advised the club that there was no more money. £2 million in debt and losing £10,000 every week, the Swans had been forced to go cap in hand to their bankers to plead for time to extricate themselves from their financial mess. Malcolm Struel resigned as chairman and his place was taken by Doug Sharpe who injected money into the club to assist in the short term. The vice chairman also left but results needed to improve rapidly or the manager would be on his way. The club had spent a staggering £2.2 million on players with only £715,000 recouped through sales.

On 29 October 1983 Toshack left Swansea City by 'mutual consent'. He still had eighteen months of a reputed £48,000 a year contract to run but refused any compensation. In fact when he left the club he made a gift of £1,000 to help develop the club's youngsters. Kennedy's contract was terminated at the same time and football secretary Tony Howard was made redundant.

Doug Livermore took over the hot seat and was charged with selling any player good enough to merit a fee. He restored Latchford and Neil Robinson to the first team but had to do without Hughes who decided to hang up his boots for a second time. Livermore felt that by using the carrot rather than the stick that had been much in evidence during the latter part of Toshack's reign, the players would respond and results would improve.

Portsmouth agreed to pay £95,000 for Charles but the player decided on a move to Queens Park Rangers for a similar fee. While new chairman Sharpe was negotiating with Rangers he received the welcome news that Liverpool had generously decided to waive the £300,000 outstanding from Swansea in unpaid transfer fees. Sunderland were still interested in Latchford and Curtis, while Liverpool were keeping tabs on Pascoe and Gale. While the North Easterners were debating their options, Southampton stepped in and wrapped up Curtis's signature for a miserly £85,000. Livermore was philosophical about losing players but the pressure became too great for him and he quit the post in the middle of December.

In another bizarre twist, Toshack returned to carry on where he had left off. Les Chappell became his assistant and Wyndham Evans assumed the role of player-coach. Toshack selected himself for the Boxing Day fixture at Cardiff and scored one of the Swansea goals in their 2-3 defeat. Three days later he handed free transfers to Latchford, Stanley and Chivers.

As 1983 drew to a close the club propped up the Second Division, eleven points adrift of safety. The year had started off with a game at Arsenal – how times had changed.

It was now a tale of woe and more woe. Rimmer would play no further part in the season as he required surgery on his hand. Stanley lightened the wage-bill in January by joining Portsmouth. Toshack scored an own-goal in an embarrassing 1-6 defeat to leaders Sheffield Wednesday, signalling the end of his playing days.

There was a little light relief when the club embarked on a short six-nation Malayan tournament in January. The Far East jaunt netted a welcome £10,000, together with the Kuala Lumpur Cup.

One the club's return Latchford fixed himself up with a contract to play in the Dutch Second Division for NAC Breda. When the Wales squad to play Scotland on 28 February was announced there was not one Swansea player included in the sixteen-strong party.

The Swans were served with a writ on behalf of the Inland Revenue claiming £102,000 in unpaid income tax and national health contributions. Chairman Sharpe was pinning his hopes on agreeing an instalment payment schedule. To help towards it the club received £15,000 from the Save Our Swans Appeal Fund. Rimmer was transfer-listed at £30,000 in the hope of raising more cash but that was dashed when a specialist advised him not to touch a ball for a further three weeks.

Toshack gave up the fight a second time on 5 March and Les Chappell took over as caretaker manager. Chappell was already up against it as

Irwin was still having knee problems, Gale was out with a broken leg, and Walsh had turned his ankle in yet another training ground accident. Chris Marustik asked for a transfer and was put on the list at a staggering £250,000.

There was a glimmer of hope when Ante Rajkovic secured his release from Sarajevo and was back in Swansea awaiting a work permit. He eventually returned on 14 April in a 0-3 defeat at Grimsby. Dean Saunders (2) and Ian Walsh scored as the Swans defeated Cardiff 3-2 a week later but it was far too late and a second successive relegation was confirmed when Swansea lost 0-2 at Shrewsbury on 24 April.

Rajkovic promptly went back to Yugoslavia nursing a thigh strain, but before leaving he signed a one-year contract.

The final game of a sorry season was at Portsmouth who slammed the dispirited Swans 5-0. They had not won a League match away from the Vetch Field for two whole seasons, not since 8 May 1982.

On 16 May, Colin Appleton threw in his lot with Swansea City after resigning from a similar managerial post at Hull on the night they missed out on promotion from Division Three by a single goal. He was faced with the same problems as his predecessor Chappell, no money and a very inexperienced squad with only Rimmer, Robinson and Rajkovic seasoned campaigners.

It was a threadbare squad that started the 1984-85 season in Division Three. There was crowd trouble at Millwall in the opening match and the referee was forced to take both sides off the field until the police had restored control. Blame was attributed to visiting Chelsea National Front supporters.

Worse was to follow in the first home match when promoted York went ahead after only nine seconds. Chairman Bobby Jones announced his resignation for 'personal reasons', becoming the third chairman to quit inside a year. His place was taken by Winston Rees.

Appleton was forced to try his luck with triallists and players unable to gain contracts elsewhere. His situation worsened when Robinson joined Grimsby for £20,000, yet another link with the club's heyday in Division One now having departed.

On 3 October, the Swans won 2-1 at Bournemouth to record their first away victory for thirty months. Orient were beaten in the next match but at Newport Dudley Lewis and Paul Richardson were dismissed during the 0-2 defeat. Making his home debut for County was former Swan David Giles who was on loan from Birmingham City: 'I had been left to train with the schoolboys and was completely ignored by Ron Saunders. All he had to say was whether he wanted me to stay or not.'

With ten games played the Swans were languishing in twentieth place, but Appleton had a trump card up his sleeve. He announced that former England international Gerry Francis was joining the club to add his experience to the fight. Unfortunately Francis only played three matches for the Swans, all defeats, before moving on to Portsmouth.

The Swans sank even lower when Bognor Regis Town knocked them out of the FA Cup 3-1 in a replay after drawing 1-1 at the Vetch. Rajkovic had already decided that coming back was a mistake and he returned to Yugoslavia having played in only four league and cup games. Appleton's situation was desperate. At the end of November he received the dreaded vote of confidence, while at the same time being asked to prune his playing staff. True to form he was sacked a few days later, claiming that he was not given enough time to turn things around.

With money at a premium the Swansea board astounded everyone by appointing the flamboyant John Bond to the manager's position. After watching his first game the new man said 'This is the worst squad I have ever worked with'. The League had still not lifted the transfer embargo so Bond was forced to sift through the ranks of free transfer and cast-offs. Paul Price joined in the New Year after a spell with Minnesota Kicks in the American League.

Bond had clearly not done his homework when he agreed to take the job on: 'Swansea are in an awful lot of trouble and it has gone beyond a football job. The club's future in the league is in doubt. I just cannot understand the policy which went into running the club.'

By the end of January he had brought in Ray McHale and Derek Parlane, the same Parlane who scored Leeds' goal when they lost 5-1 at the Vetch in the opening game in Division One back in 1981.

A reasonable run of results pulled the club up to third from bottom. Bond reckoned they needed to win five of their last seven home matches to stay up but that became a tall order after Newport won 3-0 to do the double over their close rivals.

Bond released leading scorer Dean Saunders who moved along the M4 to Cardiff on a free transfer. Saunders had scored nine League goals and three in the cup so it was a mystifying decision. Alan Waddle returned in March and scored as the Swans thumped Preston 4-1 for their biggest league win since defeating Norwich 4-0 back in September 1982.

Six victories and three draws in their last eleven matches were just enough to stave off relegation, though they needed at least a point in their final match against Bristol City to make sure. It was achieved with a battling 0-0 stalemate to leave Bond drawing on a large cigar and feeling very pleased with himself.

The build-up to the new 1984-85 season was hardly inspiring as Phil Williams was sent off in a friendly against Newport, along with the Gwent side's Tony Pulis. Leighton James was in the County line-up. In another friendly against Ebbw Vale it was Ray McHale's turn for an early bath. In fact, that season Swansea would have seven players sent off to collect 216 penalty points and warrant a fine from the Welsh FA who also warned the club as to their future conduct.

Another bitter blow came when the 2,000-seater West Stand was closed for safety reasons, while the West Terrace had its capacity reduced from 4,500 to 800 until major safety works were carried out.

Chairman Rees and Vice-Chairman Doug Sharpe resigned, Rees becoming the fourth chairman in two years to quit after another board-room split. Also leaving was Glyn Hammond, the financial director appointed in October 1983. One of the issues that forced the departures was a deal brokered by one of the directors, Mel Nurse, and Swansea County Council by which the club would start paying off £36,000 in owed arrears at the rate of £6,000 per month. Rees was at a loss to know why that had been agreed when they didn't have enough money to pay existing creditors.

As 11,500 fans had packed into the Vetch to see the final game of 1984-85 against Bristol City, the directors were confident that a good crowd would be enticed for the first match of the 1985-86 campaign. Their optimism was misplaced as Wigan attracted just 4,700. It was the same old story on the field as the first four games were lost and attendances dipped even lower.

It was decided to run the club with a five-man committee instead of appointing a chairman and vice chairman. This committee consisted of Peter Howard, Harry Hyde, Bobby Jones, Mel Nurse and David Savage. Goalkeeper Rimmer accepted a longer contract in exchange for a wages cut, reputed to be around £200 per week. He was the last of the big signings and still on Division One money. Rimmer and his family were happily settled on the Gower and had no wish to leave.

On 9 September director Hyde revealed that the club was 'bleeding to death'. The Inland Revenue were owed £150,000 and the club was likely to face a winding-up order. He reckoned that the directors could probably find enough cash to delay matters for a month but that was all: 'What we need is 8-10,000 bodies through the gate on match days,' he said. He added that £350,000 was needed at once to keep the club alive. There was only enough money to pay wages for four more weeks. As the Swans still had a transfer embargo on them, they were not even allowed to negotiate loan deals. All they could do was take on out-of-work players.

By the end of September 1985 the Swans were third from the bottom of Division Three. The club limped through October and November, even managing to lose 0-6 to fellow relegation strugglers Darlington.

Doug Sharpe was given executive powers to steer the Swans through the crisis. The acting-chairman's first job was to try and strike a deal with Inland Revenue to pay off the £102,000 tax arrears over a six month period. The club was also facing the threat of a winding-up order instituted by the Vetch Residents Association who were still owed £30,000.

On 14 December 1985 Swansea beat second-placed York 1-0 at the Vetch in front of a crowd of only 2,779. Sharpe offered to put up some money, but only if the current directors resigned. The stumbling block appeared to be Barclays Bank who were owed £730,000 but in a reconciliatory move they offered to freeze the outstanding amount for five years. That left Sharpe gambling that the city council would weigh in with an offer to help. The Inland Revenue winding-up petition was adjourned once again, this time until 20 December. If the outstanding monies had not been paid by then the court would be unlikely to grant any further stay of execution.

On Friday, 20 December 1985, Swansea City Football Club was wound up in the High Court in London with Justice Harman saying that the club had failed to meet any of their obligations or promises. The following day's home match against Walsall was called off, laying the club open to expulsion from the Football League. Bond and all the players were dismissed, even the apprentices, and the Swans were in the hands of the liquidators. PFA secretary Gordon Taylor felt it would need a miracle to save a club which had already received £7,000 from the Association to pay wages for two weeks in November.

A rescue package was worked out with the intention of putting the club into receivership rather than liquidation. The High Court gave the Official Receiver permission to carry on trading for at least a three-week period. This meant that the Boxing Day match at Cardiff could go ahead. The Bluebirds won 1-0 and only Wolves were keeping the Swans off the bottom of Division Three, but at least they were still in business.

Tommy Hutchison was put in temporary control of playing affairs, assisted by coaches Fred Davies and Jimmy Rimmer. Almost 7,000 were in the Vetch for the New Year's Day 1-1 draw with Bournemouth and two home victories followed against Walsall and Blackpool.

On 13 January 1986 the club showed that since being in the hands of the receiver they were actually trading at a profit. A 28-day reprieve was confirmed and the Swansea delegates rushed back to the Vetch where Manchester United had sent a full-strength team to help out. Over 18,000 turned up to support the club and takings of around £40,000 swelled the Swansea City coffers. United won 5-1 against a team which included former sons, Alan Curtis and Bob Latchford.

Meanwhile former manager Bond was claiming wrongful dismissal as he had been the only one to be kicked out. He had a case as even his assistant Fred Davies had been re-instated.

There was still much to do but the supporters now believed that their club could continue in business. Many had contributed to its recovery, from shareholders right down to youngsters who sent their pocket money. The effort and dedication of Doug Sharpe went a long way to galvanising everyone into action.

The 28-day reprieve came and went with the club still operating successfully, off the field at least. Only four more League matches were won and the Swans ended 1985-86 at the bottom of Division Three, so suffering a third relegation in four seasons. They had ended up back in Division Four where it had all started just seven years previously.

The seeds of disaster had been sown in those glory days when the club marched through the Football League to the top division. To sustain that success the club overspent, believing that they would recoup the money through the gates, but the fans never turned up in numbers and not once was the ground filled to capacity.

There are several reasons why it all ended in heartache:
(a) The fault lay with over-ambitious directors who believed there was a pot of gold at the end of the rainbow.
(b) The apathy of the Swansea City supporters who seemed to turn their back on the club. After all, 23,500 turned up for the first game against Leeds in Division One, yet the second home match two weeks later drew a gate of only 14,391. The following season only 12,389 were at the Vetch for the visit of Arsenal and the average attendance dropped to 11,681.
(c) The cruel number of injuries to star players that prevented the best side from being put out week after week.

The truth is probably a mixture of all three, and when you are on the downward spiral it is difficult to arrest the fall. Even now, some twenty years later, League clubs are still being confronted by the same problems. Despite everything that happened in such a short space of time, Swansea City were lucky that they were able to continue as a Football League club. Since that day there have been many more occasions when the future looked bleak but they have continued to survive and are now enjoying the good times once again in a superb, brand new stadium – but supporters will never forget that brief period when their club enjoyed their seasons in the sun.

GUIDE TO SEASONAL SUMMARIES

Col 1: Match number (for league fixtures); Round (for cup-ties).
e.g. 4R means 'Fourth round replay.'

Col 2: Date of the fixture and whether Home (H), Away (A), or Neutral (N).

Col 3: Opposition.

Col 4: Attendances. Home gates appear in roman; Away gates in *italics*.
Figures in **bold** indicate the largest and smallest gates, at home and away.
Average home and away attendances appear after the final league match.

Col 5: Respective league positions of Swansea and opponents after the game.
Swansea's position appears on the top line in roman.
Their opponents' position appears on the second line in *italics*.
For cup-ties, the division and position of opponents is provided.
e.g. 2:12 means the opposition are twelfth in Division 2.

Col 6: The top line shows the result: W(in), D(raw), or L(ose).
The second line shows Swansea's cumulative points total.

Col 7: The match score, Swansea's given first.
Scores in **bold** show Swansea's biggest league win and heaviest defeat.

Col 8: The half-time score, Swansea's given first.

Col 9: The top line shows Swansea's scorers and times of goals in roman.
The second line shows opponents' scorers and times of goals in *italics*.
A 'p' after the time of a goal denotes a penalty; 'og' an own-goal.
The third line gives the name of the match referee.

Team line-ups: Swansea's line-ups appear on top line, irrespective of whether
they are home or away. Opposition teams are on the second line in *italics*.
Players of either side who are sent off are marked !
Swansea's players making their league debuts are displayed in **bold**.

LEAGUE DIVISION 2 — Manager: John Toshack — SEASON 1980-81

No	Date	Opponent	Att	Pos	Pt	F-A	H-T	Scorers, Times, and Referees	1	2	3	4	5	6	7	8	9	10	11	12	sub used
1	16/8	A WATFORD	11,316		L 0	1-2	1-1	James R 25p / *Poskett 30, 77* / Ref: C Newsome (Broseley)	Stewart	Marustik	Rushberry	Jackett	Attley	Stevenson	Phillips	Giles*	James R	James L	Charles	Robinson	Mahoney
		(Watford)							*Steele*	*Henderson*	*Jackett*	*Patching*	*Sims*	*Bolton*	*Blissett*	*Poskett*	*Jenkins*	*Train*	*Rostron*		
2	19/8	H SHREWSBURY	12,754	11	W 2	2-1	0-0	Attley 60, Giles 65 / *King 75* / Ref: A Glasson (Salisbury)	Stewart	Marustik	Rushberry	Jackett	Attley	Stevenson	Phillips	Giles	James R	James L	Charles*	Robinson	Craig
		(Shrewsbury)							*Wardle*	*King*	*Leonard*	*Turner*	*Griffin*	*Keay*	*Tong*	*Atkins*	*Biggins*	*Dungworth*	*Petts*		
3	23/8	A QP RANGERS	10,854	12	D 3	0-0	0-0	Ref: K Baker (Rugby)	Stewart	Robinson	Rushberry	Jackett	Attley	Stevenson	Phillips	Giles	James R	James L	Charles		Craig
		(QP Rangers)							*Woods*	*McCreery*	*Gillard*	*Waddock*	*Wicks*	*Roeder*	*Hill*	*Shanks*	*Walsh**	*Currie*	*Burke*		*Neal*
4	30/8	H CAMBRIDGE	11,112	12	D 4	1-1	1-0	Fallon 26 (og) / *Finney 66* / Ref: J Martin (Alton)	Stewart	Evans	Rushberry	Jackett	Attley	Stevenson	Phillips	Giles	James R	James L	Charles*	Robinson	Mahoney
		(Cambridge)							*Webster*	*Donaldson*	*Murray*	*Smith*	*Fallon*	*Gibbins*	*Streete*	*O'Neill*	*Reilly**	*Finney*	*Christie*		*Evans*
5	6/9	A BRISTOL CITY	9,528	5	W 6	1-0	1-0	James L 20 / Ref: R Challis (Tonbridge)	Stewart	Attley	Hadziabdic	Mahoney	Stevenson	Phillips	Giles	Waddle	James R	James L	Charles	Robinson	
		(Bristol City)							*Cashley*	*Sweeney*	*Tainton*	*Gow*	*Hay*	*Merrick*	*Whitehead*	*Ritchie*	*Mabbutt*	*Doyle*	*Garland**		*Pritchard*
6	13/9	H NOTTS CO	10,921	7	D 7	1-1	1-0	Stevenson 26 / *Kilcline 71* / Ref: E Read (Bristol)/ R Gifford (Hengoed)	Stewart	Attley	Hadziabdic	Mahoney	Stevenson	Phillips	Giles	Waddle	James R	James L	Charles	Robinson	
		(Notts Co)							*Avramovic*	*Benjamin*	*O'Brien*	*Kelly*	*Kilcline*	*Richards*	*McCulloch*	*Masson*	*Christie*	*Hunt*	*Mair**		*Hooks*
7	20/9	A BOLTON	9,419	4	W 9	4-1	3-0	Waddle 28, 41, James L 23, / *Whatmore 72* [Robinson 64] / Ref: A Saunders (Newcastle)	Stewart	Attley	Hadziabdic	Mahoney	Stevenson	Phillips	Giles	Waddle*	James R	James L	Charles	Robinson	Craig
		(Bolton)							*Peacock*	*Clement*	*Cantello*	*Gowling*	*Walsh*	*Novak*	*Whatmore*	*Wilson*	*Kidd*	*Hoggan*	*Craig*		
8	27/9	H SHEFFIELD WED	9,764	5	L 9	2-3	1-1	Giles 20, Charles 59 / *Hornsby 18, Pearson 57, McCul'ch 64 Cox* / Ref: D Lloyd (Worcester)	Stewart	Attley	Hadziabdic	Marustik*	Stevenson	Phillips	Giles	Waddle*	James R	James L	Charles	Robinson	Mahoney
		(Sheffield Wed)							*Blackhall*	*Grant*	*Smith*	*Pickering*	*Hornsby*	*Taylor*	*Mellor*	*Leman*	*McCulloch*	*Pearson*	*Cox*		
9	4/10	A WREXHAM	8,544	7	D 10	1-1	1-1	Giles 28 / *Edwards 29* / Ref: P Tyldesley (Stockport)	Stewart	Attley	Hadziabdic	Mahoney	Stevenson	Phillips	Giles	Waddle*	James R	James L	Charles	Robinson	James R
		(Wrexham)							*Davies D*	*Sutton*	*Jones J*	*Davies G*	*Cegielski*	*Carrodus*	*Vinter**	*Fox*	*Edwards*	*McNeil*	*Cartwright*		*Hill*
10	7/10	H OLDHAM	8,624	5	W 12	3-0	2-0	Giles 35, 85, Waddle 44 / Ref: B Stevens (Stonehouse)	Stewart	Attley	Hadziabdic	Mahoney	Stevenson	Phillips	Giles	Waddle	James R	James L	Charles	Robinson	James R
		(Oldham)							*McDonnell*	*Sinclair*	*Blair*	*Kowenicki**	*Clements*	*Hurst*	*Wilde*	*Futcher*	*Stainrod*	*Keegan*	*Atkinson*		*Steel*

Match reports

1. **Watford** — Charles is bundled over in the area to give the Swans an early penalty. Leighton James makes several darting runs down the flanks which Jackett brings to a halt with a series of strong tackles. The Swans are unable to break down the Hornets and Poskett's double takes both points.

2. **Shrewsbury** — Minutes after Craig comes on for skipper Charles, Swans move ahead. Leighton James lobs the ball into the area and Robbie James puts Attley through. A shot is beaten out by Shrews keeper Wardle and Giles picks up the loose ball to slot home. Shrewsbury reduce deficit from a corner.

3. **QP Rangers** — Swans almost score after three minutes when Woods beats out a drive by Robbie James straight to Giles, but his return was cleared off the line by former Chelsea stopper Wicks. After a good start by Swansea, Rangers come into the game and Roeder drives saves from the busy Stewart.

4. **Cambridge** — An own-goal gifts Swans the lead when Fallon diverts a Leighton James cross into his own net. Swans, with Toshack making an appearance up front, waste a number of chances to score, and they pay the penalty as the home defence fails to clear a free-kick and Finney nips in to net.

5. **Bristol City** — Hadziabdic makes his long-awaited debut. Robbie James catches Cashley off his line but his header strikes the crossbar. A mistake by the unfortunate keeper gives the Swans victory when he allows a shot from Leighton James to sneak inside the post without attempting to save.

6. **Notts Co** — Ref Eric Read collapses in the 20th minute and is taken off on a stretcher to be replaced by senior linesman Roger Gifford. Swans do most of the attacking and take the lead with a neat header from Stevenson. They are pegged back by a goal from impressive 17-year-old Brian Kilcline.

7. **Bolton** — Transfer-listed Waddle strikes twice before the interval at Burnden Park to put Wanderers on the rack. Former Man Utd star Kidd brings a superb save from Stewart as the Trotters try to get back into the game, but a late Whatmore strike is all they have to show for their efforts.

8. **Sheffield Wed** — Swansea are forced to refuse permission for any Wednesday fans to enter the ground and the all-ticket policy results in a very low turn-out. When Hornsby opens the scoring against the run of play it is the Owls' first away goal of the season. The victory lifts them above the Swans.

9. **Wrexham** — A Hadziabdic free-kick leads to a Swans goal when the ball is nodded down in the area and Giles strokes it home from close range. The Robins are lucky to level straight from the kick-off when Edwards bundles Stewart and the ball into the net. Robbie James has a lob hacked clear.

10. **Oldham** — The first home win since August for the Swans and against an Oldham side unbeaten in five. Giles scores for the third consecutive game but it is in front of the lowest gate for two seasons. Waddle's strike just before the interval puts paid to any hopes Oldham had of securing a point.

Season fixtures record (matches 11–21)

No	H/A	Opponent	Date	Att	Pos	Res	—	Pts	FT	HT	Scorers / Opposition scorers	Referee
11	H	DERBY	11/10	13,323	5	W	9	14	3-1	1-0	James L 33p, 55, 58; Osgood 70p	Ref: D Hodges (Oxford)
12	A	NEWCASTLE	18/10	16,392	4	W	10	16	2-1	1-0	Attley 27, Waddle 65; Rafferty 88	Ref: G Glover (Chorley)
13	A	LUTON	21/10	8,402	4	D	19	17	2-2	1-1	Waddle 20, 53; Stein 40, Moss 58	Ref: B Daniels (Brentwood)
14	H	GRIMSBY	24/10	12,928	4	W	18	19	1-0	0-0	Charles 87	Ref: S Bates (Bristol)
15	A	BLACKBURN	1/11	10,846	4	D	5	20	0-0	0-0		Ref: T Morris (Leeds)
16	H	ORIENT	8/11	10,922	4	L	7	20	0-2	0-0	Moores 73, Chiedozie 83	Ref: M Baker (Wolverhampton)
17	A	SHREWSBURY	11/11	5,863	5	D	14	21	0-0	0-0		Ref: A Porter (Bolton)
18	A	WEST HAM	22/11	27,376	6	L	1	21	0-2	0-0		Ref: D Hutchinson (Bournem'th)
19	H	PRESTON	28/11	9,115	5	W	15	23	3-0	1-0	Robinson 36, 83, Waddle 75	Ref: L Shapter (Newton Abbot)
20	A	CHELSEA	6/12	20,067	5	D	2	24	0-0	0-0		Ref: B Hill (Kettering)
21	H	NEWCASTLE	13/12	11,672	4	W	14	26	4-0	3-0	James R 11, 64, James L 10, [Charles 44]	Ref: L Burden (Dorset)

Line-ups (Swansea players listed first, opposition in italics)

The column positions across the grid are: Stewart, Attley, Hadziabdic, Mahoney, Stevenson, Phillips, Giles, Waddle, James L, Charles, Robinson, James R.

11 — DERBY: Stewart *Jones*, Attley *Emery*, Hadziabdic *Buckley*, Mahoney *Powell S*, Stevenson *McFarland**, Phillips *Osgood*, Giles* *Clark*, Waddle *Powell B*, James L *Hector*, Charles *Swindlehurst*, Robinson *Emson*, James R *Skivington*

Report: Hector and Waddle both have goals disallowed before Leighton James bags a hat-trick against one of his former clubs. Swans stay on the attack but the Rams gain some consolation when Stevenson brings down Hector and former Spurs midfielder Osgood nets from the spot.

12 — NEWCASTLE: Stewart *Carr*, Attley *Kelly*, Hadziabdic *Davies*, Mahoney *Martin*, Stevenson *Boam*, Phillips *Mitchell*, Giles *Shoulder*, Waddle *Wharton*, James L *Shinton*, Charles *Rafferty*, Robinson *Hibbitt*, James R

Report: The Magpies are very poor and find themselves trailing when Attley sends Giles racing down the wing. The full-back follows up at speed to slide Giles's cross into the net. Newcastle-born Waddle doubles the lead before a mistake by keeper Stewart gifts the Geordies a late goal.

13 — LUTON: Stewart *Findlay*, Attley *Stephens*, Hadziabdic *Donaghy*, Mahoney *Grealish*, Stevenson *Goodyear*, Phillips *Price*, Giles* *Hill*, Waddle *Stein*, James L *White*, Charles *Aizlewood*, Robinson *Moss*, James R

Report: Waddle puts Swans ahead but a poor back-pass from Mahoney gifts Stein an equaliser. When Waddle nets his second after the break the points look to be going to Swans, but Moss equalises with his 100th goal in league football, for the Hatters to gain only their seventh home point.

14 — GRIMSBY: Stewart *Batch*, Attley* *Stone*, Hadziabdic *Crosby*, Mahoney *Waters*, Stevenson *Wigginton*, Phillips *Moore K*, Giles *Brolly*, Waddle *Ford*, James L *Drinkell*, Charles *Mitchell*, Robinson *Cumming*, James R

Report: Attley limps off after 11 minutes on the very night that Wales team manager Mike England chooses to watch him in action. Robbie James is also carried off two minutes from time, leaving the Swans desperately holding on with ten men against last season's Division Three champions.

15 — BLACKBURN: Stewart *Butcher*, Attley *Branagan*, Hadziabdic *Rathbone*, Mahoney *Kendall*, Rushberry *Keeley*, Phillips *Fazackerley*, Giles* *Brotherston*, Waddle *McKenzie*, James L *Garner*, Charles *Speight*, Robinson *Stonehouse*, James R

Report: It needs a superb display from Stewart to keep Rovers at bay. Stonehouse, Speight and the lively Garner rain shots down on the Swans goal but Stewart is in great form. Swans rarely trouble the Rovers back line, with Keeley outstanding, but it is a poor game for a top of the table clash.

16 — ORIENT: Stewart *Day*, Attley *Fisher*, Hadziabdic *Roffey*, Mahoney *Taylor T*, Stevenson *Gray*, Phillips *Parsons*, Giles *Chiedozie*, Waddle *Moores*, James L *Mayo*, Charles *Hughton*, Robinson* *Margerison*, Craig

Report: Swans fall to a first defeat in eight games with Chiedozie a constant danger for Orient. The home forwards never threaten Day in the visitors' goal and, when former Spurs striker Moores opens the scoring, there is only going to be one winner. Stewart prevents an even heavier defeat.

17 — SHREWSBURY: Stewart *Wardle*, Attley *King*, Hadziabdic *Leonard**, Mahoney *Petts*, Stevenson *Griffin*, Phillips *Keay*, Giles *Tong*, Rushberry *Atkins*, James L* *Biggins*, Charles *Dungworth*, Robinson *Cross*, Craig *McLaren*

Report: Swans are given a fright in the second minute when Tong makes space before lashing a shot against the post. With Waddle and Robbie James both unfit, it is the Shrews who do most of the attacking and Petts misses an easy chance before Dungworth has a goal disallowed for offside.

18 — WEST HAM: Stewart *Parkes*, Attley *Stewart*, Hadziabdic* *Lampard*, Mahoney *Bonds*, Stevenson *Martin*, Phillips *Devonshire**, Craig *Holland*, Waddle *Goddard*, James R *Cross*, Charles *Brooking*, Robinson *Pike*, Loveridge *Neighbour*

Report: Rushberry heads a Brooking shot from under the crossbar as the Hammers pile on early pressure. Stewart saves superbly from Goddard, Pike and Holland, and Hadziabdic's injury leaves the Swans defence in even more disarray. It is the fourth match in a row they have failed to score.

19 — PRESTON: Stewart *Tunks*, Attley *Westwell*, Hadziabdic *Cameron*, Mahoney *Burns*, Stevenson *Baxter*, Phillips *Blackley*, James R *Bell*, Waddle *Taylor*, James L *Elliott*, Charles *Bruce*, Robinson *McGee*, Mahoney

Report: Preston are managed by World Cup star Nobby Stiles, but they show very little fight. Behind at half-time, they fail to raise their game and a superb header by Waddle from a Hadziabdic cross, and then a deflected shot for Robinson's second, gives the Swans a comfortable victory.

20 — CHELSEA: Stewart *Borota*, Attley *Locke*, Hadziabdic *Rofe*, Mahoney *Bumstead*, Stevenson *Droy*, Phillips *Chivers*, James R *Driver*, Waddle *Britton*, James L* *Lee*, Charles *Walker*, Robinson *F'des-Brown*, Craig

Report: Swans keep the same side that beat Preston and they are denied a penalty when Waddle is brought down by Droy. Second-placed Chelsea's defence are kept busy throughout the game and Borota saves brilliantly at the busy Waddle's feet and also from Leighton James and Charles.

21 — NEWCASTLE: Stewart *Carr*, Attley *Carney*, Hadziabdic *Johnson*, Rushberry *Martin*, Stevenson *Boam*, Mahoney *Mitchell*, Mahoney *Shinton*, James R *Wharton*, James L* *Cartwright*, Charles *Shoulder*, Robinson *Koenen**, Craig *Nicholson*

Report: Alan Curtis, Swansea's new signing, is paraded in front of the fans before the match. He must have wondered how he would get in the team as the Swans tear the Magpies defence to pieces, even without flu-stricken leading scorer Waddle, to claim a double over a poor Newcastle outfit.

LEAGUE DIVISION 2

Manager: John Toshack

Match summary

No		Opponent	Date	Att	Pos (Swans)	Pos (Opp)	Res	Pt	F-A	H-T	Scorers, Times, and Referee
22	H	WATFORD	16/12	13,305	3	18	W	28	1-0	0-0	Curtis 70p — Ref: V Callow (Solihull)
23	A	OLDHAM	20/12	5,486	3	18	D	29	2-2	2-1	James R 25, Curtis 36 / Steel 20, Wylde 73 — Ref: D Owen (Wirral)
24	H	BRISTOL ROV	26/12	15,135	2	22	W	31	2-1	2-0	Stevenson 3, James R 26 / Emmanuel 88 — Ref: A Seville (Birmingham)
25	A	CARDIFF	27/12	21,239	2	17	D	32	3-3	2-1	Robinson 40, Curtis 42, James L 73 / Stevens 13, Kitchen 85, Buchan' 86 — Ref: J Bray (Hinckley)
26	H	WEST HAM	10/1	22,110	2	1	L	32	1-3	0-2	Curtis 48 / Brooking 24, Pike 33, Cross 59 — Ref: M Scott (Nottingham)
27	A	CAMBRIDGE	17/1	5,121	2	10	L	32	1-3	1-1	Curtis 43 / Spriggs 19p, 73, Streete 60 — Ref: A Grey (Great Yarmouth)
28	H	QP RANGERS	31/1	12,518	4	8	L	32	1-2	1-2	Stevenson 27 / Langley 23, King 35 — Ref: D Webb (Radcliffe)
29	A	NOTTS CO	7/2	8,628	5	2	L	32	1-2	0-2	Robinson 83 / Masson 8, McCulloch 14 — Ref: G Courtney (Spennymoor)
30	A	SHEFFIELD WED	21/2	17,887	8	7	L	32	0-2	0-1	Sterland 11, McCulloch 71 — Ref: J Hough (Macclesfield)
31	H	BOLTON	28/2	9,468	8	15	W	34	3-0	1-0	James L 16p, 58p, 68 — Ref: J Warner (Wednesbury)

Line-ups (S = Swansea, O = Opponent)

No	Team	1	2	3	4	5	6	7	8	9	10	11	12 sub used
22	S	Stewart	Attley	Hadziabdic	Rushberry	Stevenson	Phillips	Mahoney	James R	James L*	Charles	Robinson	Curtis
22	O	Sherwood	Rice	Harrison	Taylor	Sims	Jackett	Ward*	Blissett	Armstrong	Train	Poskett	Jenkins
23	S	Stewart	Attley	Hadziabdic	Mahoney	Stevenson	Phillips	Curtis	James R	James L	Charles	Robinson	
23	O	Platt	Sinclair	Blair	Keegan	Clements	Hurst	Wylde	Futcher	Steel	Gardner	McDonough	
24	S	Stewart	Attley	Hadziabdic	Rushberry	Stevenson	Phillips	Mahoney	James R	James L*	Charles	Robinson	Curtis
24	O	Thomas	Jones	Bater	McCaffrey	Mabbutt	Emmanuel	Williams S*	Pulis	Lee	Williams D	Barrett	Barrowcl'gh
25	S	Stewart	Attley	Hadziabdic	Mahoney	Stevenson	Phillips	Curtis	James R	James L	Charles	Robinson	
25	O	Healey	Jones	Lewis	Hughes	Pontin	Dwyer*	Bishop	Kitchen	Stevens	Ronson	Buchanan	Giles P
26	S	Stewart	Attley	Hadziabdic	Mahoney	Stevenson	Phillips	James R	Curtis	James L*	Charles	Robinson	Giles
26	O	Parkes	Stewart	Lampard	Bonds	Martin	Devonshire	Holland	Goddard	Cross	Brooking	Pike	
27	S	Stewart	Attley	Hadziabdic	Rushberry	Stevenson	Phillips	Giles	James R	Curtis	Charles	Robinson*	Rushberry
27	O	Key	Donaldson	Murray	Smith	Fallon	Finney	Streete	Spriggs	Reilly	Taylor	Christie	
28	S	Stewart	Attley	Hadziabdic	Mahoney	Charles	Stevenson	Giles*	James R	Curtis	Toshack	Robinson	
28	O	Burridge	Shanks	Gillard	Fenwick	Wicks	Roeder	Langley	King	Stainrod*	Currie	Silkman	Waddock
29	S	Stewart	Attley	Hadziabdic	Lewis	Stevenson	Phillips	Craig	Mahoney	James L*	Curtis	Robinson	Giles
29	O	Leonard	Benjamin	O'Brien	Kelly	Kilcline	Richards	McCulloch	Masson	Hunt	Christie	Hooks	
30	S	Stewart	Robinson	Hadziabdic	Rushberry	Charles	Phillips	Giles*	James R	Curtis	Charles	Mahoney	Stevenson
30	O	Bolder	Blackhall	Grant*	Smith	Shirtliff	Sterland	Mirocevic	Taylor	Leman	McCulloch	King	Pearson
31	S	Stewart	Evans	Hadziabdic	Lewis	Charles	Stevenson	Craig	James R	James L*	Mahoney		Stevenson
31	O	Poole	Graham	McElhinney	Burke	Jones	Brennan	Nikolic	Whatmore	Hoggan*	Thomas	Gowling	Thompson

Match notes

22 — Watford (H): Curtis has to be content with a seat on the bench as Toshack keeps faith with a winning side. Two minutes after coming on, he begins paying back the £175,000 fee by netting a penalty after Robbie James has been brought down by Harrison. Blissett hits a late chance wide of the post.

23 — Oldham (A): Swans should have gone behind in the opening minutes but Stewart saves brilliantly at the feet of Gardner. After Robbie James cancels out Steel's opener, Curtis scores to put the Swans ahead for a second time, but a Futcher free-kick is headed in by Wylde for the equaliser.

24 — Bristol Rovers (H): Robbie James nips in between Jones and goalkeeper Thomas to put the Swans two up following Stevenson's early header. Swansea-born Emmanuel pulls one back for Rovers with a late header from a Barrett centre, but it is not enough for the club propping up the whole division.

25 — Cardiff (A): A number of fans are arrested for threatening behaviour before and during the match. With both sides unbeaten in their last six outings, it was always going to be a hard-fought game. Paul Giles, brother of Swansea's David, comes on for Cardiff in place of injured skipper Dwyer.

26 — West Ham (H): More than 500 pigeons and balloons are released before the match to celebrate the opening of the new stand. Parkes keeps the Swans at bay and the FA Cup holders take the lead when Lampard slips Brooking through the middle to score. Curtis nets his fourth goal in five matches.

27 — Cambridge (A): Leighton James misses out through injury and Giles takes over. Stevenson brings down Reilly in the box for a Spriggs penalty and, although Curtis nets his fifth goal since his return to the club, skipper Spriggs scores his second from a corner and Cambridge are worthy winners.

28 — QP Rangers (H): Toshack's first appearance since September fails to inspire the Swans, who have skipper Charles and Hadziabdic booked early on. Toshack joins them in the book in a niggling encounter and the winner comes from King, after four shots had been cleared off the Swansea goal-line.

29 — Notts Co (A): Despite making four changes it is the same old story as two quick goals put the Swans on the back foot. They never recover despite Robinson's fifth of the season. It is a fourth consecutive defeat for Toshack's side and only the brave goalkeeping of Stewart keeps them in the game.

30 — Sheffield Wed (A): Three more changes as the Swans battle to avoid five successive defeats. After King, Pearson and Taylor go close early on, and Yugoslav international Mirocevic misses an open goal, it looks odds on another defeat, particularly when Sterland beats the offside trap to net the opener.

31 — Bolton (H): A home debut for 18-year-old Lewis and a return for long-serving Evans does the trick. Leighton James strokes home a penalty when Curtis is brought down, and repeats the dose when McElhinney floors Robbie James. A 30-yard drive that dips under the bar seals a brilliant hat-trick.

No		Date	Opponent	Attendance		Res	Score	HT	Pos	Pts
32	H	6/3	WREXHAM	12,103	4	W	3-1	1-1	16	36
33	H	17/3	BRISTOL CITY	10,832	7	D	0-0	0-0	21	37
34	A	28/3	GRIMSBY	12,166	11	L	0-1	0-0	3	37
35	A	31/3	DERBY	16,210	5	W	1-0	0-0	7	39
36	H	4/4	BLACKBURN	12,011	3	W	2-0	0-0	5	41
37	A	11/4	ORIENT	4,984	4	D	1-1	1-0	13	42
38	H	18/4	CARDIFF	19,038	4	D	1-1	1-0	20	43
39	A	21/4	BRISTOL ROV	8,250	4	W	2-1	2-0	22	45
40	H	25/4	CHELSEA	16,063	4	W	3-0	2-0	10	47
41	H	27/4	LUTON	21,354	3	D	2-2	2-1	5	48
42	A	2/5	PRESTON	18,970	3	W	3-1	2-0	20	50

Home Average 13,098   Away 12,264

---

32. WREXHAM (H) 3-1
Scorers: James R 8, James L 64p, Stev'son 66 — McNeil 38
Ref: B Stevens (Stonehouse)
Swansea: Stewart, Evans, Hadziabdic, Lewis, Charles, Stevenson, Craig, James R, Curtis*, James L, Mahoney, Robinson
Wrexham: Davies, Dowman, Dwyer, Jones J, Cagelski, Carradus, Fox, Sutton, Vinter, McNeil, Cartwright*, Hill
Robbie James takes advantage of a dreadful mix-up between Dai Davies and McNeil to score his first goal in two months. Craig wins a penalty when he trips over the body of Dowman lying on the ground. It is a very bruising and often ugly match where a lot of tackles go unpunished.

33. BRISTOL CITY (H) 0-0
Ref: A Hamil (Wolverhampton)
Swansea: Stewart, Evans, Hadziabdic, Rajkovic, Charles, Stevenson, Craig, James R, Curtis*, James L, Mahoney, Robinson
Bristol City: Moller, Stevens, Hay, Aitken, Marshall, Sweeney, Tainton, Fitzpatrick, Mabbutt, Pritchard, Whitehead
Rajkovic makes long-awaited debut, after work permit delays, in place of Lewis, who plays for the Youth side. The Robins make light of their league position with neat play and deserve to get something from the game. Mabbutt is tackled from behind by Rajkovic who is cautioned.

34. GRIMSBY (A) 0-1
Scorer: Whymark 55
Ref: T Mills (Barnsley)
Swansea: Stewart, Evans, Hadziabdic, Charles, Stevenson, Lewis, James R, Curtis, James L, Mahoney, Robinson*, Giles
Grimsby: Batch, Stone, Crombie, Waters, Wigginton, Moores K, Brolly, Whymark, Drinkell, Mitchell, Steeples*, Kilmore
Swans play with five at the back to shut out the Mariners midfield. Stewart has only one save to make in a dull first half. Grimsby, with just four goals conceded at home this season, take both points when former Ipswich striker Whymark works free to beat Stewart from close range.

35. DERBY (A) 1-0
Scorer: Charles 65
Ref: M Dimblebee (Stevenage)
Swansea: Stewart, Evans, Hadziabdic*, Attley, Stevenson, Lewis, Giles, James R, James L, Charles, Curtis
Derby: Jones, Emery, Buckley, Powell S, McFarland*, Powell B, Wilson, Hector, Duncan, Swindlehurst, Emson, Sheridan
The Rams start the match with an ambitious 4-2-4 formation which Swansea counter with five in midfield. Leighton James and Giles have the home defence at full stretch. Giles creates the goal with a strong burst to the by-line, and his accurate cross is turned into the net by Charles.

36. BLACKBURN (H) 2-0
Scorers: Stevenson 57, James L 65
Ref: M Heath (Stoke)
Swansea: Stewart, Evans, Hadziabdic, Attley, Stevenson, Lewis, Giles, James R, James L, Charles, Curtis
Blackburn: Arnold, Branagan, Rathbone, Kendall, Keeley, Fazackerley, Garner, Busby, Lowey, Round*, Speight, Stonehouse
Leighton James is in inspired form and, after supplying the cross for the first goal, he nets the second himself to make it 12 league goals for the season. Rovers, under player-manager Kendall, never get to grips with the wing play of James.

37. ORIENT (A) 1-1
Scorers: Craig 23 — Godfrey 49
Ref: J Hunting (Leicester)
Swansea: Stewart, Evans, Hadziabdic, Attley, Stevenson, Lewis, Giles*, James R, James L, Charles, Curtis
Orient: Day, Fisher, Roffey, Taylor T, Gray, Moores, Godfrey, Jennings, Mayo, Bowles, Taylor P, Curtis
Stewart is forced to make a string of fine saves as Orient pile on the pressure and one block from a close-range Jennings header is world class. Charles finds the unmarked Craig in space and the Swans take the lead, but Bowles and P Taylor combine to leave Godfrey free to equalise.

38. CARDIFF (H) 1-1
Scorers: James L 42 — Kitchen 85
Ref: D Civil (Birmingham)
Swansea: Stewart, Evans, Hadziabdic, Rajkovic, Stevenson, Curtis, James R, James L, Charles, Craig, Giles*
Cardiff: Healey, Jones, Sullivan, Grapes, Pontin, Dwyer, Kitchen, Lewis, Stevens, Ronson, Giles*, Micallef
A 69th-minute penalty save by Healey proves costly for the Swans. With the scores level Pontin is penalised for handball but Leighton James's spot-kick is pushed away superbly by Healey. It is his first penalty miss for Swansea but he had netted in the first half after Curtis struck a post.

39. BRISTOL ROV (A) 2-1
Scorers: James R 6, Curtis 11 — Barrett 75
Ref: A Robinson (Waterlooville)
Swansea: Stewart, Evans, Hadziabdic, Giles, Stevenson, Curtis, James R, James L, Charles*, Craig, Mahoney, Robinson
Bristol Rov: Gillies*, McCaffrey, Hughes, Emmanuel, Williams D, Barrett, Penny, Williams G
Rovers are caught in the opening minutes with a double salvo. Robbie James strikes after Lewis hoists a high ball into Rovers danger area and Curtis doubles the lead with a well-placed header from a Leighton James cross. Barrett outpaces the Swans defence for a late consolation score.

40. CHELSEA (H) 3-0
Scorers: Robinson 22, Hadz'ic 35, James R 68
Ref: E Read (Bristol)
Swansea: Stewart, Evans, Hadziabdic, Giles, Stevenson, Curtis, James R, James L, Charles*, Craig, Mahoney, Robinson
Chelsea: Borota, Pates, Wilkins, Bumstead, Nutton*, Chivers, Locke, Britton, Lee, Walker, R'des-Brown, Fillery
Chelsea's defence fail to clear Craig's free-kick and Robinson's shot is parried into the net by Borota. A Hadziabdic rocket signals his first goal for the club. Chelsea are never in the hunt and Robbie James deflects a Curtis shot into the visitors' net to complete a comprehensive victory.

41. LUTON (H) 2-2
Scorers: Craig 3, James L 22 — Hill 29, 50
Ref: C Newsome (Broseley)
Swansea: Stewart, Evans, Hadziabdic, Robinson, Stevenson, Curtis, James R, James L, Charles, Craig, Mahoney
Luton: Findlay, Stephens, Donaghy, West, Saxby, Price, Hill, Stein, White, Antic, Moss
Swans have the best start possible and by half-time promotion is looking a near certainty. The Hatters move up a gear and pull one back when Antic sets Hill free and, with Vetch Field nerves jangling, Hill nips through a hesitant defence before clipping the equaliser beyond Stewart.

42. PRESTON (A) 3-1
Scorers: James L 25, Craig 27, Charles 85 — Bruce 78
Ref: A Challinor (Rotherham)
Swansea: Stewart, Evans, Hadziabdic, Robinson, Stevenson, Lewis, James R, James L, Charles, Craig, Curtis
Preston: Tunks, Taylor, Burns*, Haslegrave, Baxter, Blackley, Coleman, Bell, Elliott, Houston, Bruce, Anderson
At least 10,000 Swansea fans are packed into Deepdale on a tense afternoon. Superb ball control by Leighton James, followed by a cross-shot, puts them in front and Craig is unmarked to slip in the second. Preston rally and Bruce reduces the deficit but Charles finally ends the tension.

LEAGUE DIVISION 2 (CUP-TIES)

Manager: John Toshack

SEASON 1980-81

League Cup

		Att		F-A	H-T	Scorers, Times, and Referees	1	2	3	4	5	6	7	8	9	10	11	12 sub used
2:1 H ARSENAL	11 D	17,036 1:11		1-1	0-0	James L 82 / Stapleton 85 — Ref: T Spencer (Salisbury)	Stewart	Marustik*	Rushberry	Mahoney	Stevenson	Philips	Giles	James R	James L	Craig	Robinson	Toshack
26/8							*Jennings*	*Devine*	*Sansom*	*Talbot*	*O'Leary*	*Young*	*Hollins*	*Sunderland*	*Stapleton*	*Price*	*Rix*	

The Swans' defence are under early pressure and Robinson hacks a Price shot off the line. They have another escape when Sunderland has a goal disallowed for offside. Leighton James beats the offside trap to score but Stapleton equalises late on with his fourth goal in four games.

		Att		F-A	H-T	Scorers, Times, and Referees	1	2	3	4	5	6	7	8	9	10	11	12 sub used
2:2 A ARSENAL	13 L	26,399 1:8		1-3	1-1	Charles 12 / Hollins 20p, Sunderl'd 52, Walford 64 — Ref: T Bune (Billingshurst)	Stewart	Attley	Hadziabdic	Rushberry	Stevenson	Phillips	Giles	James R	James L	Charles	Toshack	
2/9							*Jennings*	*Devine*	*Sansom*	*Talbot*	*Walford*	*Young*	*Hollins*	*Sunderland*	*Stapleton*	*Price*	*Rix*	

Yugoslav Hadziabdic plays his first competitive match for the Swans, who take the lead when Charles heads a Robbie James cross beyond Jennings into the roof of the net. The Gunners level when the ref rules handball, to everyone's surprise, and they take control after the interval. (Swansea lose 2-4 on aggregate)

FA Cup

		Att		F-A	H-T	Scorers, Times, and Referees	1	2	3	4	5	6	7	8	9	10	11	12 sub used
3 H MIDDLESBROUGH	2 L	18,015 1:12		0-5	0-2	/Cochrane 72/ Ashcr't 42, Angus 44, Hodgson 69, 80, Platt — Ref: J Worral (Warrington)	Stewart	Attley	Hadziabdic	Rushberry	Stevenson	Phillips	Mahoney	James R	Curtis	Charles*	Robinson	Giles
3/1							*Platt*	*Craggs*	*Bailey*	*Angus*	*Ashcroft*	*Nattrass*	*Cochrane*	*Proctor*	*Hodgson*	*Shearer*	*McAndrew*	

Swans' attack has little to offer without injured Leighton James. They put on a grim performance in front of their largest crowd to date and are caught continually on the break by the fast-moving Boro forwards. The visitors' fourth goal is a superb overhead scissors-kick by Cochrane.

Final League Table

			Home					Away					
		P	W	D	L	F	A	W	D	L	F	A	Pts
1	West Ham	42	19	1	1	53	12	9	9	3	26	17	66
2	Notts Co	42	12	6	3	26	15	6	11	4	23	23	53
3	SWANSEA	42	12	5	4	39	19	6	9	6	25	25	50
4	Blackburn	42	12	8	1	28	7	4	10	7	14	22	50
5	Luton	42	10	6	5	35	23	8	6	7	26	23	48
6	Derby	42	9	8	4	34	26	6	7	8	23	26	45
7	Grimsby	42	10	8	3	21	10	5	7	9	23	32	45
8	QP Rangers	42	11	7	3	36	12	4	6	11	20	34	43
9	Watford	42	13	5	3	34	18	6	6	12	16	27	43
10	Sheffield Wed	42	14	4	3	38	14	3	4	14	15	37	42
11	Newcastle	42	14	7	3	22	13	8	6	9	8	32	42
12	Chelsea	42	8	6	7	27	15	6	6	9	19	26	40
13	Cambridge	42	13	1	7	36	23	4	5	12	17	42	40
14	Shrewsbury	42	9	7	5	33	22	2	10	9	13	25	39
15	Oldham	42	7	9	5	19	16	5	6	10	20	32	39
16	Wrexham	42	5	8	8	22	24	7	6	8	21	21	38
17	Orient	42	9	8	4	34	20	4	4	13	18	36	38
18	Bolton	42	10	5	6	40	27	4	5	12	21	39	38
19	Cardiff	42	7	7	5	23	24	5	5	11	21	36	36
20	Preston	42	8	7	6	28	26	3	7	11	13	36	36
21	Bristol City	42	6	5	10	19	15	1	6	14	10	36	30
22	Bristol Rov	42	4	8	8	21	24	4	4	16	13	41	23
		924	217	144	101	668	405	101	144	217	405	668	924

Odds & ends

Double wins: (5) Bolton, Derby, Newcastle, Preston, Bristol Rov.
Double losses: (2) Sheffield Wed, West Ham.
Won from behind: (0).
Lost from in front: (2). Watford (a), Arsenal Lcup (a).
High spots: Eight-match unbeaten finish to secure promotion. Only one goal conceded in last ten league games.
Low spots: Heavy home defeat by Middlesbrough in FA Cup. A four-match sequence without scoring in league.
Ever present: (1) Dave Stewart.
Hat-tricks: (2) Leighton James.
Opposing hat-tricks: (0).
Penalties for: (6) Leighton James 4, Robbie James 1, Alan Curtis 1.
Penalties against: (2) K Osgood (Derby), S Spriggs (Cambridge).
Penalty misses for: (1) L James (v Cardiff).
Penalty misses against: (0).
Leading scorer: Leighton James (15).

Appearances and Goals

Player	Lge	Sub	LC	Sub	FAC	Sub	Goals Lge	FAC	Tot
Attley, Brian	32						2		2
Charles, Jeremy	37	5	1		1		5	1	6
Craig, Tommy	14	5	1		1		3		3
Curtis, Alan	16	4			1		6		6
Evans, Wyndham	13								
Giles, David	24	3	2			1	5		5
Hadziabdic, Dzemal	38		1		1		1		1
James, Leighton	40		2		1		15	1	16
James, Robbie	30		2				8		8
Lewis, Dudley	12	1							
Loveridge, Jimmy		1							
Marustik, Chris	3		1						
Mahoney, John	31	4	1		1				
Phillips, Leighton	29		2		1				
Rajkovic, Ante	2								
Robinson, Neil	33	3	1		1		6		6
Rushbury, Dave	11	1	2		1				
Stevenson, Nigel	39	1	2		1		5		5
Stewart, Dave	42		2		1				
Toshack, John	3	1	1						
Waddle, Alan	13	1	1				7		7
(own-goals)							1		1
21 players used	**462**	**30**	**22**	**1**	**11**	**1**	**64**	**2**	**66**

LEAGUE DIVISION 1 — SEASON 1981-82

Manager: John Toshack

No	Date	Att	Pos	Pt	F-A	H-T	Scorers, Times, and Referees	1	2	3	4	5	6	7	8	9	10	11	12 sub used
1	H LEEDS 29/8	23,489		W 3	5-1	1:1	Charles 5, Latchford 46, 50, 55, [Curtis 70]	Davies	Robinson	Hadziabdic	Rajkovic	Irwin	Mahoney	Curtis	James R	James L	Charles	Latchford	Attley
							Parlane 26 — Ref: S Bates (Bristol)	Lukic	Hird	Gray F	Flynn	Hart	Cherry	Harris	Graham	Parlane	Gray E	Barnes	Smith
2	A BRIGHTON 1/9	19,885	1	W 6	2:1	2:1	James L 10, Latchford 14	Davies	Robinson	Hadziabdic	Rajkovic	Irwin	Mahoney	Curtis	James R	James L*	Charles	Latchford	Attley
			15				Ritchie 36 — Ref: D Vickers (Ilford)	Moseley	Shanks	Williams	Greaish*	Foster	Stevens	Case	Ritchie	Robinson	McNab	Ryan	Smith
3	A WEST BROM 5/9	18,063	6	L 6	1-4	0-1	Robinson 76	Davies	Robinson	Hadziabdic	Rajkovic	Irwin	Mahoney	Curtis	James R	James L	Charles*	Latchford	Attley
			15				Regis 18, 68, 73, MacKenzie 69 — Ref: R Bridges (Deeside)	Godden	Batson	Statham	Moses	Wile	Robertson	Robson	Mills	Regis	Owen	MacKenzie	
4	H NOTTS CO 12/9	14,391	2	W 9	3:2	2-0	Curtis 21, James L 36, Latchford 51	Davies	Robinson	Hadziabdic	Rajkovic	Irwin	Mahoney	Curtis	James R	James L	Thompson	Latchford	
			6				O'Brien 65p, McCulloch 85 — Ref: T Spencer (Salisbury)	Avramovic	Benjamin	O'Brien	Goodwin*	Kilcine	Richards	Chiedozie	McCulloch	Christie	Hunt	Lahtinen	
5	A MANCHESTER U 19/9	47,309	4	L 9	0:1	0:1	Birtles 38	Davies	Robinson	Hadziabdic	Rajkovic	Irwin	Mahoney	Curtis	James R	Attley	Thompson	Latchford*	Giles
			17				Ref: G Napthine (Loughborough)	Bailey	Gidman	Albiston	Wilkins	McQueen	Buchan	Coppell	Birtles	Stapleton	Macari	McIlroy*	Moses
6	H TOTTENHAM 22/9	22,206	3	W 12	2:1	0-0	James R 62, Curtis 74	Davies	Robinson	Hadziabdic*	Rajkovic	Irwin	Mahoney	Curtis	James R	James L	Thompson	Latchford	Charles
			8				Hoddle 65p — Ref: D Civil (Birmingham)	Clemence	Hughton	Miller	Roberts	Villa	Perryman	Ardiles	Archibald	Galvin	Hoddle	Falco	
7	H SUNDERLAND 26/9	17,826	3	W 15	2-0	0-0	Curtis 56, James L 82p	Davies	Robinson	Hadziabdic	Rajkovic	Irwin	Mahoney	Curtis	James R	James L	Charles*	Latchford	Thompson
			20				Ref: R Baker (Wolverhampton)	Siddall	Hinnigan	Elliott	Buckley	Clarke	Hindmarch	Arnott	Cummins	Ritchie	Rowell	Pickering*	McCoist
8	A LIVERPOOL 3/10	48,645	3	D 16	2:2	1-0	James L 15p, Latchford 57	Davies	Robinson	Hadziabdic*	Rajkovic	Irwin	Mahoney	Curtis	James R	James L	Thompson	Latchford	Charles
			13				McDermott 50p, 63p — Ref: A Challinor (Rotherham)	Grobbelaar	Neal	Kennedy A	Thompson	Lawrenson	Whelan	Dalglish	Lee	Johnson*	McDermott	Souness	Sheedy
9	H ARSENAL 10/10	20,600	2	W 19	2-0	1-0	James L 38, Thompson 83	Davies	Robinson	Hadziabdic	Rajkovic	Irwin	Mahoney	Curtis	James R	James L	Thompson	Latchford*	Charles
			18				Ref: L Robinson (S'n Coldfield)	Jennings	Devine	Sansom	Talbot	O'Leary	Young	Davis	Sunderland	Hawley	Nicholas	Hollins	
10	A STOKE 17/10	14,665	1	W 22	2:1	0:1	Stanley 67, Latchford 81	Davies	Robinson	Hadziabdic	Rajkovic	Irwin	Mahoney	Curtis	James R	James L*	Thompson	Latchford	Stanley
			17				Griffiths 36 — Ref: D Scott (Burnley)	Fox	Evans	Hampton	Dodd	O'Callaghan	Smith	Griffiths	Chapman	Heath	Bracewell	Maguire	

Match reports:

1. Playing against his old club, Curtis brings a smart save from Lukic in the opening minutes and a neat dummy gives Swans their first goal in the top flight. Parlane equalises from a cross by Harris but a Latchford hat-trick and superb Curtis strike gives the club a great start to the season.

2. Swans begin well and fully deserve early lead when a slip by Foster leaves Leighton James with time and space. Latchford converts a Charles cross for the second, and although Robinson and Curtis go close, Ritchie pulls one back for the Seagulls, who then lay siege to the Swans goal.

3. Regis fires a hat-trick on his first appearance of the season. Both Charles and Curtis go close early on, but Swans are caught square for the first goal. Charles fails to come out after the interval and three goals in five second-half minutes sinks the Swans, despite a late strike by Robinson.

4. Thompson makes his Swansea debut after signing from Blackpool for £20k. A rare header from Leighton James increases the Swans' lead and Latchford's fifth goal in four games should have sealed a comfortable victory, but the Magpies strike back to make it an edgy last few minutes.

5. United were bottom of the table before the match and Birtles' first goal in 30 outings for the club lifts them up a couple of places. His 25-yard volley gives Davies no chance and, although Giles skims a post with Bailey beaten and Robbie James misses an easy chance, it's United's day.

6. FA Cup holders Spurs defend well until half-time. Then two superb goals light up a packed Vetch Field. Robbie James strikes a clean volley beyond Clemence and, after Hoddle levels from the spot, Curtis turns in a flash and fires a 35-yard shot into the net.

7. Latchford has a goal disallowed for offside in a poor first half offering few chances. Charles goes close on his 22nd birthday, and a rebound from one of his shots gives Curtis the opener. But they need a late penalty from Leighton James to make sure of beating the lowly Wearsiders.

8. A minute's silence is held before the match in memory of the late Bill Shankly. Swans win a penalty after Thompson brought down Robinson, and the unfortunate England defender lets in Latchford for the second. Two disputed penalties in four minutes gifts Liverpool a lucky draw.

9. An inswinging corner from Hollins on Arsenal's first league visit to the Vetch sees Robinson hack clear off the line. Hawley has the ball in the net for the Gunners but it is disallowed for handball. Thompson volleys the clincher in great style following a free-kick conceded by Nicholas.

10. A Griffiths header from a corner gives the Potters a shock lead. Swans improve after the interval and Mahoney goes close before substitute Stanley lashes in an equaliser. Stanley's free-kick is then headed home by Latchford to take Swans to the top of the division for the first time.

Match-by-match record (matches 11–21)

---

11. A COVENTRY — 24/10 · Att 14,050 · Pos 3 (Opp 11, Pts 22) · **L 1-3** (HT 0-2)
Curtis 74
Hateley 36, 52, Kaiser 38
Ref: M Lowe (Sheffield)

Swansea: Davies, Robinson, Stanley, Rajkovic, Irwin, Mahoney, Curtis, James R, James L, Thompson*, Latchford, Marustik
Coventry: Blyth, Thomas, Roberts, Jacobs, Dyson, Gillespie, Kaiser, Whitton, Thompson, Hateley, Hunt

Two goals in a devastating two-minute spell sees Swans quickly knocked off top spot. Hateley fires in a brace to make it four goals in five appearances and Dutchman Kaiser knocks in a loose ball that Davies should have claimed. 20-year-old Marustik is booked after first challenge.

---

12. H WOLVES — 31/10 · Att 17,750 · Pos 4 (Opp 21, Pts 23) · **D 0-0** (HT 0-0)
Ref: E Read (Bristol)

Swansea: Davies, Stanley, Attley, Rajkovic, Irwin, Mahoney, Curtis, James R, James L, Stevenson, Latchford
Wolves: Bradshaw, Palmer, Parkin, Daniel, Brazier, Berry, Birch*, Atkinson, Eves, Richards, Matthews, Clarke

Irwin almost slices an Eves cross into his own net and Richards heads straight at Davies from point-blank range as lowly Wolves make the early running. Berry, hoping to impress watching Wales boss Mike England, hooks the ball out from under the crossbar after a Stanley corner.

---

13. A IPSWICH — 7/11 · Att 24,190 · Pos 3 (Opp 2, Pts 26) · **W 3-2** (HT 1-0)
Curtis 7, Latchford 62, Stanley 82
Mariner 53, Muhren 80
Ref: K Salmon (Barnet)

Swansea: Davies, Robinson, Stanley, Rajkovic, Irwin, Stevenson, Curtis, James R, James L, Mahoney, Latchford
Ipswich: Cooper, Mills, McCall, Thijssen, Osman, Butcher, Wark, Muhren, Mariner, Brazil, Gates

Second-placed Ipswich have England hopefuls Osman and Butcher at the heart of defence but they are rocked when Swans take an early lead. Wark blasts over when well-placed but Cooper is the busier keeper. Swans' five-man midfield holds the key and Stanley hits deserved winner.

---

14. A MANCHESTER C — 21/11 · Att 34,744 · Pos 4 (Opp 8, Pts 26) · **L 0-4** (HT 0-1)
Tueart 40p, 85, Reeves 63, 82
Ref: G Courtney (Spennymoor)

Swansea: Davies, Hadziabdic*, Stanley, Rajkovic, Irwin, Stevenson, Curtis, James R, James L, Mahoney, Latchford, Giles
Manchester C: Corrigan, Ranson, McDonald, Reid, Bond, Caton*, Tueart, Reeves, Francis, Hartford, Hutchison, Hareide

Blues' striker Reeves almost gives his side a dream start but the £1.3m signing hits his shot against the post. City stay on the attack and just before the interval McDonald goes down pole-axed in area to win a penalty. There is a rude awakening for Swansea in a one-sided second half.

---

15. H BRIGHTON — 24/11 · Att 14,459 · Pos 3 (Opp 11, Pts 27) · **D 0-0** (HT 0-0)
Ref: K Baker (Wolverhampton)

Swansea: Davies, Stanley, Hadziabdic, Rajkovic*, Irwin, Mahoney, Curtis, James R, James L, Thompson, Latchford, Charles
Brighton: Moseley, Shanks, Nelson, Grealish, Foster, Gatting, Case, Smith, Robinson, McNab, Thomas

Swans attacks break down against solid Brighton defending and they are limited to two Leighton James chances. Thomas shaves a post with a snapshot that flies across the face of the goal and McNab goes close. Swansea end with ten men as Charles is forced off with a knee injury.

---

16. H BIRMINGHAM — 28/11 · Att 15,097 · Pos 2 (Opp 20, Pts 30) · **W 1-0** (HT 0-0)
James R 66
Ref: D Hutchinson (Bourn)

Swansea: Davies, Robinson, Stanley*, Rajkovic, Irwin, Mahoney, Curtis, James R, James L, Thompson, Latchford, Hadziabdic
Birmingham: Coton, Langan, Dennis, Curtishley, v d Hauwe, Todd, Dillon, Whatmore, Worthington, Gemmill, Van Mierlo*, Handysides

The match is switched for an evening kick-off to avoid clash with the rugby international. Swans use three-man back line, with transfer-listed Stevenson outstanding. Robbie James heads in at near post from Leighton James' corner and Davies saves well from Worthington and Dillon.

---

17. A EVERTON — 5/12 · Att 23,860 · Pos 4 (Opp 13, Pts 30) · **L 1-3** (HT 0-0)
Latchford 78
Sharp 48, O'Keefe 61, 66
Ref: K Redfern (Whitley Bay)

Swansea: Davies, Robinson, Hadziabdic, Rajkovic, Irwin, Mahoney, Curtis, James R, James L, Thompson*, Latchford, Stanley
Everton: Arnold, Stevens, Ratcliffe, Walsh, Lyons, Kendall, McMahon, Ross, Sharp, Biley, O'Keefe

Curtis rounds Ratcliffe only to have his shot bundled off line by Lyons. A high ball into box by Ross gives Sharp the opener and a brace in five minutes by O'Keefe seals the points for the mid-table Toffees. A late Latchford score cannot disguise a lacklustre performance by the Swans.

---

18. H NOTT'M FOREST — 12/12 · Att 17,550 · Pos 4 (Opp 6, Pts 30) · **L 1-2** (HT 1-0)
James R 34
Young 78, Robertson 89p
Ref: D Lloyd (Fernhill Heath)

Swansea: Davies, Robinson, Marustik, Rajkovic, Irwin, Mahoney, Curtis, James R, James L, Thompson, Latchford, Robertson
Nott'm Forest: Shilton, Anderson, Gunn, McGovern, Young, Needham, Rober, Wallace, Fashanu, Proctor, Robertson

The coldest night since 1883 fails to stop the match starting, although Forest's train is delayed and the game kicks off seven minutes late. Robbie James snatches the lead but debut-making Young equalises and a Robertson penalty after Robinson handles clinches Forest a late win.

---

19. H ASTON VILLA — 15/12 · Att 15,191 · Pos 1 (Opp 17, Pts 33) · **W 2-1** (HT 2-1)
James R 12, 43
Thompson 14 (og)
Ref: A Glasson (Salisbury)

Swansea: Davies, Marustik, Hadziabdic*, Rajkovic, Stevenson, Mahoney, Curtis, James R, James L, Thompson, Latchford, Linton
Aston Villa: Rimmer, Swain, Gibson, Evans, Williams, Deacy*, Bremner, Shaw, Geddis, Cowans, Morley, Linton

Swans set the pace against the league champions but Rimmer is at his best for Villa, keeping Leighton James and Latchford at bay. A Robbie James header from a Stanley cross is cancelled out when Thompson slices into his own net, but James scores a second just before the interval.

---

20. A SOUTHAMPTON — 28/12 · Att 22,703 · Pos 3 (Opp 2, Pts 33) · **L 1-3** (HT 1-1)
Rajkovic 14
Armstrong 3, Keegan 50, 67
Ref: L Shapter (Newton Abbot)

Swansea: Davies, Stanley, Hadziabdic*, Rajkovic, Irwin, Mahoney, Curtis, James R, James L, Thompson, Latchford, Ball
Southampton: Katalinic, Golac, Holmes, Williams, Nicholl, Waldron, Keegan, Channon, Moran, Armstrong, Ball

Keegan makes his 400th league appearance but misses a first-half spot-kick after being felled by Hadziabdic. An Armstrong free-kick gives Saints an early lead but Rajkovic's powerful header leaves it all square at the interval. Two Davies handling errors gifts Keegan a double.

---

21. A LEEDS — 16/1 · Att 18,709 · Pos 5 (Opp 14, Pts 33) · **L 0-2** (HT 0-1)
Stevenson 17, Butterworth 48
Ref: N Wilson (Morecambe)

Swansea: Davies, Stanley, Marustik, Rajkovic, Irwin, Mahoney, Curtis, James R, James L, Thompson*, Latchford, Greenhoff
Leeds: Lukic, Cherry, Gray F, Stevenson, Hart, Burns, Gray E, Graham*, Butterworth, Hanson, Hird, Greenhoff

Elland Road is in poor condition but Leeds adapt far better in the early stages. Curtis, back at a previous club, causes the home defence some problems but Hart and Burns are in control. Wales international Stevenson scores from a Graham cross and Butterworth slides in the second.

LEAGUE DIVISION 1 — Manager: John Toshack — SEASON 1981-82

No	Date	Venue / Opponent	Att	Pos	Pt	Res	F-A	H-T	Scorers, Times, and Referees
22	30/1	H MANCHESTER U	23,900	6	36	W	2-0	0-0	Curtis 54, James R 56 · Ref: J Martin (Alton)
23	6/2	A NOTTS CO	10,070	5	39	W	1-0	1-0	James L 12p · Ref: N Midgley (Salford)
24	13/2	A MIDDLESBROUGH	11,209	6	40	D	1-1	1-0	Kennedy 36, McAndrew 68g · Ref: D Webb (Radcliffe)
25	16/2	H LIVERPOOL	22,604	4	43	W	2-0	0-0	James L 74, Curtis 89 · Ref: V Callow (Solihull)
26	20/2	A SUNDERLAND	13,163	3	46	W	1-0	1-0	James L 22 · Ref: R Nixon (West Kirby)
27	27/2	A ARSENAL	29,724	2	49	W	2-0	1-0	Kennedy 17, James L 65p · Ref: H Taylor (Oadby)
28	6/3	H STOKE	11,811	2	52	W	3-0	1-0	James R 34, 87, Charles 72 · Ref: L Burden (Wimborne)
29	13/3	H COVENTRY	16,425	2	53	D	0-0	0-0	Ref: T Spencer (Salisbury)
30	20/3	A WOLVES	14,158	1	56	W	1-0	1-0	Walsh 35 · Ref: T Fitzharris (Bolton)
31	27/3	H IPSWICH	20,750	2	56	L	1-2	1-1	James R 32p, Brazil 20, Gates 88 · Ref: C Newsome (Broseley)

Line-ups (Swansea top row, opponents in italics)

No	1	2	3	4	5	6	7	8	9	10	11	12 (sub used)
22	Davies	Stanley	Marustik	Irwin	**Kennedy**	Rajkovic	Curtis	James R	Latchford	Thompson	Robinson*	James L
	Bailey	*Duxberry*	*Alliston*	*Wilkins*	*Moran*	*McQueen**	*Robson*	*Birtles*	*Stapleton*	*Macari*	*Coppell*	*Gidman*
23	Davies	Stanley	Marustik	Irwin	Kennedy	Rajkovic	Curtis	James R	James L	Thompson	Robinson	
	Avramovic	*Benjamin*	*O'Brien*	*Goodwin**	*Kilcline*	*Richards*	*Chiedozie*	*Masson*	*McCulloch*	*Hooks*	*Mair*	*Christie*
24	Davies	Marustik	Hadziabdic	Irwin	**Kennedy**	Rajkovic*	Curtis	James R	James L	Stanley	Charles	Robinson
	Platt	*Craggs*	*Bailey*	*Angus*	*Baxter*	*Nattrass*	*Cochrane*	*Otto*	*Hodgson*	*Ashcroft*	*McAndrew*	
25	Davies	Stanley	Marustik	Irwin	Kennedy	Rajkovic	Curtis	James R	James L	Thompson	Charles	
	Grobbelaar	*Neal*	*Lawrenson*	*Kennedy*	*Whelan*	*Hansen*	*Dalglish*	*Lee*	*Rush*	*McDermott*	*Souness*	
26	Davies	Stanley	Marustik	Irwin	Kennedy	Rajkovic	Curtis	James R	James L	Stevenson	Charles	
	Siddall	*Hinnigan*	*Munro*	*Hindmarch*	*Clarke*	*Elliott*	*Buckley*	*McCoist*	*Brown*	*McGinley*	*Cummins*	
27	Davies	Stanley	Marustik	Irwin	Kennedy	Rajkovic	Curtis	James R	James L*	Stevenson	Robinson	**Walsh**
	Wood	*Hollins*	*Sansom*	*Talbot*	*O'Leary*	*Whyte*	*Vaessen**	*Sunderland*	*Davis*	*Nicholas*	*Rix*	*Meade*
28	Davies	Robinson	Marustik	Irwin	Kennedy	Rajkovic	Curtis	James R	James L	Thompson	Charles	
	Fox	*Kirk**	*Hampton*	*Dodd*	*Watson*	*McAutrie*	*McIlroy*	*O'Callaghan*	*Chapman*	*Bracewell*	*Maguire*	*Griffiths*
29	Davies	Robinson	Marustik	Irwin	Kennedy	Rajkovic	Curtis	James R	James L	Thompson	Charles*	Stanley
	Sealey	*Thomas*	*Roberts*	*Jacobs*	*Dyson*	*Gillespie*	*Hendrie*	*Francis*	*Hateley*	*English*	*Whitton*	
30	Davies	Stanley	Hadziabdic	Irwin	Kennedy	Rajkovic	Curtis	James R	Walsh	Stevenson	Robinson	
	Bradshaw	*Humphrey*	*Palmer*	*Matthews*	*Pender*	*Coy*	*Hibbitt*	*Carr*	*Gray*	*Eves*	*Clarke*	
31	Davies	Stanley	Marustik	Irwin	Kennedy	Stevenson	Curtis	James R	James L	Thompson	Mahoney	
	Sivell	*Burley*	*McCall*	*Mills*	*Osman*	*Steggles*	*Wark*	*Muhren*	*D'Avray*	*Brazil*	*Gates*	

Match reports

22. Swans are flying off on a sunshine break to Spain after toppling the league leaders. Kennedy makes a big contribution on his debut after not playing for two months as Swans take control in second half. Marginally offside Curtis puts them in front and Robbie James taps in the other.

23. A superb performance from Dai Davies helps Swans to victory at Meadow Lane. Under heavy pressure in the second half, particularly from Kilcline and McCulloch, Davies stands firm and Swans hold out. The penalty is awarded early on when Curtis is brought down in the area.

24. Lowest league gate of season sees a mistake-ridden match. A foul on Curtis gives Swans a free-kick and Leighton James's inswinger is met by a brave header from Kennedy. Stanley hauls down Hodgson and McAndrew scores from spot to give Middlesbrough their first goal in 1982.

25. Leighton James celebrates his 29th birthday with a spectacular goal. Hansen fouls Curtis 30 yards out and James beats Grobbelaar for pace. Curtis clinches victory with his 100th goal for the club after a jinking run. The European Champions are well beaten but Davies plays well.

26. Davies is forced to save from Brown as the striker is free on goal but Swans win it with a speculative 25-yard shot from Leighton James that goes into corner of net without Siddall attempting to save. The match is delayed as two visiting fans are removed from pitch by police officers.

27. Toshack completes four years at Vetch with his side up to second place after completing the double over Gunners, who were on a seven-match unbeaten run. Nicholas slips to let Kennedy score against his old club, and Walsh wins penalty on debut after being brought down by O'Leary.

28. Charles comes back after injury to score first goal in six months. Chapman and O'Callaghan have chances at other end, but Robbie James seals a place in Wales team to play Spain with a superb performance and two well-taken goals. Davies is alert as Stoke look for consolation.

29. In a poor display, the nearest Swansea come to scoring is a Kennedy header which flashes just past the post. They are lucky not to fall behind when the lively Whitton strikes the underside of the crossbar with Davies stranded. Coventry were seeking their first win in twelve games.

30. Relegation strugglers Wolves bring Swans down to their level in a dour match. Gray misses early chance and Hibbitt goes close. While Gray is signalling to referee, Curtis crosses to Walsh who heads firmly into net. Clarke strikes post as Wolves try to hit back but Swans defence is firm.

31. The loss of Rajkovic through suspension proves expensive for Swans, who lose to a brilliantly struck volley by Gates at the death. Swansea level Brazil's opener from the spot after Wark handles, but just as it seems they have earned a point, up pops Gates with his wonder strike.

Match 32 — WEST HAM (H), 30/3

Davies	Robinson	Hadziabdic*	Irwin	Kennedy	Rajkovic	Curtis	James R	James L	Stevenson	Latchford	Stanley
Parkes	Stewart	Lampard	Orr	Martin	Devonshire	Van der Elst	Goddard	Cross	Brooking	Allen	

Pos 4 · 0-1 · L · 56 · 20,272 · 10

Van der Elst 9
Ref: B Stevens (Stonehouse)

Swans' title aspirations suffer a blow when they go down to a second successive defeat. Belgian international Van der Elst spots Davies off his line and cleverly lifts the ball over him. Swans press for equaliser and Parkes makes a number of saves before Brooking almost makes it.

Match 33 — WEST BROM (H), 6/4

Davies	Marustik	Hadziabdic	Irwin	Kennedy	Rajkovic	Curtis	James R	James L	Stevenson	Latchford	Stanley
Grew	Arthur	Statham	Bennett	Wile	Robertson	Zondervan	Cross*	Regis	Owen	Mackenzie	Brown

Pos 4 · 3-1 · W · 59 · 15,744 · 15

Marustik 58, Curtis 80, Latchf'd 89 · *Mackenzie 44*
Ref: R Milford (Bristol)

Marustik's first league goal of the season levels it up after Albion take the lead with their first attack. Curtis collects a rebound from a Kennedy shot to put Swans ahead and in the closing stages leading scorer Latchford hammers in a third. Regis has little luck with several good attempts.

Match 34 — WEST HAM (A), 10/4

Davies	Marustik*	Hadziabdic	Irwin	Kennedy	Rajkovic	Curtis	James R	James L	Stevenson	Latchford	Stanley	
Parkes	Stewart	Lampard*	Orr	Martin	Devonshire	Van der Elst	Goddard	Cross	Brooking	Allen	Robinson	Neighbour

Pos 3 · 1-1 · D · 60 · 26,566 · 8

James R 32 · *Goddard 87*
Ref: A Robinson (Portsmouth)

A superb strike by Robbie James gives Swans a first-half advantage at Upton Park. He sends a shot scorching into the roof of the net, leaving Parkes helpless. They hold out until the final stages when they fail to clear a Devonshire corner and the unmarked Goddard scores with ease.

Match 35 — SOUTHAMPTON (H), 13/4

Davies	Robinson	Hadziabdic	Irwin	Kennedy	Rajkovic	Curtis	James R	James L	Stevenson	Latchford*	Stanley
Katalinic	Baker	Holmes	Williams	Nicholl	Whitlock	Keegan	Channon	Cassells	Armstrong	Ball	

Pos 3 · 1-0 · W · 63 · 23,771 · 5

Curtis 28
Ref: A Hamil (Wolverhampton)

Swans are forced to hang on after Curtis holds off Whitlock's challenge to score. Channon has a couple of chances but Davies produces some magnificent saves. Keegan and debut-making Cassells rarely trouble the Swansea rearguard and Latchford should have extended the lead.

Match 36 — MANCHESTER C (H), 17/4

Davies	Hadziabdic	Marustik	Stanley	Kennedy	Rajkovic	Curtis	James R	James L	Stevenson	Latchford	Walsh
Williams	Ranson	McDonald	Reid	Bond	Caton	May*	Reeves	Francis	Hartford	Kinsey	Hareide

Pos 3 · 2-0 · W · 66 · 19,212 · 8

Stanley 11, Latchford 37
Ref: K Baker (Rugby)

Corrigan is a late absentee for the Blues, giving Williams only his fourth league start. Bond has a shot cleared off the line by Hadziabdic but a 35-yard curler from Stanley sets the Swans on the way. After Curtis clips a post, Latchford deflects a Robbie James shot for a comfortable win.

Match 37 — BIRMINGHAM (A), 24/4

Davies	Marustik	Hadziabdic	Irwin*	Kennedy	Rajkovic	Curtis	James R	James L	Stevenson	Stanley	Walsh	
Coton	Langan	Hawker	Stevenson*	v d Hauwe	Curbishley	Van Mierlo	Dillon	Harford	Broadhurst	Evans	Whatmore	

Pos 3 · 1-2 · L · 66 · 14,973 · 16

Walsh 55 · *Broadhurst 31, Harford 79*
Ref: C White (Harrow)

The Blues are gifted the lead when Swansea fail to clear a corner and Broadhurst strikes the bar. Walsh outpaces Stevenson before firing over Coton for the equaliser, but Harford's fourth strike in six games sends Swans crashing to a costly defeat.

Match 38 — EVERTON (H), 1/5

Davies	Marustik	Hadziabdic	Irwin	Kennedy*	Rajkovic	Curtis	James R	James L	Stevenson	Latchford	Stanley
Southall	Stevens	Walsh	Higgins	Wright	McMahon	Irvine	Heath	Sharp	Rimmer*	Ross	Richardson

Pos 4 · 1-3 · L · 66 · 16,243 · 8

James R 76 · *Sharp 55p, 65, Heath 26*
Ref: D Hedges (Oxford)

Everton do the double over Swans, with Heath and Sharp too clever for the home defence. After Heath opens the scoring, Marustik pulls down McMahon for a penalty. Sharp nets another shortly after and a Robbie James header from a Leighton James cross is all Swansea can muster.

Match 39 — TOTTENHAM (A), 5/5

Davies	Robinson	Marustik	Evans*	Mahoney	Rajkovic	Curtis	James R	James L	Stevenson	Walsh	Stanley
Aleksic	Hughton	Corbett	Roberts	Lacey	Perryman	O'Reilly	Archibald	Falco	Brooke	Crook*	Jones

Pos 5 · 1-2 · L · 66 · 36,348 · 4

James L 76 · *Brooke 26, 57p*
Ref: L Shapter (Newton Abbot)

Evans is brought in for his Division One debut but it only lasts 22 minutes before he is carried off with knee damage. Davies keeps his side in the game, but a Brooke double, including a penalty after Stanley bowls him over, puts Spurs on top. Leighton James' side-footer is not enough.

Match 40 — NOTT'M FOREST (A), 8/5

Davies	Robinson	Hadziabdic	Thompson	Mahoney	Rajkovic	Curtis	James R	James L	Stevenson	Latchford*	Marustik
Shilton	Anderson	Gunn	Needham	Young	Bowyer	Rober	Proctor*	Davenport	Wallace	Robertson	Walsh

Pos 5 · 2-0 · W · 69 · 15,037 · 13

James R 1, 83
Ref: K Barratt (Coventry)

Swans end losing run with a solid display at Forest. They score almost direct from the kick-off and are in control throughout. Stevenson and Thompson are booked for challenges on Davenport, Forest's only danger. Transfer-listed Shilton is beaten by a low shot to tie up the victory.

Match 41 — MIDDLESBROUGH (H), 15/5

Davies	Marustik	Hadziabdic	Thompson	Kennedy	Rajkovic	Walsh*	James R	James L	Stevenson	Latchford	Stanley
Platt	Craggs	Bailey	Ashcroft	Baxter	Bolton	Thomson	Otto	McAndrew	McDonald	Thomas*	Currie

Pos 6 · 1-2 · L · 69 · 12,961 · 22

Latchford 77 · *Otto 81, Stanley 89 (og)*
Ref: D Letts (Aldershot)

Toshack is booked for ungentlemanly conduct as his side slips back into their old bad habits. But when Latchford touches home a Stevenson cross in the closing stages it looks good. Boro have other ideas and Otto hooks in the equaliser before Stanley deflects a cross into his own net.

Match 42 — ASTON VILLA (A), 21/5

Sander	Richards	Irwin*	Rajkovic	Loveridge	Walsh*	James R	Mahoney	Stevenson	Latchford	Gale	
Rimmer	Swain	Williams	Evans	McNaught	Mortimer	Bremner	Geddis	Withe	Cowans	Morley	

Pos 6 · 0-3 · L · 69 · 18,294 · 11

Morley 37, Bremner 43, Withe 65
Ref: M Dimblebee (Stevenage)

Latchford strikes the woodwork twice and Swans miss chance of toppling the European Cup finalists. 19-year-old Sander, in goal for Davies, is chipped by Morley and then beaten by a long shot. Irwin is forced off injured and Gale becomes the fifth teenager to make Division One debut.

Home Average 18,202 · Away 22,684

LEAGUE DIVISION 1 (CUP-TIES)

Manager: John Toshack

Match details

		Date	Att	Pos	Res	F-A	H-T	Scorers, Times, and Referees
Milk Cup								
2:1	A BARNSLEY	6/10	12,793 2:13	3	L	0-2	0-0	Riley 47, Evans 74; Ref: A Banks (Manchester)
2:2	H BARNSLEY	27/10	9,800 2:9	3	W	3-2	1-0	James L 18(p), Irwin 66, Curtis 73; Glavin 46, Cooper 113; Ref: A Seville (Birmingham) (Swansea lose 3-4 on aggregate)
FA Cup								
3	H LIVERPOOL	2/1	24,179 1:12	3	L	0-4	0-2	Hansen 35, Rush 44, 75; [Lawrenson 73]; Ref: C White (Harrow)
Cup-Winners' Cup								
1:1	H LOKOMOTIV LEIPZIG (E Germany)	16/9	10,295		L	0-1	0-0	Kinne 70; Ref: M Joel Quiniou (France)
1:2	A LOKOMOTIV LEIPZIG	30/9	22,000		L	1-2	0-2	Charles 78; Kinne 13, Moldt 22; Ref: M Ciulli (Italy) (Swansea lose 1-3 on aggregate)

Line-ups (Swansea in roman, opponents in *italic*)

Match	1	2	3	4	5	6	7	8	9	10	11	12 sub used
2:1	Davies	Robinson	Lewis	Marustik	Irwin	Charles	Curtis	Stanley	James L*	Thompson	Latchford	Attley
2:1	*Horn*	*Joyce*	*Chambers*	*Glavin*	*Banks*	*McCarthy*	*Evans*	*Parker*	*Riley*	*McHale*	*Campbell**	*Barrowcl'gh*
2:2	Davies	Robinson !	Marustik	Rajkovic	Irwin	Mahoney	Curtis	James R	James L	Stanley	Latchford*	Stevenson
2:2	*Horn*	*Joyce*	*Chambers*	*Glavin**	*Banks*	*McCarthy*	*Evans*	*Parker*	*Aylott*	*McHale*	*Campbell !*	*Cooper*
3	Davies	Stanley	Marustik*	Rajkovic	Irwin	Stevenson	Curtis	James R	James L	Mahoney	Latchford	Thompson
3	*Grobbelaar*	*Neal*	*Lawrenson*	*Thompson*	*Whelan*	*Hansen*	*Dalglish*	*Kennedy*	*Rush*	*McDermott*	*Souness*	
1:1	Davies	Robinson	Hadziabdic	Stevenson	Attley*	Rajkovic	Curtis	James L^	James R	Latchford	Mahoney	Evans/Giles
1:1	*Muller*	*Joachim*	*Baum*	*Demnstedt*	*Zotzsche*	*Kinne*	*Moldt*	*Liebers*	*Altmann*	*Schoene*	*Kuhne*	
1:2	Davies	Robinson	Hadziabdic	Stevenson*	Mahoney	Rajkovic	Curtis !	Charles	James L	Latchford	James R	Latchf'd^ Evans/Giles
1:2	*Muller*	*Baum*	*Fritzsche*	*Demnstedt*	*Zotzsche*	*Kinne*	*Moldt*	*Liebers*	*Altmann*	*Bornschein**	*Kuhne^*	*Sch/ne/Gros'm'n*

Match reports

2:1 Barnsley (a): The Tykes make better use of the rain-soaked turf and Davies turns away a stinging drive from Parker. Horn saves well from Latchford and Thompson. Riley deservedly opens scoring and Wales international Evans gets another to leave Swans facing a difficult task in the second leg.

2:2 Barnsley (h): Eight players are booked and two dismissed as Swans crash out. Robinson and Campbell are sent off as the game explodes in the second period of extra-time. The match is held up after a linesman was struck by a firework and Barnsley manager Hunter has to appeal to his fans for calm.

3 Liverpool (h): Both sides find themselves under early pressure on the waterlogged pitch but Mahoney goes close with a couple of shots. Hansen chips in a rare goal from a Whelan cross. Although Davies saves well from Dalglish and Rush, Liverpool take complete control and canter to easy win.

1:1 Lokomotiv Leipzig (h): The East Germans funnel back in defence to blot out the Swans attack. James is heavily tackled and replaced by Giles, who becomes the first player to appear for three Welsh sides in Europe. Davies spills a shot from Moldt and Kinne pokes the winner over the line from close range.

1:2 Lokomotiv Leipzig (a): Within a minute of the start Bornschein is injured and replaced by Schoene. Kinne steals in on blindside of Mahoney to head in first and Kuhne sets up second when Davies fumbles his cross and Moldt taps in. Curtis was dismissed in the 41st minute after an ugly scuffle with Fritzsche.

League Table

		P	Home					Away					Pts
			W	D	L	F	A	W	D	L	F	A	
1	Liverpool	42	14	3	4	39	14	12	6	3	41	18	87
2	Ipswich	42	17	1	3	47	25	9	4	8	28	28	83
3	Manchester U	42	12	6	3	27	9	10	6	5	32	20	78
4	Tottenham	42	12	4	5	41	26	8	7	6	26	22	71
5	Arsenal	42	13	5	3	27	15	7	6	8	21	22	71
6	SWANSEA	42	13	3	5	34	16	8	3	10	24	35	69
7	Southampton	42	15	2	4	49	30	4	7	10	23	37	66
8	Everton	42	11	7	3	33	21	6	7	10	23	29	64
9	West Ham	42	9	10	2	42	29	5	6	10	24	28	58
10	Manchester C	42	9	7	5	32	23	6	6	9	17	27	58
11	Aston Villa	42	9	6	6	28	24	6	6	9	27	29	57
12	Nott'm Forest	42	7	7	7	19	20	8	5	8	23	28	57
13	Brighton	42	8	7	6	30	24	5	6	10	13	28	52
14	Coventry	42	9	4	8	31	24	4	7	10	25	38	50
15	Notts Co	42	8	5	8	32	33	5	3	13	29	36	47
16	Birmingham	42	8	6	7	29	25	2	8	11	24	36	44
17	West Brom	42	6	6	9	24	25	5	5	11	22	32	44
18	Stoke	42	9	2	10	27	28	3	6	12	17	35	44
19	Sunderland	42	6	5	10	19	26	5	6	10	19	32	44
20	Leeds	42	6	11	4	23	20	4	1	16	16	41	42
21	Wolves	42	8	5	8	19	20	2	5	14	13	43	40
22	Middlesbro'	42	5	9	7	20	24	3	6	12	14	28	39
		924	214	121	127	672	501	127	121	214	501	672	1265

Odds & ends

Double wins: (4) Arsenal, Notts Co, Stoke, Sunderland.
Double losses: (1) Everton.
Won from behind: (2) Stoke (a), West Brom (h).
Lost from in front: (2) Nott'm Forest (h), Middlesbrough (h).
High spots: Topping the First Division on three separate occasions. A nine-match unbeaten run, including seven victories.
Low spots: Five defeats in last six games. The home defeat by Liverpool in FA Cup.
Ever present: (1) Robbie James (League only).
Hat-tricks: (1) Bob Latchford.
Opposing hat-tricks: (1) C Regis.
Penalties for: (5) Leighton James 3, Robbie James 2.
Penalties against: (8) 2 T McDermott (Liverpool), G Hoddle (Spurs), D Tueart (Man City), J Robertson (Notts Co), G Sharp (Everton), T McAndrew (Middlesbrough), G Brooke (Spurs).
Penalty misses for: (0).
Penalty misses against: (1) K Keegan (Southampton).
Leading scorer: (14) Robbie James.

Appearances and Goals

Player	Appearances								Goals					
	Lge	Sub	LC	Sub	FAC	Sub	Eur	Sub	Lge	Sub	LC	FAC	Eur	Tot
Attley, Brian	9	2					1	1						
Charles, Jeremy		4	1		1		1	1	2				1	3
Curtis, Alan	40		2		1		2		10				1	11
Davies, Dai	41		2		1		2							
Evans, Wyndham	1							2		2				
Gale, Darren		1												
Giles, David		2						2		2				
Hadziabdic, Dzemal	25	1	2			2	2							
Irwin, Colin	37		2		1		2		1					1
James, Leighton	34	4	2		1	1	2		9		1			10
James, Robbie	42		1		1		2		14					14
Kennedy, Ray	18							2	2					2
Latchford, Bob	31		2		1		2	2	12					12
Lewis, Dudley	1		1					1						
Loveridge, Jimmy	1													
Mahoney, John	25		1		1		2							
Marustik, Chris	19	3	2		1			2			1			1
Rajkovic, Ante	40		1		1		2				1			1
Richards, Gary	1													
Robinson, Neil	27	2	2		2		2		1					1
Sander, Chris	1													
Stanley, Gary	22	7	2		1		2		3					3
Stevenson, Nigel	20	1	1	1	1			2						
Thompson, Max	22	1		1	1				1					1
Walsh, Ian	3	2							2					2
25 players used	462	29	22	2	11	1	22	4	58	3	3		1	62

LEAGUE DIVISION 1

Manager: John Toshack

SEASON 1982-83

No		Pos		Pt	F-A	H-T	Scorers, Times, and Referees	1	2	3	4	5	6	7	8	9	10	11	12 sub used
1	A NOTTS CO 28/8	–	8,061	D 1	0-0	0-0	Ref: B Hill (Kettering)	Davies / *Avramovic*	Marustik / *Benjamin*	Hadziabidic / *Worthington*	Irwin / *Hunt*	Mahoney / *Kilcline*	Stanley / *Richards*	James L / *McParland**	James R / *Harkouk*	Charles / *Christie*	Stevenson / *Chiedozie*	Latchford / *Mair*	Curtis / *Lahtinen*
2	H COVENTRY 31/8	7	11,712	10 W 4	2-1	0-1	James R 60p, Latchford 64, *Whitton 13*, Ref: D Letts (Aldershot)	Davies / *Suckling*	Marustik* / *Thomas !*	Hadziabidic / *Roberts*	Irwin / *Jacobs*	Mahoney / *Dyson*	Rajkovic / *Gillespie*	James L / *Singleton**	James R / *Francis*	Charles / *Hateley*	Stevenson / *Thompson G*	Latchford / *Whitton*	Curtis / *Hormansch'k*
3	H NORWICH 4/9	2	11,694	19 W 7	4-0	3-0	Latchford 13, 30, 81, James R 41, Ref: B Stevens (Stonehouse)	Davies / *Woods*	Marustik / *Haylock*	Hadziabidic / *Smith*	Irwin / *McGuire*	Stevenson / *Walford*	Rajkovic / *Watson*	Curtis / *Barham*	James R* / *O'Neill*	James L / *Deehan*	Charles / *Bertschin*	Latchford / *Mendham*	Stanley
4	A WATFORD 7/9	7	15,535	4 L 7	1-2	0-1	Stevenson 88, *Blissett 45p, Callaghan 70*, Ref: M Taylor (Deal)	Davies / *Sherwood*	Marustik / *Rice*	Hadziabidic / *Rostron*	Irwin / *Taylor*	Rajkovic / *Bolton*	Rajkovic / *Jackett*	James L / *Callaghan*	James R / *Armstrong*	Charles / *Jenkins**	Stevenson / *Blissett*	Latchford* / *Barnes*	Curtis / *Lohman*
5	A STOKE 11/9	10	14,058	6 L 7	1-4	1-1	Latchford 12 [*Maguire 80p*], *Watson 15*, Davies 56 (og), *Thomas 60*, Ref: N Wilson (Morecambe)	Davies / *Fox*	Marustik* / *Parkin D*	Hadziabidic / *Hampton**	Irwin / *Bracewell*	Kennedy / *Watson*	Rajkovic / *Berry*	Curtis / *Maguire*	James R / *McIlroy*	Charles / *O'Callaghan*	Stevenson / *Thomas*	Latchford / *Chamberlain*	Charles / *Griffiths*
6	H LIVERPOOL 18/9	16	20,322	2 L 7	0-3	0-2	*Rush 15, 22, Johnston 85*, Ref: A Hamil (Wolverhampton)	Davies / *Grobbelaar*	Marustik* / *Neal*	Hadziabidic / *Kennedy A*	Irwin / *Thompson*	Kennedy / *Lawrenson*	Rajkovic / *Johnston*	Curtis / *Dalglish*	James R / *Lee*	Charles / *Rush*	Stevenson / *Hodgson**	Latchford / *Souness*	James L / *McDermott*
7	A ASTON VILLA 25/9	17	21,246	8 L 7	0-2	0-2	*Mortimer 32, Evans 44*, Ref: T Fitzharris (Bolton)	Davies / *Rimmer*	Stanley / *Jones*	Hadziabidic / *Williams*	Irwin* / *Evans*	Kennedy / *McNaught*	Mahoney / *Mortimer*	Loveridge / *Bremner*	James R / *Shaw*	Charles / *Withe*	Stevenson / *Cowans*	Latchford / *Morley*	Marustik
8	H TOTTENHAM 2/10	14	16,381	10 W 7	2-0	0-0	Thompson 60, Latchford 71, Ref: A Seville (Birmingham)	Davies / *Clemence*	Marustik / *Hughton*	Lewis / *Lacy*	Charles / *Price*	Kennedy / *Brooke**	Mahoney / *Perryman*	Curtis / *Mabbutt*	James R / *Archibald*	James L / *Hazard*	Thompson / *Villa*	Latchford / *Crooks*	James L / *O'Reilly*
9	A BRIGHTON 9/10	15	11,050	12 D 11	1-1	0-1	Lewis 70, *Foster 2*, Ref: D Vickers (Ilford)	Davies / *Moseley*	Lewis / *Stevens*	Hadziabidic / *Shanks*	Charles / *Grealish**	Kennedy / *Foster*	Stevenson / *Gatting*	Curtis / *Case*	James R / *Ritchie*	James L / *Robinson*	Thompson / *McNab*	Mahoney* / *Smith*	Gale / *Smillie*
10	H EVERTON 16/10	17	11,183	10 L 11	0-3	0-1	Stevenson 1 (og), *Richardson 64*, [*Bailey 78*], Ref: K Barratt (Coventry)	Davies / *Southall*	Lewis / *Borrows*	Mahoney / *Bailey*	Charles / *Higgins*	Kennedy / *Wright*	Thompson / *McMahon*	Curtis / *Richardson*	James R / *Johnson*	Charles / *Sharp*	Stevenson / *King*	Stevenson* / *Sharp*	Latchford / *Sheedy* *Walsh*

Match notes

1. Swans are without five regulars and on the defensive in the opening minutes when Stevenson almost slices a Kilcline cross-shot into his own net. Chiedozie and Harkouk shoot wide when well-placed, Charles has goal disallowed, and Harkouk strikes a post as County press late on.

2. Thomas is sent off in 52nd minute after tangling with Leighton James. 16-year-old Suckling becomes the busier keeper. Whitton gives the Sky Blues an early lead but when Charles was fouled by Whitton, Robbie James nets from the spot. Latchford scores winner from Rajkovic break.

3. Curtis returns in place of Mahoney and newly-promoted Norwich are given a painful lesson. Latchford heads in crosses from Marustik and Leighton James before shooting home for a hat-trick. The Canaries are outclassed in all departments and Robbie James completes the rout.

4. Irwin brings down Barnes in area but Blissett's spot-kick hits a post. The referee calls for a re-take and this time Blissett beats Davies. Toshack and Boersma have words with the ref at interval. The tricky Callaghan nets from a Blissett pass before Stevenson heads in from a late corner.

5. Latchford strikes his fourth in five games to give Swans the lead but a deflected goal brings the Potters level. Wales international Thomas is in thick of things for Stoke and his fierce drive puts them ahead. A mistake by Davies gifts them another and a Maguire penalty seals big victory.

6. Liverpool dominate the early stages and, when Stevenson deflects Alan Kennedy's shot, Davies fumbles and Rush nips in to score. Dalglish takes ball to by-line before crossing for Rush to add his second. Johnston gathers a Dalglish pass and shoots past Davies to complete the score.

7. Mortimer fires in a superb left-foot volley for his fourth of the season. Swans force a couple of quick corners but Cowans crosses to Evans, who heads firmly past Davies. Latchford has a goal ruled out for pushing, just before Irwin is stretchered off following a challenge from Shaw.

8. Lewis is a shock inclusion at full-back in place of Hadziabidic. Swans play without a sweeper, although Kennedy remains in a deep position. Clemence saves full length from Leighton James and a free-kick is headed beyond the England keeper by Thompson to set Swans on their way.

9. Without an away win in four matches, Swans are hit by a goal in 75 seconds. Case flights over a corner for Gatting but his shot is palmed away by Davies straight to the waiting Foster. Swans level when Lewis ghosts in to head Leighton James's centre over Moseley and into the net.

10. For the second match running, Swans are hit by a quick goal as Everton take the lead in only 35 seconds. A cross from Richardson is missed by Sharp and Stevenson slices a Kennedy header off his line and Latchford goes close but it is not enough.

Match 11 — H SOUTHAMPTON, 23/10 — Pos 15 — W 3-2
Score: Rofe 50(og), James R 51, Latchf'd 87 / Fashanu 43, Wallace 53
Att: 10,694 (21, 14) — Ref: M Heath (Stoke)

Davies	Lewis	Evans	Hadziabdic	Kennedy	Rajkovic	Curtis	James R	Latchford	Stanley	Mahoney*	Loveridge
Wells	Rofe	Williams	Holmes	Nicholl	Wright	Ball	Moran	Fashanu	Armstrong	Wallace	

Evans, back in side for first game of season, is booked after nine minutes. Wells, deputising for the injured Shilton, saves well from Curtis and Mahoney. Phil Boersma is booked after a half-time tunnel incident sparking three goals in three minutes, but Latchford pops in a late winner.

Match 12 — A MANCHESTER C, 30/10 — Pos 17 — L 1-2
Score: Latchford 65 / Tueart 16, Hartford 65
Att: 25,021 (6, 14) — Ref: K Redfern (Whitley Bay)

Davies	Stanley	Charles	Hadziabdic	Mahoney	Rajkovic	Walsh	James R	James L*	Stevenson	Latchford	Curtis
Corrigan	Ranson	McDonald	Bond	Power	Caton	Tueart	Reeves	Cross	Hartford	Baker	

A superb strike from Tueart puts Swans in early trouble. It comes from a free-kick after Reeves was obstructed. A diving header by Latchford almost levels but Hartford doubles the home side's advantage before a looping header from Latchford, his eighth of the season, reduces deficit.

Match 13 — H SUNDERLAND, 6/11 — Pos 14 — W 3-0
Score: Curtis 9, 65, James R 45
Att: 10,034 (20, 17) — Ref: R Milford (Bristol)

Davies	Lewis	Charles	Marustik*	Mahoney	Rajkovic	Curtis	James R	Walsh	Stevenson	Stanley	James L
Turner	Nicholl	Hindmarch	Munro	Chisholm	Pickering	Buckley*	Rowell	McCoist	West	Venison	Atkins

Curtis finally nets his first of the season for the Swans. They are without injured Latchford, who fails a late fitness test. Walsh sets up Robbie James to double the lead on the interval and with the Wearsiders wilting, Curtis nets with a header from a deflected Leighton James shot.

Match 14 — A WEST BROM, 13/11 — Pos 12 — D 3-3
Score: James L 68, Charles 75, James R 85 / Cross 24, Jol 41, Eastoe 46
Att: 12,432 (8, 18) — Ref: R Nixon (West Kirby)

Davies	Stanley	Charles	Hadziabdic	Kennedy*	Rajkovic	James L	James R	Mahoney	Stevenson	Latchford	Robinson
Godden	Whitehead	Statham	Zondervan	Wile	Robertson	Jol	Cross	Regis	Owen	Eastoe	

Swansea's search for a first away win of the season suffers a blow when Cross opens the scoring, then Jol's shot seems to drift past Davies. Former Swindon striker Eastoe meets Jol's pass to put Albion further ahead, and Cross strikes the bar before a tremendous Swans fight-back.

Match 15 — H ARSENAL, 20/11 — Pos 15 — L 1-2
Score: Latchford 59 / Woodcock 73, Chapman 88
Att: 12,389 (13, 18) — Ref: G Napthine (Loughborough)

Davies	Stanley	Charles	Hadziabdic	Lewis	Rajkovic	Loveridge	James R	Mahoney	Stevenson	Latchford	
Wood	O'Shea	Sansom	Talbot	O'Leary	Whyte	Davis	Sunderland	Robson	Woodcock*	Rix	Chapman

Sunderland and Woodcock go close early on and Talbot watches his shot brush the post. Loveridge, in his first game of the season, links up well but Davis has a goal disallowed for handball. Latchford chases a long ball and scores with a left-foot shot but Chapman hits a late winner.

Match 16 — A IPSWICH, 27/11 — Pos 16 — L 1-3
Score: James L 83 / Osman 22, Burley 35, Wark 65
Att: 17,849 (8, 18) — Ref: J Moules (Ongar)

Davies	Stanley	Charles	Hadziabdic	Lewis	Rajkovic	Loveridge	James R	Mahoney	Stevenson	Latchford	
Cooper	Burley	Gernon	Thijssen	Osman	Butcher	Wark	McCall	Mariner	Brazil	Gates	

Wark strikes the post and Osman's first of the season sees Swans trailing. They should have equalised, but Latchford's shot is blocked by Gates. Ipswich pepper Davies in the Swans goal to lengthen their lead but a deflected shot by Leighton James pulls one back for Swansea.

Match 17 — H LUTON, 4/12 — Pos 14 — W 2-0
Score: Curtis 51, Latchford 83
Att: 9,556 (19, 21) — Ref: C Newsome (Broseley)

Davies	Stanley	Charles	Hadziabdic	Kennedy	Rajkovic	Curtis*	James R	Mahoney	Stevenson	Latchford	James L
Findlay	Stephens	Money	Horton	Goodyear	Donaghy	Hill	Stein	Walsh	Turner*	Moss	Antic

Kennedy and Curtis return from injury and Latchford's drive rattles the upright. The Hatters rarely trouble the home defence and a Curtis header from Stanley's accurate cross puts Swansea ahead. A brilliant Robbie James run into the danger area sets up Latchford for the clincher.

Match 18 — A NOTT'M FOREST, 11/12 — Pos 17 — L 1-2
Score: James R 77 / Walsh 25, Proctor 58
Att: 14,585 (3, 21) — Ref: K Salmon (Cuffley)

Davies	Stanley	Charles	Hadziabdic	Kennedy*	Rajkovic	Curtis	James R	Mahoney	Stevenson	Latchford	James L
Sutton	Swain	Bowyer	Gunn	Young	Walsh	Proctor	Wallace	Birtles	Turner*	Hodge	Robertson

Robbie James's right-footer is turned round the post by Sutton but Forest come back for Birtles to rattle the woodwork. Walsh opens the scoring and Proctor's drive is saved by Davies. Wallace and Young combine for Proctor to double the lead and it's yet another away defeat.

Match 19 — H MANCHESTER U, 18/12 — Pos 17 — D 0-0
Att: 15,748 (2, 22) — Ref: T Bune (Yattenden)

Davies	Stanley	Charles	Hadziabdic	Evans	Rajkovic	Curtis*	James R	Mahoney	Stevenson	Latchford	James L
Bailey	Duxbury	Albiston	Moses	Moran	McQueen	Robson	Muhren	Stapleton	Whiteside	Coppell	

Swans are in jittery mood and have some lucky goalmouth escapes before letting their own good opportunities go begging. Evans is brought in for his 350th league game in place of the injured Kennedy. Bailey makes a couple of saves and Coppell has a goal disallowed for offside.

Match 20 — A WEST HAM, 27/12 — Pos 18 — L 2-3
Score: Latchford 26, 38 / Goddard 86, Stewart 49p, Van der Elst 68
Att: 23,843 (4, 22) — Ref: I Borrett (Eye)

Davies	Stanley	Hadziabdic	Robinson	Evans	Rajkovic	James L	James R	Mahoney	Charles	Latchford	
Parkes	Stewart	Brush	Orr	Martin	Devonshire	Van der Elst	Goddard	Clark	Allen	Pike	

Swans take a two-goal lead into the interval, with Latchford dummying Parkes for the first, then sliding the ball past the keeper for the second. Stanley brings down Devonshire for a spot-kick. Rajkovic deflects Goddard's shot for winner after both sides seem content with the draw.

Match 21 — H BIRMINGHAM, 29/12 — Pos 17 — D 0-0
Att: 11,840 (21, 23) — Ref: A Glasson (Salisbury)

Davies	Robinson	Hadziabdic	Mahoney	Evans	Rajkovic	Curtis	James R	Mahoney	Charles*	Latchford	Stevenson
Coton	Langan	v d Hauwe	Blake	Broadhurst	Dillon	Harford	Ferguson	Curbishley	Handysides		

Points are precious for both sides which leads to a tense match and Charles goes off injured before the interval. Robbie James is carried off for attention but ten-man Swans battle away until his return. Leighton James almost wins it with a shot Coton fails to hold, but the ball is cleared.

LEAGUE DIVISION 1 — Manager: John Toshack — SEASON 1982-83

Match summary

No	Date	V	Opponent	Pos	Res	F-A	H-T	Att	Opp Pos	Pt
22	1/1	A	ARSENAL	17	L	1-2	0-2	25,237	14	23
23	3/1	A	NORWICH	19	L	0-1	0-0	16,296	17	23
24	15/1	H	NOTTS CO	18	W	2-0	0-0	8,992	16	26
25	22/1	A	COVENTRY	18	D	0-0	0-0	9,964	5	27
26	6/2	H	WATFORD	19	L	1-3	1-0	14,461	3	27
27	12/2	A	TOTTENHAM	19	L	0-1	0-1	24,632	8	27
28	26/2	A	EVERTON	19	D	2-2	1-1	17,112	7	28
29	1/3	H	BRIGHTON	19	L	1-2	1-1	8,825	20	28
30	5/3	A	SOUTHAMPTON	20	L	1-2	0-0	16,842	6	28
31	12/3	H	MANCHESTER C	18	W	4-1	3-0	9,884	17	31

Line-ups (Swansea on first line, opponents on second)

No	Team	1	2	3	4	5	6	7	8	9	10	11	12 sub used
22	Swansea	Davies	Robinson	Hadziabdic	Evans	Mahoney	Rajkovic	Curtis*	Lewis	James L	Stevenson	Latchford	Stanley
22	Arsenal	Jennings	Hollins	Sansom	Talbot	O'Leary	Robson	Davis	Sunderland*	Woodcock	Rix	Chapman	Petrovic
23	Swansea	Davies	Robinson*	Hadziabdic	Charles	Evans	Rajkovic	Gale	James R	Mahoney	Stevenson	Latchford	Stanley
23	Norwich	Woods	Haylock	Downes	Mendham	Walford	Watson	Barham	O'Neill	Channon	Bertschin	Deehan	
24	Swansea	Davies	Robinson	Hadziabdic	Charles	Stevenson	Rajkovic	Curtis	James R	Mahoney	Stanley*	Latchford	Gale
24	Notts Co	Avramovic	Benjamin	Worthington	Hunt	Kilcline	Richards	McParland	Fashanu	McCulloch	Goodwin	Mair	Christie
25	Swansea	Davies	Robinson	Marustik	Charles	Stevenson	Rajkovic	Gale	James R	Mahoney	Stanley	Latchford	Latchford
25	Coventry	Sealey	Thomas	Roberts	Butterworth	Dyson	Gillespie	Whitton	Francis	Hateley	Melrose*	Hunt	Thompson
26	Swansea	Davies	Robinson	Marustik	Charles*	Stevenson	Rajkovic	Curtis	James R	Gale	Kennedy	Latchford	Stanley
26	Watford	Sherwood	Rice	Rostron	Taylor	Sims	Bolton	Callaghan	Blissett	Barnes	Jackett	Lohman	
27	Swansea	Davies	Clemence	Hadziabdic	Charles	Kennedy	Rajkovic*	Curtis	James R	Mahoney	Stanley	Latchford	Gale
27	Tottenham	Clemence	Hughton*	Lacy	Price	Villa	Perryman	Galvin	Mabbutt	Gibson	Brooke	Crooks	Falco
28	Swansea	Davies	Robinson	Hadziabdic	Lewis	Kennedy	Richards	Loveridge	James R	Gale	Mahoney	Latchford	Mahoney
28	Everton	Arnold	Stevens	Bailey	Ratcliffe	Higgins	Richardson	Irvine*	King	Sharp	Heath	Sheedy	Johnson
29	Swansea	Davies	Robinson	Hadziabdic	Lewis	Kennedy	Richards	Mahoney*	James R	Gale	Loveridge	Latchford	**Pascoe**
29	Brighton	Moseley	Ramsey	Gatting	Grealish	Foster	Stevens	Case	Ritchie	Robinson	Ryan	Smillie	
30	Swansea	Davies	Marustik	Richards	Charles	Kennedy*	Lewis	Loveridge	Robinson	James R	Rajkovic	Gale	Hadziabdic
30	Southampton	Shilton	Agboola	Mills	Williams	Nicholl	Wright	Holmes	Baird	Moran	Armstrong	Wallace	
31	Swansea	Davies	Marustik	Richards	Charles	Lewis	Rajkovic	Loveridge	James R	Walsh*	Stanley	Latchford	Gale
31	Manchester C	Corrigan	Golac	McDonald	Reid	Bond	Caton	Tueart	Reeves	Cross	Hildersley*	Baker	May

Scorers, Times, and Referees

22 — Arsenal: Curtis 63 / Sunderland 4, Woodcock 6 / Ref: D Hedges (Oxford)

The Gunners are fortunate to take an early lead when Sunderland's shot is deflected to wrong-foot Davies. They add another when debut-making Petrovic sends Woodcock through the middle. Swans are up against it but they pull one back with a Curtis header from a fifth corner.

23 — Norwich: Channon 58 / Ref: C Downey (Hounslow)

Disappointing Swans are in serious trouble following this defeat by their fellow strugglers. Former England international Channon pounces when Davies fumbles a shot from Deehan. O'Neill goes close with a header and Mendham fires in a shot that flashes over the Swans crossbar.

24 — Notts Co: Gale 81, Latchford 84 / Ref: D Lloyd (Fernhill Heath)

Swans are desperate for victory after only gaining two points from last six games but Kilcline clears from Latchford as the striker goes for goal. One of smallest crowds of the season see Swans gain in confidence after the break and late goals from Gale and Latchford seal the victory.

25 — Coventry: Ref: A Robinson (Portsmouth)

Robinson brings fine save from Sealey as Swans go on attack. Hateley almost scores for high-flying Coventry but Marustik hacks off goal-line. Sealey blocks Latchford, who then heads wide from a good position. Gale almost snatches a late win but his first-time shot drifts past far post.

26 — Watford: Latchford 37 / Blissett 56, 89, Barnes 81 / Ref: N Ashley (Nantwich)

Switched to Sunday to avoid rugby international, Swans get a boost with Latchford's 200th league goal. But they pay the penalty for defensive blunders. Barnes moves in on Stevenson's short back-pass for the lead and Blissett scores his second when Davies misses a Jackett centre.

27 — Tottenham: Crooks 35 / Ref: J Hunting (Leicester)

Crooks nets his 15th goal of the season to give Spurs the lead when he comes in unmarked at the far post to meet Gibson's cross with a firm header. Galvin almost increases the lead with a crisp shot and Davies saves from Falco and Price. Brooke has a late goal ruled out for offside.

28 — Everton: James 41, Gale 81 / King 23, 84 / Ref: P Tyldesley (Stockport)

Swans field four youngsters and have 17-year-old Pascoe on the bench but find themselves trailing when Irvine sets up King. A spectacular shot from James levels and Gale collects an Arnold fumble to put Swans ahead. King's shot goes in off a post to square the match for Everton.

29 — Brighton: Latchford 19 / Robinson 16, Case 70 / Ref: E Crickmore (Plymouth)

Brighton's first away win in a year plunges Swans into desperate trouble. Robinson fires home a rebound but Latchford nets his 24th of the season. Veteran Case fires home a rocket for the winner. Despite plenty of youthful effort they cannot match the Seagulls' greater experience.

30 — Southampton: Loveridge 61 / Baird 63, Armstrong 77 / Ref: M Taylor (Deal)

Davies is busy as Saints pile on the early pressure. Gale shoots into side netting in a rare breakaway. Swans take shock lead when James feeds Loveridge and his shot beats Shilton. A Wallace centre is headed in by the abrasive Baird and Armstrong converts a Mills cross for the winner.

31 — Manchester C: Latch'd 8, Walsh 37, 51, James R 44p / McDonald 63 / Ref: L Shapter (Torquay)

Swans throw everyone forward and are rewarded when Corrigan pushes away a James shot and Latchford is on hand. Walsh doubles the score and then Bond brings down James who rifles in the spot-kick. Swans end the match with ten men after Charles is forced to hobble off the pitch.

32 A SUNDERLAND 17,445 — 19/3 — 1-1 D — 19 · 16 32
Marustik 51 / Rowell 82
Ref: R Banks (Manchester)

Sander	Marustik	Richards	Robinson	Lewis	Rajkovic	Loveridge	James R	Gale	Stanley	Latchford
Turner	Nicholl	Pickering	Atkins	Chisholm	Proctor	Venison	Rowell	Worthington	James	Cummins* McCoist

Former Swan Leighton James has his old club in trouble and a well-struck shot is palmed round the post by Sander. Marustik puts Swansea ahead against the run of play when he picks up a clearance from Atkins to chip Turner. Once again, however, they cannot hold onto their lead.

---

33 H WEST BROM 11,222 — 26/3 — 2-1 W — 18 · 8 35
James R 36, Latchford 54 / Thompson 89
Ref: L Burden (Poole)

Sander	Marustik	Richards	Stevenson	Lewis	Rajkovic	Loveridge	James R	Walsh*	Stanley	Latchford
Barron	Webb	Statham	Zondervan	Wile	Robertson	Jol	Thompson	Regis	Owen	Whitehead* Cross (Curtis)

Boxing hero Colin Jones leads out Swans at start and his influence rubs off as James puts his side ahead. Stanley's free-kick beats the Albion defence and James nets with a low drive. Latchford makes it two with an unstoppable header but Thompson pulls one back for a tense finish.

---

34 A BIRMINGHAM 13,591 — 2/4 — 1-1 D — 18 · 20 36
Latchford 80, Stevenson 87p
Ref: R Bridges (Deeside)

Sander	Marustik	Richards	Stevenson	Lewis	Rajkovic	Loveridge	James R	Walsh	Stanley	Latchford
Coton	Hagan	Dennis	Stevenson	Blake	v d Hauwe	Gayle*	Phillips	Harford	Halsall	Hopkins Handysides

This is a relegation dogfight and nerves get to both sides in opening half. Lewis, watched by Wales manager Mike England, cuts off moves by Gayle and Hopkins. Walsh and Loveridge go close before Latchford scores, but Richards brings down Hopkins to give Blues a late spot-kick.

---

35 H WEST HAM 13,303 — 5/4 — 1-5 L — 19 · 10 36
Walsh 2 / [Dickens 82, 88] Pike 24, 72, Devonshire 43
Ref: D Civil (Birmingham)

Sander	Marustik	Richards	Stevenson	Lewis	Rajkovic	Loveridge	James R	Walsh*	Stanley	Latchford
Parkes	Stewart	Lampard	Bonds	Martin	Devonshire	Van der Elst	Goddard	Orr	Dickens	Pike Gale

Walsh gives Swans an early lead when he climbs above Pike and Martin for a firm header but the Hammers rip them apart in a devastating display. They break down Swansea's defence too easily and inflict the biggest defeat of the season, with Devonshire and Dickens outstanding.

---

36 A LIVERPOOL 30,010 — 9/4 — 0-3 L — 20 · 1 36
Rush 57, Lee 72, Fairclough 86
Ref: J Lovatt (Crewe)

Sander	Marustik	Richards	Robinson	Rajkovic	Lewis	Loveridge	James R	Walsh	Stanley	Pascoe*
Grobbelaar	Neal	Kennedy	Lawrenson	Whelan	Hansen	Dalglish	Lee	Rush	Johnston*	Souness Charles Fairclough

Top of table Liverpool are in no mood to do any favours for Toshack's side, yet Swans battle bravely for almost an hour. Rush misses several good chances before scoring from a Rajkovic slip. The busy Lee increases the lead and super-sub Fairclough is put in by Lee for the third.

---

37 H STOKE 10,100 — 16/4 — 1-0 W — 20 · 6 37
Charles 39 / Thomas 59
Ref: S Bates (Bristol)

Sander	Marustik	Richards	Charles	Lewis	Rajkovic	Loveridge	James R	Walsh*	Robinson	Latchford
Fox	Bould	Hampton	Bracewell	Watson	Berry	Painter	McIlroy	O'Callaghan	Thomas	Chamberlain Stevenson

Charles is back in the side after five-week absence and he celebrates with a header from a Loveridge corner. Walsh has ball in net but it is ruled out for handball. Potters equalise against run of play when Wales international Thomas heads in. Loveridge has a shot cleared off line by Berry.

---

38 A LUTON 11,561 — 23/4 — 1-3 L — 22 · 18 37
Latchford 85 / Walsh 55, 74, 86
Ref: A Hamil (Wolverhampton)

Sander	Marustik	Richards	Charles	Lewis	Rajkovic	Loveridge	James R	Robinson*	Kennedy	Latchford
Godden	Stevens	Money	Horton	Elliott	Donaghy	Hill	Aylott	Walsh	Antic	Moss Pascoe

Swans revert to five at the back in another relegation six-pointer. Marustik has a goal ruled out for a foul on Godden. A superb Walsh hat-trick gives Hatters a notable victory and although Latchford nets a late consolation, the defeat means the Swans have dropped to bottom place.

---

39 H IPSWICH 8,568 — 30/4 — 1-1 D — 22 · 11 38
Rajkovic 76 / Mariner 54
Ref: V Callow (Solihull)

Sander	Marustik	Richards	Charles	Lewis	Rajkovic	Loveridge*	James R	Gale	Kennedy	Latchford
Cooper	Burley	McCall	Putney	Steggles*	Butcher	Wark	Gernon	Mariner	D'Avray	O'Callaghan Turner Pascoe

Ipswich are forced into an early change when Steggles goes off with a hamstring injury. Cooper saves from Loveridge but O'Callaghan outwits Charles and crosses from by-line for Mariner to score. Swans then throw everyone forward and a Pascoe corner-kick yields a welcome point.

---

40 H ASTON VILLA 9,173 — 2/5 — 2-1 W — 21 · 5 41
Pascoe 9, Gale 49 / Shaw 29
Ref: D Hedges (Oxford)

Sander	Marustik	Richards	Charles	Kennedy	Lewis	Pascoe	James R	Gale	Stanley	Latchford
Spink	Williams	Gibson	Evans	McNaught	Mortimer	Curbishley	Shaw	Walters	Cowans	Morley

Swans lift themselves off the bottom with goals from teenagers Pascoe and Gale. Robbie James misses a second-half penalty against the new European champions that would have taken him to 100 league goals. Kennedy has his best game for the club and Lewis shines in defence.

---

41 A MANCHESTER U 35,724 — 7/5 — 1-2 L — 21 · 3 41
Latchford 89 / Robson 22, Stapleton 77
Ref: P Willis (Meadowfield)

Sander	Marustik	Richards	Charles	Kennedy	Lewis	Pascoe	James R	Gale	Stanley	Latchford
Bailey	Duxbury	Grimes	Wilkins*	Moran	McQueen	Robson	Muhren	Whiteside	Stapleton	Cunningham Davies

Home fans taunt Swans with shouts of 'going down' but they still try to play football against second-placed United. Robson misses an easy chance before heading in Whiteside's cross, and Cunningham, Whiteside and Robson combine to increase the lead before Latchford's reply.

---

42 H NOTT'M FOREST 9,226 — 14/5 — 0-3 L — 21 · 5 41
Wallace 11, 37, Anderson 65
Ref: J Martin (Alton)

Sander	Lewis	Richards	Rajkovic	Stevenson	Lewis	Loveridge	Stanley	Gale	Kennedy	Pascoe*
V Breukelen	Anderson	Swain	Gunn	Young	Bowyer	Hodge	Wallace	Davenport*	Walsh	Robertson Wigley Lake

Swans make a sad exit from top flight and but for Sander it would have been far worse. He makes a series of top-class saves to deny Clough's men and even saves a second-half penalty from Robertson but strikes by Wallace and an Anderson header brings the curtain down for Swans.

Average 11,681 — Home — Away 18,195

LEAGUE DIVISION 1 (CUP-TIES) Manager: John Toshack SEASON 1982-83

Milk Cup

Rd	Date	V	Opponent	Pos		F-A	H-T	Att	Scorers, Times, and Referees	1	2	3	4	5	6	7	8	9	10	11	12 sub used
2:1	5/10	A	BRISTOL ROV	14	L	0-1	0-0	9,279 3:6	Parkin 89 — Ref: M James (Horsham)	Davies	Marustik	Lewis	Charles	Kennedy	Mahoney	Curtis	James R	Loveridge	Thompson	Latchford	
										Kite	*Slatter*	*Williams B*	*Williams G*	*Parkin*	*McCaffrey*	*Holloway*	*Williams D*	*Kelly*	*Randall**	*Barrett**	*Stephens*

Swans are beaten by a dramatic last-minute goal from centre-half Parkin, who headed in after a Holloway cross. Rovers more than matched Swansea, who were on the defensive for most of the game. Holloway hits war bar with Davies beaten and Barrett almost gets through the defence.

Rd	Date	V	Opponent	Pos		F-A	H-T	Att	Scorers, Times, and Referees	1	2	3	4	5	6	7	8	9	10	11	12 sub used
2:2	26/10	H	BRISTOL ROV	15	W	3-0	1-0	9,755 3:2	Latchford 11, 51,78	Davies	Evans	Lewis	Charles	Kennedy	Rajkovic	Curtis	James R	James L	Stanley	Latchford	
										Kite	*Slatter*	*Williams B*	*Williams G*	*Parkin*	*McCaffrey*	*Holloway*	*Williams D*	*Withey*	*Randall**	*Barrett**	*Channon*

Ref: L Robinson (Sut' Coldfield) — (Swansea win 3-1 on aggregate)

Latchford strikes a superb hat-trick to put Swans in next round. His first is an angled shot from a Charles pass and his other two are similar bullet headers from crosses by Stanley and Curtis. Former England international Channon makes a late appearance for Rovers, but it is no use.

Rd	Date	V	Opponent	Pos		F-A	H-T	Att	Scorers, Times, and Referees	1	2	3	4	5	6	7	8	9	10	11	12 sub used
3	9/11	A	BRENTFORD	14	D	1-1	1-1	15,261 3:8	Latchford 13 / Roberts 31	Davies	Stanley	Hadziabdic	Charles	Kennedy	Rajkovic	Curtis	James R	Mahoney	Stevenson	Latchford	
										Roche	*Rowe**	*Harris*	*McNichol*	*Whitehead*	*Hurlock*	*Kamara*	*Joseph*	*Mahoney*	*Bowles*	*Roberts*	

Ref: T Spencer (Salisbury)

Several players are booked in an ill-tempered match. Veteran defender Harris uses his experience to marshal Bees defence but Swans take lead when Roche pushes out a header and Latchford pounces. Kamara's run puts Bowles in the clear and Rhyl-born Roberts nets with a rising drive.

Rd	Date	V	Opponent	Pos		F-A	H-T	Att	Scorers, Times, and Referees	1	2	3	4	5	6	7	8	9	10	11	12 sub used
3R	17/11	H	BRENTFORD	12	L	1-2	0-1	6,676 3:12	Loveridge 84 / Roberts 1, Mahoney T 83	Davies	Stanley	Hadziabdic	Charles	Robinson*	Rajkovic	James L	James R	Mahoney	Stevenson	Latchford	Loveridge
										Roche	*Rowe*	*Harris*	*McNichol*	*Whitehead*	*Hurlock*	*Kamara*	*Joseph*	*Mahoney*	*Bowles*	*Roberts*	

Ref: E Read (Bristol)

Swans are in trouble 19 seconds from kick-off when Roberts sweeps home a Joseph cross. The Bees net again through Tony Mahoney after Joseph hits an upright and all sad Swansea have to offer is a tap-in from substitute Loveridge after Roche fumbled Latchford shot.

FA Cup

Rd	Date	V	Opponent	Pos		F-A	H-T	Att	Scorers, Times, and Referees	1	2	3	4	5	6	7	8	9	10	11	12 sub used
3	8/1	A	NORWICH	20	L	1-2	1-2	13,222 1:18	Gale 14 / Bertschin 24, 35	Davies	Richards	Hadziabdic	Rajkovic	Charles	Lewis	Curtis	James R*	Gale	Marustik	Latchford	Mahoney
										Woods	*Haylock*	*Downes*	*Mendham*	*Walford*	*Watson*	*Barham*	*O'Neill*	*Deehan*	*Bertschin*	*Van Wyk*	

Ref: L Robinson (Sut' Coldfield)

Swans gamble with four changes and new-boy 19-year-old Gale gives them a dream start. The Canaries regroup and a mistake by Rajkovic gifts them an equaliser before Davies saves Bertschin's penalty. Barham's cross is headed in by Bertschin. Curtis just fails to find a response.

Cup-Winners' Cup

Rd	Date	V	Opponent			F-A	H-T	Att	Scorers, Times, and Referees	1	2	3	4	5	6	7	8	9	10	11	12 sub used
P:1	17/8	H	BRAGA (Portugal)		W	3-0	1-0	10,614	Charles 42, 87, Cordoso 65 (og)	Davies	Marustik	Hadziabdic	Irwin	Rajkovic	Stevenson*	Kennedy	James L	James R	Charles	Latchf'rd^	Thomp'n/Walsh
										Helder	*Artur*	*Cordoso*	*Nelito*	*Guedes*	*Serra*	*Oliviera*	*Paris*	*Gomes**	*Manoel*	*Santos*	*Malheiro*

Ref: A Thomas (Netherlands)

Charles opens the scoring after Irwin's mis-kick comes back off the post. Kennedy has a header pushed over by Helder but from the corner, Braga skipper Cordoso turns into his own net. In the driving rain, Charles makes sure of Swansea's first win in Europe with his second strike.

Rd	Date	V	Opponent			F-A	H-T	Att	Scorers, Times, and Referees	1	2	3	4	5	6	7	8	9	10	11	12 sub used
P:2	25/8	A	BRAGA		L	0-1	0-0	18,000	Marustik 88 (og)	Davies	Marustik	Hadziabdic	Irwin	Rajkovic	Mahoney	James L	James L	Charles	Stanley	Latchford	
										Helder	*Artur*	*Cordoso*	*Paris*	*Guedes*	*Serra*	*Oliviera*	*Spencer**	*Manoel^*	*Gomes*	*Santos*	*Fontes/Malheiro*

Ref: J Baumann (Switzerland) — (Swansea win 3-1 on aggregate)

Leighton James is the sole Swansea striker as they aim to soak up the pressure. The Portuguese win on the night when Marustik slices a goalmouth clearance beyond his own keeper.

Rd	Date	V	Opponent			F-A	H-T	Att	Scorers, Times, and Referees	1	2	3	4	5	6	7	8	9	10	11	12 sub used
1:1	15/9	H	SLIEMA WANDERERS (Malta)		W	12-0	4-0	5,130	Ch' 16,77, Lov' 18,65, Ir' 22, Lat' 42, Raj'88 [Had'62, Wal' 75,79,86, St' 87, Raj'88]	Davies	Marustik	Hadziabdic	Rajkovic	Stevenson	Irwin	Loveridge*	James R	Loveridge*	Charles	Latchford^	Kennedy, James L/Walsh
										Zammitt	*Losco*	*Camilleri*	*Tortell*	*Schembri*	*Portelli*	*Caruana*	*Fabri*	*Tabone*	*Buttigieg*	*Aquilina*	

Ref: G Biguet (France)

The poor attendance is put down to increased ticket prices but the fans who stay away miss a goal feast. Charles sets the wheels in motion and Loveridge hooks the ball over his shoulder for the second. Walsh takes the field as a late substitute and nets a hat-trick in just eleven minutes.

Rd	Date	V	Opponent			F-A	H-T	Att	Scorers, Times, and Referees	1	2	3	4	5	6	7	8	9	10	11	12 sub used
1:2	29/9	A	SLIEMA WANDERERS		W	5-0	3-0	2,000	Curtis 19, 45, Gale 38, 74, Toshack 90	Sander	Lewis	Hadziabdic	Stevenson	Marustik	Charles	Curtis*	Gale	Stanley	Loveridge	Kennedy	Toshack
										Zammitt	*Theuma*	*Camilleri*	*Losco*	*Schembri*	*Portelli*	*Butigieg*	*Fabri*	*Tortell*	*Aquilina*	*Oherno*	

Ref: E Barbaresco (Italy) — (Swansea win 17-0 on aggregate)

Sliema's only goal-attempt comes in the first minute when Sander spills Aquilina's free-kick and Lewis heads behind for a corner. Toshack sets himself on for Curtis on the hour for his first competitive match in 20 months to score the fifth goal in the final minute of the game.

2:1 H PARIS ST GERMAIN	**L 0-1 0-0**		
20/10 (France) 9,505	*Toko 71*		
	Ref: U Eriksson (Sweden)		

Davies	Marustik*	Hadziabdic	Evans	Mahoney	Lewis	Stanley	Curtis	Kennedy	Latchford^	James R	James L/Walsh
Baratelli	*Fernandez*	*Pilorget*	*Bathenay*	*Lemoult*	*Guillochan*	*Dahleb*	*Ardiles*	*Zaremba*	*Toko*	*Kist*	*Kist*

Despite Ardiles being in the visiting line-up it is a poor attendance for this round two tie. Evans is brought in to cover for the loss of four centre backs. Kennedy and Robbie James go close but the French side gain the advantage when Zaremba slips the ball to Chad-born Toko who scores.

2:2 A PARIS ST GERMAIN	**L 0-2 0-1**		
3/11 49,700	*Kist 5, Fernandez 75*		
	Ref: S Kirschen (Germany)		
	(Swansea lose 0-3 on aggregate)		

Davies	Hadziabdic*	Stanley	Rajkovic	Evans	Stevenson	Mahoney	James L	Charles	Latchford	James R	Lewis
Baratelli	*Col*	*Pilorget*	*Bathenay*	*Bathenay*	*Guillochan*	*Lemoult*	*Zaremba*	*Fernandez*	*Toko*	*Kist**	*N'Gom*

Gate receipts are a staggering £380,000, compared to Swansea's £25,000. Toshack named himself as substitute to beat an FA of Wales touchline ban. Hopes are dashed early on when Dutch international Kist scores. Swans plug away in the Paris fog and Stevenson strikes a post.

Appearances / Goals

	Appearances								Goals					
	Lge	Sub	LC	Sub	FAC	Sub	Eur	Sub	Lge	Sub	LC	FAC	Eur	Tot
Charles, Jeremy	30	2	2		1		5		2				4	6
Curtis, Alan	17	4	3		1		3		4				2	6
Davies, Dai	30		4		1		5							
Evans, Wyndham	6		1				1							
Gale, Darren	10	5					1		3		1		2	6
Hadziabdic, Dzemal	24	1	3		1		6		1					1
Irwin, Colin	8						3		1					1
James, Leighton	14	5	2				3		2					2
James, Robbie	40		4		1		5		9					9
Kennedy, Ray	21		3				4							
Lake, Huw		1												
Latchford, Bob	38		4		1		5		20		4	1		25
Lewis, Dudley	23		1				2		1					1
Loveridge, Jimmy	16	1	1		1	1	3		2				2	4
Mahoney, John	24		3				5							
Marustik, Chris	22	1	1		1	1			1					1
Pascoe, Colin	4	3												
Rajkovic, Ante	33		3		1		4		1				1	2
Richards, Gary	15													
Robinson, Neil	17	1	1		1		1							
Sander, Chris	12													
Stanley, Gary	24	4	3				4							
Stevenson, Nigel	24	2	2		1		4		1			1		2
Thompson, Max	3		1						1					1
Toshack, John	7	1							1					1
Walsh, Ian	7	1							3		3			6
(own-goal)														2
26 players used	462	31	44	2	11	1	66	7	51		5	1	20	77

League Table

	P	W	D	L	F	A	W	D	L	F	A	Pts
			Home						**Away**			
1 Liverpool	42	16	4	1	55	16	8	6	7	32	21	82
2 Watford	42	16	2	3	49	20	6	3	12	25	37	71
3 Manchester U	42	14	7	0	39	10	6	10	5	17	28	70
4 Tottenham	42	15	4	2	50	15	5	5	11	15	35	69
5 Nott'm Forest	42	12	5	4	34	18	8	4	9	28	32	69
6 Aston Villa	42	17	2	2	47	15	4	3	14	15	35	68
7 Everton	42	13	6	2	43	19	5	4	12	23	29	64
8 West Ham	42	13	3	5	41	23	7	1	13	27	39	64
9 Ipswich	42	11	3	7	39	23	4	10	7	25	27	58
10 Arsenal	42	11	6	4	36	19	5	4	12	22	37	58
11 West Brom	42	11	5	5	35	20	4	7	10	16	29	57
12 Southampton	42	11	5	5	36	22	4	7	10	18	36	57
13 Stoke	42	13	4	4	34	21	3	5	13	19	43	57
14 Norwich	42	10	6	5	30	18	4	6	11	22	40	54
15 Notts Co	42	12	4	5	37	25	3	5	12	18	46	52
16 Sunderland	42	7	10	4	30	22	5	4	12	18	39	50
17 Birmingham	42	9	7	5	29	24	3	7	11	11	31	50
18 Luton	42	7	7	7	34	33	5	6	10	31	51	49
19 Coventry	42	10	5	6	29	17	3	4	14	19	42	48
20 Manchester C	42	9	5	7	26	23	5	7	14	21	47	47
21 SWANSEA	42	10	4	7	32	29	4	7	14	19	40	41
22 Brighton	42	8	7	6	25	22	1	6	14	13	46	40
	924	255	111	96	810	454	96	111	255	454	810	1275

Odds & ends

Double wins: (0)

Double losses: (5) Watford, Liverpool, Arsenal, Nott'm For, West Ham.

Won from behind: (2) Coventry (h), Southampton (h).

Lost from in front: (7) West Ham (h/a), Watford (h), Stoke (a), Arsenal (h), Southampton (a), Norwich (FAC).

High spots: Four-match unbeaten run.
Beating Norwich 4-0 and Manchester City 4-1.

Low spots: Losing at home 1-5 to West Ham.
Failing to win a match away from home.

Ever presents (0).

Hat-tricks: (2) Bob Latchford.

Opposing hat-tricks: (1) P Walsh (Luton).

Penalties for: (2) Robbie James.

Penalties against: (4) L Bissett (Watford), P Maguire (Stoke), R Stewart (West Ham), B Stevenson (Birmingham).

Penalties missed (for): (1) Robbie James (v Aston Villa).

Penalties missed (against): (1) J Robertson (Nott'm Forest).

Leading scorer: (20) Bob Latchford.

THE RISE AND FALL OF SWANSEA CITY 1977-86

Season	P	W	D	L	F	A	Pts	Div	Pos	Ave Att	Highest	Lowest
1977-78	46	23	10	13	87	47	56	4	Pro	8,054	16,140	4,253
1978-79	46	24	12	10	83	61	60	3	Pro	13,633	22,341	7,983
1979-80	42	17	9	16	48	53	43	2	12th	14,315	21,400	10,352
1980-81	42	18	14	10	64	44	50	2	Pro	13,098	21,354	9,468
	176	82	45	49	282	205	209					
1981-82	42	21	6	15	58	51	69	1	6th	18,202	24,115	11,811
1982-83	42	10	11	21	51	69	41	1	Rel	11,681	20,322	8,568
1983-84	42	7	8	27	36	85	29	2	Rel	7,114	10,900	3,648
1984-85	46	12	11	23	53	80	47	3	20th	4,443	11,709	2,380
1985-86	46	11	10	25	43	87	43	3	Rel	4,323	6,989	2,779
	176	40	40	96	183	321	160					

WITH THANKS TO THE FOLLOWING
AND THEIR CHOICE OF FAVOURITE SWANSEA CITY PLAYER 1981-83

Andy Bowen	Robbie James
Leon Gelleburn	Alan Curtis
Huw Grove	Robbie James
D Lynne Jones	Robbie James
Geraint Jones	Dzemal Hadziabdic
Howard Peters	Ante Rajkovic
Andy Philpin	Bob Latchford
Trevor Rees	Robbie James
Andrew Webber	Robbie James
Marc Winchester	Robbie James